W9-AAN-921

3 1611 00327 1365

VISIT US AT

www.syngress.com

Syngress is committed to publishing high-quality books for IT Professionals and delivering those books in media and formats that fit the demands of our customers. We are also committed to extending the utility of the book you purchase via additional materials available from our Web site.

SOLUTIONS WEB SITE

To register your book, visit www.syngress.com/solutions. Once registered, you can access our solutions@syngress.com Web pages. There you may find an assortment of value-added f̶ ̶ ̶ ̶ ̶ ̶ ̶ ̶ ̶ ̶ ̶ ̶ as free e-books related to the topic of this book, URLs of related Web ̶ tes from the author(s).

ULTIMATE CD

Our Ultimate C̶ ̶ ̶ ̶ ̶ ̶ ̶ ̶ ̶ ̶ ̶ ̶ ̶ ̶ ̶ npilations of some of our b̶ ̶ ̶ ̶ ̶ ̶ ̶ ̶ ̶ ̶ ̶ ̶ ̶ ̶ ̶ are the perfect way to extend ̶ ̶ ̶ ̶ ̶ ̶ ̶ ̶ ̶ ̶ ̶ ̶ ̶ area of expertise, including ̶ ̶ ̶ ̶ ̶ ̶ ̶ ̶ ̶ ̶ ̶ ̶ ̶ tration, CyberCrime In̶ ̶ ̶ ̶ ̶ ̶ ̶ ̶ ̶ ̶ ̶ ̶ ̶ ation, to name a few.

DOWNLOAD

For readers wh̶ ̶ ̶ ̶ ̶ ̶ ̶ ̶ ̶ ̶ ̶ ̶ ̶ ̶ n download-able Adobe PE̶ ̶ ̶ ̶ ̶ ̶ ̶ ̶ ̶ ̶ ̶ ̶ ̶ ̶ e hard copies, and are priced ̶ ̶ ̶ ̶ ̶ ̶ ̶ ̶ ̶ ̶ ̶ ̶

SYNGRESS O

Our outlet sto̶ ̶ ̶ ̶ ̶ ̶ ̶ ̶ ̶ ̶ ̶ ̶ ̶ r slightly hurt books at sign̶ ̶ ̶ ̶ ̶ ̶ ̶ ̶ ̶ ̶ ̶ ̶

SITE LICENS

Syngress has ̶ ̶ ̶ ̶ ̶ ̶ ̶ ̶ ̶ ̶ ̶ ̶ ̶ ̶ ts onto servers in corporation̶ ̶ ̶ ̶ ̶ ̶ ̶ ̶ ̶ ̶ ̶ ̶ ntact us at sales@syngre̶ ̶ ̶ ̶ ̶ ̶ ̶ ̶

CUSTOM PU

Governors State University
Library
Hours:
Monday thru Thursday 8:30 to 10:30
Friday and Saturday 8:30 to 5:00
Sunday 1:00 to 5:00 (Fall and Winter Trimester Only)

DEMCO

Many organizations welcome the ability to combine parts of multiple Syngress books, as well as their own content, into a single volume for their own internal use. Contact us at sales@syngress.com for more information.

SYNGRESS®

SYNGRESS®

CD and DVD
Forensics

GOVERNORS STATE UNIVERSITY
UNIVERSITY PARK
IL 60466

Paul Crowley

Dave Kleiman Technical Editor

Syngress Publishing, Inc., the author(s), and any person or firm involved in the writing, editing, or production (collectively "Makers") of this book ("the Work") do not guarantee or warrant the results to be obtained from the Work.

There is no guarantee of any kind, expressed or implied, regarding the Work or its contents. The Work is sold AS IS and WITHOUT WARRANTY. You may have other legal rights, which vary from state to state.

In no event will Makers be liable to you for damages, including any loss of profits, lost savings, or other incidental or consequential damages arising out from the Work or its contents. Because some states do not allow the exclusion or limitation of liability for consequential or incidental damages, the above limitation may not apply to you.

You should always use reasonable care, including backup and other appropriate precautions, when working with computers, networks, data, and files.

Syngress Media®, Syngress®, "Career Advancement Through Skill Enhancement®," "Ask the Author UPDATE®," and "Hack Proofing®," are registered trademarks of Syngress Publishing, Inc. "Syngress: The Definition of a Serious Security Library"™, "Mission Critical™," and "The Only Way to Stop a Hacker is to Think Like One™" are trademarks of Syngress Publishing, Inc. Brands and product names mentioned in this book are trademarks or service marks of their respective companies.

KEY	SERIAL NUMBER
001	HJIRTCV764
002	PO9873D5FG
003	829KM8NJH2
004	GF98366VHH
005	CVPLQ6WQ23
006	VBP965T5T5
007	HJJJ863WD3E
008	2987GVTWMK
009	629MP5SDJT
010	IMWQ295T6T

HV
8079
.C65
C76
2007

PUBLISHED BY
Syngress Publishing, Inc.
800 Hingham Street
Rockland, MA 02370

CD and DVD Forensics

Copyright © 2007 by Syngress Publishing, Inc. All rights reserved. Except as permitted under the Copyright Act of 1976, no part of this publication may be reproduced or distributed in any form or by any means, or stored in a database or retrieval system, without the prior written permission of the publisher, with the exception that the program listings may be entered, stored, and executed in a computer system, but they may not be reproduced for publication.

Printed in Canada
1 2 3 4 5 6 7 8 9 0
ISBN-10: 1-59749-128-4
ISBN-13: 978-1-59749-128-0

Publisher: Andrew Williams
Acquisitions Editor: Erin Heffernan
Technical Editor: Dave Kleiman
Cover Designer: Michael Kavish

Page Layout and Art: Patricia Lupien
Copy Editor: Judy Eby
Indexer: Odessa&Cie

Distributed by O'Reilly Media, Inc. in the United States and Canada.
For information on rights, translations, and bulk sales, contact Matt Pedersen, Director of Sales and Rights, at Syngress Publishing; email matt@syngress.com or fax to 781-681-3585.

Acknowledgments

Syngress would like to acknowledge the following people for their kindness and support in making this book possible.

Syngress books are now distributed in the United States and Canada by O'Reilly Media, Inc. The enthusiasm and work ethic at O'Reilly are incredible, and we would like to thank everyone there for their time and efforts to bring Syngress books to market: Tim O'Reilly, Laura Baldwin, Mark Brokering, Mike Leonard, Donna Selenko, Bonnie Sheehan, Cindy Davis, Grant Kikkert, Opol Matsutaro, Steve Hazelwood, Mark Wilson, Rick Brown, Tim Hinton, Kyle Hart, Sara Winge, Peter Pardo, Leslie Crandell, Regina Aggio Wilkinson, Pascal Honscher, Preston Paull, Susan Thompson, Bruce Stewart, Laura Schmier, Sue Willing, Mark Jacobsen, Betsy Waliszewski, Kathryn Barrett, John Chodacki, Rob Bullington, Kerry Beck, Karen Montgomery, and Patrick Dirden.

The incredibly hardworking team at Elsevier Science, including Jonathan Bunkell, Ian Seager, Duncan Enright, David Burton, Rosanna Ramacciotti, Robert Fairbrother, Miguel Sanchez, Klaus Beran, Emma Wyatt, Krista Leppiko, Marcel Koppes, Judy Chappell, Radek Janousek, Rosie Moss, David Lockley, Nicola Haden, Bill Kennedy, Martina Morris, Kai Wuerfl-Davidek, Christiane Leipersberger, Yvonne Grueneklee, Nadia Balavoine, and Chris Reinders for making certain that our vision remains worldwide in scope.

David Buckland, Marie Chieng, Lucy Chong, Leslie Lim, Audrey Gan, Pang Ai Hua, Joseph Chan, June Lim, and Siti Zuraidah Ahmad of Pansing Distributors for the enthusiasm with which they receive our books.

David Scott, Tricia Wilden, Marilla Burgess, Annette Scott, Andrew Swaffer, Stephen O'Donoghue, Bec Lowe, Mark Langley, and Anyo Geddes of Woodslane for distributing our books throughout Australia, New Zealand, Papua New Guinea, Fiji, Tonga, Solomon Islands, and the Cook Islands.

Author

Paul Crowley is the founder and lead developer at InfinaDyne. InfinaDyne is one of a small number of companies publishing software specifically targeted at the forensic examiner. Paul has been working in the software development field since 1975. His career includes experience that spans computer hardware from the very smallest home video-game console to the largest IBM mainframes. Paul began working with CD recording technology in 1994 and is one of a small number of respected authorities on this technology. The first CD data recovery software product was written by Paul and has led the market for such tools since 1997. InfinaDyne has been offering CD and DVD Forensics training classes since 2005 and has held classes in the U.S. and Australia. Attendees at these classes have included members of the FBI, US Department of Defense, and the Australian Federal Police.

Technical Editor

Dave Kleiman (CAS, CCE, CIFI, CISM, CISSP, ISSAP, ISSMP, MCSE) has worked in the information technology security sector since 1990. Currently, he is the owner of SecurityBreachResponse.com and is the Chief Information Security Officer for Securit-e-Doc, Inc. Before starting this position, he was Vice President of Technical Operations at Intelliswitch, Inc., where he supervised an international telecommunications and Internet service provider network. Dave is a recognized security expert. A former Florida Certified Law Enforcement Officer, he specializes in computer forensic investigations, incident response, intrusion analysis, security audits, and secure network infrastructures. He has written several secure installation and configuration guides about Microsoft technologies that are used by network professionals. He has developed a Windows operating system lockdown tool, S-Lok (www.s-doc.com/products/slok.asp), which surpasses NSA, NIST, and Microsoft Common Criteria Guidelines.

Dave was a contributing author to *Microsoft Log Parser Toolkit* (Syngress Publishing, ISBN: 1-932266-52-6). He is frequently a speaker at many national security conferences and is a regular contributor to many security-related newsletters, Web sites, and Internet forums. Dave is a member of several organizations, including the International Association of Counter Terrorism and Security Professionals (IACSP), International Society of Forensic Computer Examiners® (ISFCE), Information Systems Audit and Control Association® (ISACA), High Technology Crime Investigation Association (HTCIA), Network and Systems Professionals Association (NaSPA), Association of Certified Fraud Examiners (ACFE), Anti Terrorism Accreditation Board (ATAB), and ASIS International®. He is also a Secure Member and Sector Chief for Information Technology at The FBI's InfraGard® and a Member and Director of Education at the International Information Systems Forensics Association (IISFA).

Contents

Foreword xxi

Chapter 1 Physical Characteristics of CD and DVD Media 1

CD Features 4

    CD Sizes and Shapes 6

    CD and DVD Types 7

    CD and DVD Colors 8

    CD–R Dyes 9

    Information Storage on CDs and DVDs 11

    CD and DVD Organization and Terminology 12

        Border Zone 12

        Lead In 13

        Lead Out 13

        Philips CD Text .13

        RZone 14

        Sector 14

        Session 14

        Sony CD Text 14

        TOC 14

        Track 14

    CD and DVD Sectors 15

    R–W Subchannels 16

    CD and DVD Differences 19

    CD-ROM Manufacturing Process 20

    Inside a CD–ROM Drive 23

    External Interfaces 26

    Drive Firmware 27

Chapter 2 CD and DVD Logical Structure 29

Writing to a CD or DVD 30

Logical File Systems 32

CD and DVD File Systems 35

    Red Book Audio 35

    HSG 36

ISO 9660 37

Joliet 39

Rock Ridge 40

UDF 43

HFS 46

HFS+ 47

El Torito 47

Space Allocation by CD and DVD File Systems 48

Disc Accessibility Problems 50

ISO 9660/Joliet File Systems 50

UDF File Systems 51

Other File Systems 51

Chapter 3 Forensic Binary Images 53

Reproducing Forensic Images 55

Chapter 4 Collecting CD and DVD Evidence 57

Recognizing CD and DVD Media 58

Collection Considerations 58

Marking Discs 59

Transporting Discs 60

Documenting and Fingerprinting Discs 61

Officer Safety 62

Chapter 5 Preparing for Disc Examination 63

Forensic Hardware 64

Forensic Software 65

Forensic Workstation 66

Validation 67

Disc Triage 67

Chapter 6 CD/DVD Inspector - The Basics 73

CD/DVD Inspector Installation 74

CD/DVD Inspector Facts 74

Getting Started with CD/DVD Inspector 75

Data Window Usage 80

Disc Memory 81

Useful Tools 83

Analysis 83

Compute Disc MD5 83
Compute MD5 Hash 84
Disc Map 84
Disc Report 84
Hardware Information 84
Scan Files 84
Sector Display 84
TOC 85
View Image 85
Write Image File 86
Searching 86
Scan Files 87
Producing a Forensic Image 92
Copying Files from the Media 95
User Preferences 96
Options Settings 96
Remove Version Marker from Files 97
Show Analysis File Details 97
Save Window Position 98
Sort Initial Display by Name 98
Accept All Errors without Prompting 98
Always Prompt for Filename on Copy 99
Force-intensive UDF Examination 99
Keep Duplicate Files from UDF Examination 99
Automatically Examine Disc at Startup 100
Enable Special Features .100
Recover without Prompts 100
Show Extents in Disc Reports 101
Disable Disc Memory Feature 101
Forensic Use 101
Use 64-bit .zip Extensions for .zip Image Files 101
Disc Memory Settings 102
Keep Last Discs in Disc Memory 102
Empty Button 102
Click to Delete a Single Item 103
Disc Memory Catalog 103
The Analysis Tool 103

name File System in Track nn Recorded as Part of
Session nn 104

nnnnn Sectors are Used Out
of nnnnn Available Sectors 104

type (media) load nnnn at
0xnnnn from Sector nnnn .104

A Properly Written Post-gap
was Found For This Track .105

All Linked Files (nnnn) in
this Session Came from Session nn 105

Application Identification .105

ATIP Reference Power = nn,
Reference Speed = nn 106

Blank Disc with nnnnn Free Sectors 106

Bootable Disc Information
Found, Boot Catalog at Sector nnn 106

Bootable Media from company, platform=platform   106

The CDDB Key for this CD is xxxxxxxx 106

Data Preparer Identification: sssssss 107

Disc is a DVD-kind Type is type 107

Disc Manufacturer: ssssss Type: ssssss 107

DVD Manufacturer is ssssss 107

Error nnn in Manufacturer Determination,
Manufacturer Information Not Available 107

Error Reading Boot Catalog, Sense=0xnn 0xnn 108

Error Reading File System Data
from Disc, No Further Information Available 108

Error Reading Sector nnnnn in
Track nn, Analysis of Track Skipped 108

Error Returned Obtaining
ISRC Code, Sense = ss ss .108

File ssssss is Linked to Track nnn, Session nn 109

HFS Volume Name ssssss .109

Image File in type Format: ssssss 109

Invalid Boot Catalog Found,
Key Values = 0xnn 0xnn .109

Lead-out Track Starts at Sector nnnnn 109

Little-endian Block Size (nnnn)
Not Equal to Big-endian Block Size (nnnn) 109
Little-endian Volume Size (nnnnn)
Not Equal to Big-endian Volume Size (nnnnn) 110
Media Catalog Number for this Disc is ssssss 110
Minimum Recording Speed = nnX,
Maximum Recording Speed = nnX 110
Mismatched File Counts Between
this File System and the ssssss File System 111
Next Writable Location on Disc is nnnnn 111
No Directory Was Found for This File System 111
No ISRC/RID Code Present for This Track 111
No Manufacturer Information
was Returned for This Disc 111
None of the Files in This Session
Are Linked to Prior Sessions 112
Note: Directory Depth of nn May
Cause Problems on Some MSCDEX Versions 112
Note: Directory Depth of nn Violates
ISO-9660 Limit of Eight 112
One or More Files are Using
Characters Which MS-DOS Cannot Access 112
One or More Files Do Not
Have a Trailing Version Identifier (";1") 113
Partition Name: ssssss 113
Publisher Identification 113
Rock Ridge Extension Information is Present 113
Table of Contents 113
The "." Directory Entry is Missing
From One or More Directories 114
The ".." Directory Entry is Missing
From One or More Directories 114
The tttttt Code for This Track is cccccc 114
The Block Size is nnnn, Not 2048 as
Would Be Expected 114
The Directory in This File System
Qualifies as Using the setname Character Set 115

The Disc Is Not Recorded in XA Mode,
But This File System is Marked for XA Mode 115
The Disc Is Recorded in XA Mode,
But This File System Is Not Marked for XA Mode .115
The File "ssssss" Appears in
the Directory But is Not Present 116
The Files ssssss and ssssss Overlap
and One or Both are Destroyed 116
The Last Track in the
Table of Contents is Not the Lead-out 116
The Mastering Program for this Disc Did Not Place
Version Numbers (";1") After the Filenames 117
The Post-gap for This Disc is Either
Missing or Invalid. nnn Trailing Sectors Found 117
The System Identifier in the ISO-9660 Volume
Descriptor Contains Other Than "a" Characters 117
The Volume Identifier in the ISO-9660 Volume
Descriptor Contains Other Than "d" Characters 117
The Volume Identifier is
Blank. This May Cause Problems 118
There Appear To Be Additional
Boot Definitions Present 118
There are nnn Files in the Directory
Which Are Not Recorded in This File System 118
There are nnn Accessible Files and nnn
Directories Contained in This File System 119
There are nnn Directories in This File System 119
There are nnn Files in This File System 119
There are nnn Files Linked from Session nn 119
There are nnn Files That Could
Not Be Connected to a Filename 119
There are nnnn Free Sectors in This Track 119
There is a Total of nnn File Systems on Disc 120
This Disc Appears to be "Open" and Can
Have Data Added to It. The Pointer is nnnnn 120
This Disc Has nn Layers 120

This Disc Is Still "Open" and
Can Have Data Added To It 120
This File System Contains Compressed Data 120
This File System Was Written by ssssss 121
This File System Was Written
by Packet-writing Software 121
This Track Contains Audio with Pre-emphasis 121
This Track Contains Audio without Pre-emphasis . .121
This Track Contains Data
and Contains ssssss File System(s) 121
This Track Contains Data from
the File System in the Prior Track 122
This Track Has Been Recorded in XA Mode 122
This Track is Marked as Being Blank 122
Track nn Has Been Added to
Represent an Open Session 122
Track nn is an Audio Track 123
Track nn Occupies nnn sectors
(nn Min, nn Sec, nn Frames) 123
Track Contains MCN of nnnnnn 123
Track Image Written with nnnn Byte Sectors 123
Track Was Written with Fixed-
length Packets nnnn Bytes in Length 123
Track Was Written with Variable-length Packets 123
UDF Examination Error: ssssss 124
UDF Partition Exceeds Size of
Track According To Disc Information 124
Volume Create Date date 124
Volume Size Appears Suspicious;
Header Says nnnnn While Track is nnnnn Sectors . .124
Warning: One or More Checksum
Errors were Detected in the UDF Structures 124
Warning: Root Directory Length is Specified as Zero125
Warning: This Disc is Marked as
Having a Sparable Partition, But
No Sparing Information Table is Present 125
Warning: Virtual Allocation Table Missing 125
Warning: VAT Not Found in Conventional Place . . .125

Whole Disc MD5 Hash Value xxxxxxxxxxxxxxxxxxx .126
The Hardware Information Display 126
Device Name 126
Revision 126
Date of Revision 127
Read CDDA Command 127
"RAW read" Command 127
Track Information Command 127
Using 10- Byte Commands 127
Readability Test Reason Code 128
Loading Mechanism 128
Bar Code Reading Supported 128
UPC Code is Read 128
ISRC Code is Read 128
C2 Error Pointers 128
Maximum Reading Speed 129
Multi-session Capable 129
Mode 2 Form 1 Supported 129
Mode 2 Form 2 Supported 129
Digital Output on Port 1 129
Digital Output on Port 2 129
Audio Play Supported 130
Reading CDDA Supported 130
CD-Text/CD+G Supported 130
CD-Text/CD+G Decoded 130
Accurate CDDA Positioning 130
Transfer Block Supported 131
Inactivity Spin-down 131
Device Capabilities 131
Device Buffer Size (in K) 131
Drive Serial Number 131
The Volume Information Display 131
ISO-9660 Volume Information 132
Volume ID 132
System ID 132
Volume Size 133
System Use 133
Volume Set Size 133

Volume in Set 133
Block Size (Bytes) 133
Path Table Size (Bytes) 134
Path Table (L) 134
Optional Path Table (L) 135
Path Table (M) 135
Optional Path Table (M) 135
Root Directory Sector 135
Root Directory Timestamp 135
Volume Set 135
Publisher 136
Data Preparer 136
Application 136
Copyright File 136
Abstract File 137
Bibliography File 137
Volume Created 137
Volume Modified 138
Volume Expires 138
Volume Effective 138
Volume Size 138
Volume Set Size 138
Volume in Set 138
Block Size (Bytes) 139
Path Table Size (Bytes) 139
Root Directory Sector 139
Joliet Volume Information .139
Volume ID 139
System ID 139
Volume Size 140
System Use 140
Volume Set Size 140
Volume in Set 141
Block Size (Bytes) 141
Path Table Size (Bytes) 141
Path Table (L) 141

Optional Path Table (L) 142
Path Table (M) 142
Optional Path Table (M) 142
Root Directory Sector 142
Root Directory Timestamp 143
Volume Set 143
Publisher 143
Data Preparer 143
Application 144
Copyright File 144
Abstract File 144
Bibliography File 145
Volume Created 145
Volume Modified 145
Volume Expires 146
Volume Effective 146
Volume Size 146
Volume Set Size 146
Volume in Set 146
Block Size (Bytes) 146
Path Table Size (Bytes) 146
Root Directory Sector 147
HFS and HFS+ Volume Information 147
Volume ID 147
Files 147
Directories 147
Allocation Size (Bytes) 147
Allocation Blocks 147
Free Blocks 148
Volume Created 148
Volume Modified 148
HSG Volume Information 148
UDF Volume Information 148
Volume Descriptor Sequence 148
Volume ID 148
Interchange Level 149

Volume Set Name 149
Implementation Identifier .149
Application 149
Recording Time 149
Disc Reports 149
Disc Contents by Folder 151
Disc Contents by Name 152
Disc Contents by Extension 153
Files with MD5 Hash Value 154
CSV Format Export 155
Image Reports 156

Chapter 7 Using CD/DVD Inspector 159
Examining a Disc—A Step-by-step Guide 160
Starting CD/DVD Inspector 160
Initial Observations 161
Analysis Tool 161
Disc Map 162
Quick Image Examination 162
Scan Files for Keywords 163
Other Examination Tasks 163
Create an ISO Image File .163
Create an InfinaDyne Image File 164
Determining the Writing Application 165
Date Correspondence 165
Missing Files 166
Multi-Session Hiding 167

Chapter 8 Advanced Tasks with CD/DVD Inspector. . . 169
Using Hash Matching and MD5 Hashes 170
Space Utilization Analysis 171
ISO-9660 Directory Analysis .176
Unknown Data Track Issues 179

Chapter 9 Reporting Your Findings 181
Full List of All Files on the Media 182
Image Report(s) 183
Analysis Report 183

Scan Files Results 184
Raw Search Results 184

Chapter 10 Things to Keep In Mind 185

Appendix A Disc Swap Drive Modification 187

Appendix B Downloading Additional Materials 195

Glossary 197

Index 283

Introduction

This book was originally developed as a companion for the CD and DVD Forensics class given through InfinaDyne. It has been researched and prepared by Paul Crowley, the founder and lead developer at InfinaDyne. InfinaDyne is one of a small number of companies publishing software specifically targeted at the forensic examiner.

Paul Crowley has been working in the software development field since 1975. His career includes experience that spans computer hardware from the very smallest home video-game console to the largest IBM mainframes. Crowley began working with CD recording technology in 1994 and is one of a small number of respected authorities on this technology.

InfinaDyne publishes the product CD/DVD Inspector which is featured in this book. It was developed based on a data recovery program, originally written in 1996, to assist users of CD recording in the recovery from hardware errors, software bugs and user mistakes. Today, CD/DVD Inspector is one of a small number of products which professional forensic examiners worldwide rely on to acquire evidence from CD and DVD media.

For the purposes of this book, all examples and practical exercises are based on CD/DVD Inspector version 3. Earlier versions of the product may not be capable of performing all of the functions described in the examples. Later versions of the product should be able to be used without any difficulties.

If you or your organization is interested in the CD and DVD Forensics training class please contact the InfinaDyne sales department for more information at sales@infinadyne.com.

Conventions in this Book

The term "disc" will be used to refer to optical media (CDs and DVDs) and "disk" to refer to hard drives and other magnetic media.

An effort has been made to reproduce all measurements in both metric and US terms.

A "nanometer" is a measure of length. It is equal to one billionth of a meter. One million (1,000,000) nanometers equal one millimeter.

Chapter 1

Physical Characteristics of CD and DVD Media

Little has changed in Compact Disc (CD) physics since the origin of CD audio discs in 1980. This is due in part to the desire to maintain physical compatibility with an established base of installed units, and because the structure of CD media was both groundbreaking and nearly ideal for this function.

Digital Versatile Discs (DVDs) are an evolutionary growth of CD's with slight changes. Considering the development of DVD follows the CD by 14 years, you can see that the CD was truly a revolutionary creation in its time. It is important to understand that both CDs and DVDs are electro optical devices, as opposed to nearly all other compter peripherals which are electromagnetic. There are no magnetic fields in the reading or recording of these discs, therefore, they are immune to magnetic fields of any strength, unlike hard drives

Due to its immunity to magnetic fields, CD and DVD media is unaffected by Electromagnetic Pulse (EMP) effects, X-rays, and other sources of electromagnetic radiation. The primary consideration with recordable CD media (and to a lesser extent, manufactured media) is energy transfer. It takes a significant amount of energy to affect the media that the writing laser transfers to the disc. Rewritable discs (Compact Disc - ReWriteable [CD-RW], Digital Versatile Disc - Rewriteable [DVD-RW], and Digital Versatile Disc - Rewriteable [DVD+RW]) require even more energy to erase or rewrite data.

This is in direct contrast to floppy disks and hard drives, which can be affected by electromagnetic devices such as Magnetic Resonance Imaging (MRI) machines, some airport X-ray scanners, and other devices that create a strong magnetic field. CDs and DVDs are also immune to Electromagnetic Pulse (EMPs) from nuclear detonations.

It is important to understand that CD and DVD media is *read with light*, and recordable discs are *written with heat*. Using an infrared (IR) laser, data is transferred to a CD or DVD onto a small, focused area that places all of the laser energy onto the target for transfer. It should be noted that all CD and DVD media are sensitive to heat (i.e., above 120F/49C), and recordable media is sensitive to IR, ultraviolet (UV), and other potential intense light sources. Some rewritable media are affected by Erasable Programmable Read-Only Memory (EPROM) erasers, which use an intense UV light source. Various forensic alternative light sources can provide sufficient energy to affect optical media, especially if it is focused on a small area. It is not necessarily a question of heat but one of total energy transfer, which can result in heating.

Both CD and DVD media are organized as a single line of data in a spiral pattern. This spiral is over 3.7 miles (or 6 kilometers [km]) in length on a CD, and 7.8 miles (or 12.5 km) for a DVD. The starting point for the spiral is towards the center of the disc with the spiral extending outward. This means that the disc is read and written from the inside out, which is the opposite of how hard drives organize data.

With this spiral organization, there are no cylinders or tracks like those on a hard drive. (The term "track" refers to a grouping of data for optical media.)

The information along the spiral is spaced linearly, thus following a predictable timing. This means that the spiral contains more information at the outer edge of the disc than at the beginning. It also means that if this information is to be read at a constant speed, the rotation of the disc must change between different points along the spiral.

All optical media is constructed of layers of different materials (see Figure 1.1).

Figure 1.1 CD-R Construction

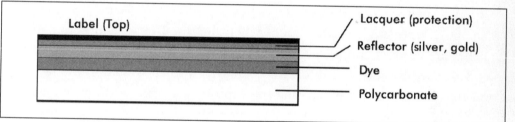

This is similar to how all optical media discs are constructed. The differences between different types of discs are:

- **CD-R** The dye layer can be written to once.

- **CD-ROM** The reflector has the information manufactured into it and there is no dye layer.

- **CD-RW** The dye is replaced with multiple layers of different metallic alloys. The alloy is bi-stable and can be changed many times between different states.

- **DVD** DVD's are constructed of two half-thickness discs bonded together, even when only one surface contains information. Each half disc contains the information layer 0.6 Millimeter (mm) from the surface of the disc.

DVD media consists of two half-thickness polycarbonate discs, each half containing information and constructed similarly to CD media. DVD write-once recordable media uses a dye layer with slightly different dyes than those used for CD-R media, but otherwise are very similar physically. Manufactured DVD media has the information manufactured into the reflector and no dye layer is present. Rewritable DVD media uses bi-stable alloy layers similar to those for CD rewritable media. The differences between manufactured, write-once, and rewritable media are physically similar between CD and DVD media.

The key to all recordable media types is the presence of a reflector with the ability to reflect laser energy. Data is represented by blocking the path to the reflector either by dye or a bi-stable metallic alloy.

The bottom of a CD is made of a relatively thick piece of polycarbonate plastic. Alternatively, the top is protected by a thin coat of lacquer. Scratches on the polycarbonate are out of focus when the disc is read, and minor scratches are ignored completely. It takes a deep scratch in the polycarbonate to affect the readability of a disc. However, even a small scratch in the lacquer can damage the reflector. Scratching the top of a disc can render it unreadable, which is something to consider the next time you place a disc on your desk top-down "to protect it."

A DVD has polycarbonate on both sides; therefore, it is difficult to scratch the reflector.

CD Features

There are a number of distinct areas on the surface of a CD or DVD. Moving from the inside to the outside of the disc, the following areas are illustrated in Figure 1.2:

- **A** Spindle hole
- **B** Clamping ring

- **C** Stacking ring

- **D** Mirror band

- **E** Beginning of data area

- **F** End of data area, slightly inside the outer edge of the disc

The CD standard has specific measurements for all of these areas; approximately 99 percent of CDs (manufactured or recordable) meet these standards. DVD measurements are similar to those for CDs and are considered identical.

Figure 1.2 Areas on a CD or DVD

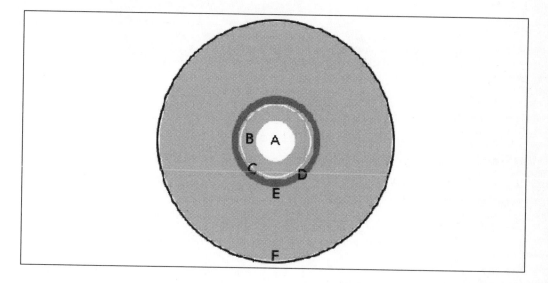

The stacking ring is used to keep the surfaces of discs separate when stacked on a spindle. Without the stacking ring, the lacquer surface of one disc would adhere to the polycarbonate surface of the one above it. This is especially true in high humidity environments. The stacking ring and proper alignment of stacked discs is important for transporting discs.

Figure 1.3 Batch Number on a CD-R

Some manufactured CDs contain identification in the mirror band, which identifies the contents of the disc. In the case of recordable or rewritable media, this is a batch number or a date code. This number is of limited value to forensic examiners, because it does not uniquely identify the disc and generally does not clearly identify the manufacturer of the disc. Finding the meaning of whatever is written here can be very difficult because there is no consistent standard for what information is placed here or how it is encoded. This information in no way uniquely identifies a single disc. It is more likely information about an entire batch of discs. It is likely there are millions of discs with the same information.

When considering marking discs for identification purposes, it is suggested that you avoid the data area of the disc and place such markings in the clamping ring area of the disc. Using solvent-based markers in the data area can dissolve the lacquer and destroy the reflector.

CD Sizes and Shapes

CDs and DVDs come in a variety of sizes and shapes. The following are the standard sizes:

- 120mm/5.25 inches
- 80mm/3.15 inches

■ Business card

Business card discs have a data area slightly smaller than that found on 80mm discs, and are rectangular in shape with either square or rounded ends. Technically, these are not specified in the standards; however, they are fairly common. Some retail stores sell recordable business card-size discs.

After the initial introduction of CDs, it was found that discs could be machined into different sizes after manufacture. The variety of shapes that can be found is as wide as your imagination—one creative machining company produced a CD in the shape of a rooster. At this point, it is rare to find other sizes of DVDs; however, it is possible to develop them. The only critical aspect is the balance of the disc to prevent vibration as the disc is read. A high-speed drive may rotate the disc at speeds above 5000 Revolutions Per Minute (RPM); any slight unbalance causes vibration and noise.

At this time, it is common to find recordable media in any of the above standard sizes and shapes. It is fairly safe to assume that any unusual shape disc is a manufactured disc. Although theoretically possible to machine recordable media into odd shapes it would be rare to find such a disc.

CD and DVD Types

Choosing the right type of disc depends on a number of factors, including the quantity of data being recorded, any additional data that must be added in the future, and how long the data must be accessible.

Not all users can read a DVD as easily as a CD. Therefore, for compatibility with the largest number of users, writing data to a CD makes the most sense. Because DVD recordable and rewritable discs are physically more robust than CD-R and CD-RW discs, this can be an important consideration.

The choice between write-once and rewritable media is not as simple as it seems. Rewritable CD-RW discs hold less data (i.e., approximately 570 megabytes [MB] instead of 700MB when used with most applications). Additionally, all rewritable media (CD and DVD) have significant problems over long periods of time. Chances are that information written to a rewritable disc may not be readable six months or a year after the disc has been written.

If the data has value after six months, using rewritable media is not recommended. Transferring data from one computer to another or short-term backups are ideal uses for rewritable media. Permanent archives, family photographs, and other such applications should only be written to write-once media.

Choosing between DVD-R and DVD+R discs should be guided by the intended use of the disc. There is some evidence that DVD-R discs are more compatible with consumer DVD recorders than DVD+R discs, however, there are consumer players that will only read DVD+R discs.

DVD-R discs are often the best choice for compatibility if the disc being produced contains data files. Early DVD-ROM drives can generally read DVD-R discs but are incapable of reading DVD+R discs. DVD writers that only write DVD+R/RW discs will read DVD-R discs.

CD and DVD Colors

CD-ROM discs and audio CDs are typically manufactured with clear polycarbonate and an aluminum reflector; however, this is not the only possibility. When the Sony Playstation® was originally released, all of its discs were black (opaque to visible light, but transparent to the IR laser light used to read the disc).

When CD-R discs originally appeared, the reflector was always gold and the dye added a greenish cast to the data side (or bottom) of the disc. However, today CD-R discs can be found with silver or gold reflectors and various dye colors that give the data side of the CD-R disc anything from a green tint to a yellow tint to a blue tint and various other shades of these colors. The specific colors are dependent on the dye formulation being used. There are a number of different dyes and many possible changes in exact formulation that give rise to the number of different colors.

Some CD-R discs have a silver reflector and the dye is a very faint yellow. Under some conditions, these discs are nearly indistinguishable to the human eye from manufactured CD-ROM or CD audio discs. Memorex® released black CD-R discs that were inspired by the Sony Playstation® discs.

CD-RW discs generally have a silver reflector and a dull silver data side.

DVD-R discs originally had a silver reflector and a purplish tint on the data side. Today, DVD-R and DVD+R discs come in a wide variety of colors with different dye formulations. Nearly all of the reflectors for DVD-R and DVD+R are silver.

DVD-RW discs appear similar to CD-RW discs, with a silver reflector and a dull silver data side.

DVD+RW discs come in a variety of colors, but most have a silver reflector and a dull silver data side. Some can be hard to tell apart from manufactured DVD-ROM discs.

The reasons for all of the different color dyes and reflectors are primarily cost, performance, and licensing. Today, there are no really expensive dyes in use, because a small difference in cost per disc can add up when you are producing millions of discs. Annually, over a half a billion recordable discs are used each year. The performance of a dye is directly related to how the disc can be written in terms of speed and laser power. It is also a factor in the longevity of a disc. Finally, licensing terms affect this, because the dyes have been patented. For the most part, the cost difference between a lower cost license and a higher cost license can be significant depending on the number of discs being manufactured.

Silk screened labels are not exclusive to manufactured discs; it is common to silk screen CD-R blanks. Some software product distribution discs in retail packaged software products are silk screened CD-R blanks that have been duplicated with the last session left open. This means that the discs can be added to.

It used to be easy to tell a recordable disc from a manufactured disc. The manufacturers made the discs in this manner, each disc as an advertisement. Today, media comes in a wide variety of colors. Similarly, manufacturers have a slightly different motivation; some are producing discs that intentionally appear to be manufactured discs.

Unless you have a lot of experience with such discs, it is not safe to assume that an investigator can tell the difference between a recordable disc and a manufactured disc. It is recommended that you do not attempt to exclude discs from being collected as evidence based on their appearance. Creating a policy of "collect everything" ensures that less experienced people are not faced with decisions regarding which discs to collect.

CD-R Dyes

The original development of CD-R discs required a bi-stable dye that could be changed from transparent to opaque by a laser. The first CD-R manufacturer, Taiyo Yuden, met this requirement by developing and patenting a cyanine organic dye. Cyanine refers to a family of organic polymer dyes that were originally formulated in 1986 for use in photography and spectroscopy. The term "organic" in this case refers to the use of chains of carbon and hydrogen atoms in the dye. The dye formulation that Taiyo Yuden created remains transparent until an IR laser heats it, at which point it changes color and is less transparent, thereby resulting in recordable CD media. CD-R technology began in the early 1990s and Sony released the first CD recorder in 1993.

Although the estimated life of the original cyanine organic dye was approximately 10 years, it is not clear if this was actually tested. Discs that were recorded in 1995 are still readable if they have been kept away from heat and UV light.

Since then, additional types of dyes have been developed, some with different properties. Also, dye developments have allowed the recording speeds to increase with dyes that are far more sensitive than the original.

It is often claimed that phthalocyanine dye is more stable than the original cyananine, and has a life of 100 years. While some testing has been done regarding this, and it is clear that it is more stable than earlier Cyanine dyes, the claims of 100-year life are yet to be proven.

The following table summarizes the types of dyes and their visible characteristics. They are listed in the order they appeared in CD-R media.

Table 1.1 CD-R Dye Information

Dye	Patent Holder	Color	Color with Gold Reflector	Color with Silver Reflector
Cyanine	Taiyo Yuden	Blue	Green	Green/Blue
Phthalo-Cyanine	Mitsui Toatsu Chemicals	Transparent	Gold	-
Metalized Azo	Verbatim/ Mitsubishi	Blue	-	Dark Blue
Advanced Phthalo-Cyanine	Mitsui Toatsu Chemicals	Transparent	Gold	-
Formazan	Kodak Japan Limited	Light Green	Green/Gold	-

"Formazan" is a hybrid Cyanine/PhthaloCyanine dye that was developed by Kodak. The appearance of the data side of a CD-R depends on the combination of dye color and reflector color. Thus, a blue dye and a gold reflector results in a green appearance on the bottom of the disc.

DVDs exhibit similar characteristics, but the dye formulations are not usually disclosed by the manufacturers. While CD-R technology was jointly shared between Sony, Philips, and Taiyo Yuden in the early 1990s, the recordable media market has become far more competitive. Today, a small change in dye formulation can make a difference in writing speed or other performance characteristics, and therefore are of significant benefit to media manufacturers. The result is that there is less sharing of information about DVD dyes than there is for CD-R dyes.

Information Storage on CDs and DVDs

The information on discs is represented by *pits* and *lands* in manufactured discs. Extremely tight focusing of the laser is used to differentiate between different heights of the reflector in the disc. The reflection from a land is in focus and in phase, whereas the reflection from a pit is out of phase. CD and DVD drive optics are designed to detect these differences.

Recordable media replaces physical pits with organic dye (such as Cyanine) that can be made to be opaque (or less transparent) by the application of heat. Instead of the light being reflected differently, there is a distinct contrast between a land on a recordable disc where the light is reflected strongly and a pit where the light is reflected less strongly. The similarity between an out-of-focus/out-of-phase pit and an opaque spot allowed CD recordable media to be read by CD-ROM drives and audio players, even though the player was designed long before recordable media existed.

Rewritable media uses a slightly different technique, since the organic dye is a one-way transformation from transparent to opaque. Instead, a metallic alloy is used that has two states: *crystalline* and *amorphous*. In a crystalline state, the alloy is more reflective than in the amorphous state; therefore, it can be used in the same manner as the pits and lands or organic dye. The difference is that additional laser power can "anneal" the alloy to return to a crystalline state. Therefore, a drive that can be used with rewritable discs has three separate power levels: *read*, *write* and *erase*.

Rewritable discs typically have one-third the reflectivity of write-once recordable media. However, the contrast difference between a pit and a land on rewritable media is similar. Adjustments to drives in order to read rewritable discs were primarily the adjustment of the sensitivity during reading. Drives that could automatically cope with the adjustments could read rewritable media, but those that could not were unable to read rewritable media.

When a disc is read, the transitions between lands and pits and pits to lands are represented as binary. The spacing between these transitions serves to fill in binary zeros between the 1s and is represented by the length of a pit. Pits come in eight sizes from 3T to 11T, where T is a unit of time. The ability of digital systems to measure time precisely allows for the determination of exactly how many binary 0s occur between each binary 1 transition. Decoding this time—which is the length of a pit—is how the data on the disc is read.

Encoding on a disc uses 14 bits to represent each 8 data bits. Each group is required to have individual 1 bits with two or more 0 bits following. The encoding of this is called Eight into Fourteen Modulation (EFM). The spacing of the 1 bits in the EFM encoding preserves the clocking of the data by not allowing either too long or too short a run of binary zeros. The translation from EFM encoding back to data bytes when reading the disc is done with a simple lookup table where each legal pattern of 14 "raw" bits from the disc has a corresponding 8-bit data byte. (This was designed circa 1980 with 8-bit 1 MHz microprocessors being common.) Complex signal processing was not required for reading CDs and is not required for reading DVDs. In the early 1980s, such signal processing was possible but too expensive for wide adoption in consumer electronics devices. Today, such signal processing is more common and less expensive; however, it is not required to read CDs and DVDs.

CD and DVD Organization and Terminology

It is important to have understand the terminology used with this technology. The following is a description of the various terms that you are likely to encounter.

Border Zone

A *Border Zone* is the area on a DVD that contains the real content of the disc, whether it is data files, music, or videos. It is roughly equivalent to a track on a CD.

A manufactured DVD is always composed of a single border zone; however, recordable discs can have multiple border zones. In some documentation, a border zone is also called a *RZone*.

While there is no Table of Contents (TOC) on a DVD, the drive can return information in the form of a TOC by listing border zone information.

Lead In

The *lead in* serves as a container for the TOC for a session on a CD. Sony-style CD Text information is also recorded in this area. Originally, this was used to help calibrate the laser and mechanical components of the drive for reading the disc.

The first (or only) session on a disc has 7,500 sectors (14.65MB) reserved for the lead in; subsequent sessions have 4,500 sectors (9 MB) reserved for the lead in. Using "Disc At Once" recording the TOC and other lead-in information is written first in this area, whereas using "Track At Once" recording in this area is reserved and written after the session is closed.

For multi-session recording, a pointer is placed in the lead-in area to indicate the next writable location on the disc. If and when the disc is finalized or closed, this pointer is recorded as either 0 or 24 bits of binary 1s. Both formats have the same effect of preventing further information from being added to the disc.

Lead Out

The *lead out* of the disc indicates the end of the CD disc or the end of a session on the disc. One use of the lead-out area is to tell an audio player to stop playing the disc.

This area is made up of a group of sectors written at the end of the disc. The lead out for the first session is 6,750 sectors (13.5 MB) and all subsequent sessions have a lead-out of 2,250 sectors (4MB).

Philips CD Text

Philips developed a technique in 1997 by which lyrics and other information could be stored on audio discs without interfering with the audio samples. Approximately 31 MB of data can be stored on a disc using this technique. This is not in common use today, unlike Sony CD Text, which stores only the disc name, artist name, and track titles.

RZone

RZone is an alternate term for a border zone.

Sector

Each CD *sector* contains 2,048 bytes of user data for data tracks and 2,352 bytes of audio samples for audio tracks.

Session

A *session* is a group of one or more tracks recorded on a CD at the same time. This corresponds to a border zone on a DVD.

Multi-session discs have more than a single session, which is usually a user-recorded disc that has been written to multiple times.

Sony CD Text

Sony developed a technique in 1997 by which the album title, artist name, and track titles could be stored in the lead-in area of an audio disc, which allows a maximum of approximately 15KB of data to be stored on a disc. Most commercial audio discs produced by Sony have this, as well as many discs produced by other manufacturers.

TOC

The *TOC* is recorded in the lead in for a session and contains only some information about the type of track (audio or data), the session number, and the starting address of the track. There is one TOC per session; therefore, multi-session discs have several independent TOCs.

Unclosed sessions do not have a TOC, which is why an unclosed session cannot be read on a CD-ROM drive.

The TOC is not a file system and cannot be read directly; it is just a list of tracks on the disc.

DVDs do not have a TOC; however, the information can be constructed from information about border zones.

Track

A *track* is a single collection of data (audio or video) on a CD. It is common to have multiple (up to 99) tracks on a CD.

On a DVD, a border zone (or RZone) is similar to a CD track with the exception that it is rare to find DVDs with multiple border zones. All manufactured DVDs have only a single border zone.

CD and DVD Sectors

There are several different types of sectors found on CD media. The most basic and original form is CD Audio or CD-DA:

2352 Bytes
588 16-bit stereo

Technically, audio discs contain "subcode blocks," not sectors. However, since circa 1996, most CD drives and all DVD drives read audio subcode blocks and return the information as a 2,352-byte sector. Each subcode block is composed of 98 frames. For data formats, these same 98 subcode frames are referred to as sectors and contain the raw 2352 bytes per sector.

Aside from the main data, subchannels P through W are available. P and Q have defined purposes and hold information to assist in determining the difference between "gap" and program material (the music) for audio discs, and also for holding information such as the time in the current track. Subchannels R through W can be used in several different ways:

- Graphics for CD+G karaoke discs

- Text information for Philips CD-TEXT

- Other information

The next format introduced was CD-ROM Mode 1. Mode 1 was developed in 1988 with the introduction of the CD-ROM format. Each sector also contains 2,352 bytes, but much of that is used for control and error correction information.

12 Bytes Sync	4 Bytes Header	2,048 Bytes User Data	4 EDC	8 Bytes Reserved	276 Bytes ECC

Devices such as CD-i® and the Kodak PhotoCD® player were introduced following Mode 1. Additional features on CDs were required to utilize the technology and the XA format was introduced. XA discs come in two formats:

Mode 2 Form 1 and Mode 2 Form 2. The Mode 2 Form 1 sector layout looks very similar to that for Mode 1:

12 Bytes Sync	4 Bytes Header	2,048 Bytes User Data	4 Bytes 4 EDC	8 Bytes Reserved	276 Bytes ECC

Mode 2 Form 2 frees up additional space in the sector for greater density, but sacrifices the second level of error correction provided by the ECC data:

12 Bytes Sync	4 Bytes Header	8 Bytes Subheader	2,324 Bytes User Data	4 Bytes

DVD sectors are much simpler, because there was no audio format to build on.

2,048 Bytes User Data

DVD sectors are composed of data frames on the physical disc. Information other than the 2,048 bytes of user data is not accessible. A DVD data frame contains 4 bytes of ID, 2 bytes of ID Error Correction Code (ECC), 6 bytes of copyright management information, 2,048 bytes of user data, and 4 bytes of Error Detection Code (EDC). Sixteen such data frames are assembled into a single 32K ECC block. It is not possible to access DVD data frames (also called ECC blocks) with consumer DVD drives.

R-W Subchannels

CDs can have up to 80 additional bytes of data in the R through W subchannels associated with each sector. For a full 80-minute disc (700 MB) this can provide more than 27 MB of additional data storage capability. The data stored in the R through W subchannels is invisible to most CD applications; therefore, it does not interfere with other uses. There are two defined uses for data for audio discs:

- **CD+G Graphics for Karaoke Discs** The Red Book standard and its extensions define the content of the R through W subchannel data for playing low-resolution graphics while playing music at the same time. This was originally used to display images on a television synchronized with Karaoke music.

■ **Philips CD-TEXT** Philips defines the content of the R through W subchannels to provide a means of storing text information with music. The primary application of this was to store the lyrics with the music, but it was never adopted.

Aside from these documented uses, the R through W subchannels can contain any other data that the creator of the disc wants to add. There are standards for how this data can be arranged and still be compatible with various CD+G players and other devices.

The R through W subchannels supply bits 5 through 0 in each byte of the 96-byte sector data. The terminology used in the Philips standards documents is as follows:

■ Each group of 6 bits (R through W) is called a SYMBOL.

■ A group of 24 SYMBOLS is called a PACK.

■ A PACKET is composed of four PACKS.

For error correction and detection purposes, the PACK data is interleaved across eight PACKS on the disc. This reduces the effects of physical damage to the disc and allows for better error correction by spreading out the effects of a physical defect across multiple PACKS. Since there are four packs to a sector, de-interleaving all of the packs for a sector requires reading three consecutive sectors. See Figure 1.5 for a diagram of how a single pack is interleaved across 8 packs on a disk.

CD/DVD Inspector (version 3.0 and later) can de-interleave this information and write a file containing all of the R through W subchannel information. This is done on a track-by-track basis using the Copy Sectors tool.

Because the R through W subchannel information only stores 6 bits for each symbol, there are two methods by which it can be decoded. The first is to use the standard CD-TEXT 6-bit character set and translate the information to standard American Standard Code for Information Interchange (ASCII). This results in the largest amount of text that can be stored in the R through W subchannel area, but restricts the text to letters, numbers, and some punctuation symbols.

The other technique for decoding the R through W subchannel information translates the 24 6-bit symbols into 16 8-bit ASCII characters, which is capable of containing any data.

CD/DVD Inspector can also output the 6-bit symbols as is without translation, with or without de-interleaving (see Figure 1.4).

Figure 1.4 R-W Subchannel Pack De-interleave

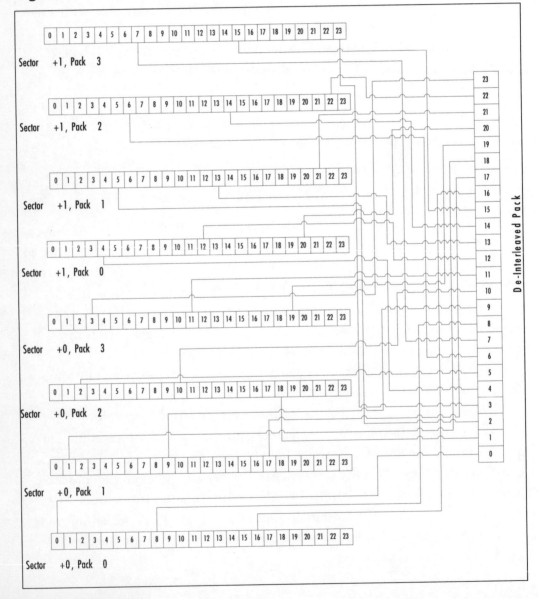

CD and DVD Differences

The principle difference between CD and DVD media is density. CD media is designed to be read with a 780 nanometers (nm) laser and the physical features on a disc are 1 to 1.5 wavelengths in width. Alternatively, DVD media is designed to be read with a 630–650 nm laser and the physical features are correspondingly smaller (see Figures 1.5 and 1.6).

Figure 1.5 CD Media at 30,000x   **Figure 1.6** DVD Media at 30,0000x

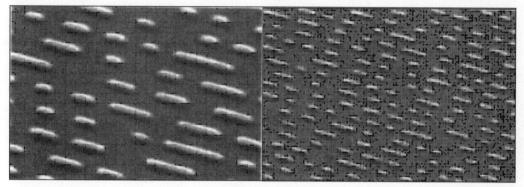

Note that the spacing of the pits and lands does not change across the radius of the disc. This means there is more information stored at the outer edge than there is at the inner edge. The track pitch is the distance between the "wraps" of the spiral. CDs can have a track pitch from 1,500 to 1,700 nm, or about two wavelengths.

As detailed above, CD media is organized into subcode blocks that contain 2,352 bytes. Each subcode block consists of 98 contiguous frames containing synchronization (SYNC) bytes, subcode information (including addressing), user data, and two levels of Cross-Interleaved Reed-Solomon Code (CIRC) that detects and corrects errors in both audio and data discs. Some CD-ROM data formats contain an additional Reed-Solomon Product Code (RS-PC) that detects and corrects severe errors that are beyond the capability of the frame level CIRC.

Conventional data discs use additional RS-PC; however, more specialized discs (e.g., Video Compact Discs [VCDs]) do not use RS-PC in order to take advantage of the additional space in the data sectors. This allows more bytes per second to be transferred to the computer.

While it is convenient to think of CD media as being broken up into sectors, it is misleading when talking about the low-level organization of a disc, because there is a considerable amount of interleaving of sector data. To minimize the effects of physical damage, the data is stored with redundancy over a large physical area and a single sector's worth of data is spread over the distance of three sectors. This is both a positive and a negative aspect. It helps minimize the effects of physical damage to the disc; however, when a sector is damaged beyond the ability of the redundancy to correct it, three sectors are rendered unreadable.

DVD media was not built on a foundation of audio players as is the case with CD-ROM technology. There is a single data format on DVD media and all sectors contain 2,048 bytes of error-corrected data. To reduce the overhead that is present on CDs, DVDs use a different mechanism whereby 16 data frames are grouped together in a single ECC block. Each data frame contains a 2,048-byte user data sector as well as some control information. This reduces the overhead considerably without sacrificing the error-correction capabilities. It implies that a DVD drive is reading and buffering at least 16 data frames (or user data sectors) at a time, whereas early CD-ROM drives would read and buffer only a single sector at a time. The result is that DVDs have significantly more capacity than they would if the same methods for CDs were used.

CD-ROM Manufacturing Process

CD-ROM and CD audio discs are manufactured by creating a glass master disc, which is then mechanically reproduced to form stamped polycarbonate discs. Aluminum is then deposited on the stamped surface to reflect the laser. The aluminum is protected by a thin coating of lacquer, usually cured by UV light from a high intensity Xenon flash lamp.

The glass master is made in much the same way as a printed circuit board or integrated circuit mask. A piece of glass is coated with a photosensitive compound, which is then exposed to a laser in much the same way a recordable disc is written to. The actual machine is called a *Laser Beam Recorder*, and differs from a consumer writer in one very important aspect – the glass master is blank when the process starts. Consumer "blank" recordable discs are not really blank before they are used. They contain a spiral pattern that the consumer writer follows to write the data. This spiral pattern is called a *pregroove*.

After the laser beam recorder has exposed the photosensitive compound on the glass master, the glass master is "developed" using a solution of sodium hydroxide, which washes away the areas that were exposed to the laser. This forms tiny pits in the surface in a spiral pattern, which become the information on the final disc. This is identical to the process used to create printed circuit boards. The glass master is then placed into a vacuum chamber where a molecules-thick layer of silver is deposited onto the disc. This is then called a *metalized glass master*.

The metalized glass master is then immersed into a tank of nickel sulfamate where an electroforming technique is used to deposit a layer of metallic nickel onto the silver surface of the disc. This takes approximately two hours, and when complete, the nickel is removed from the disc and becomes the *father disc*. The father disc is a negative (reverse) impression of what is used to form the disc.

The father disc is then put back into the electroforming tank where another layer of nickel is deposited. After approximately two hours, this new layer of nickel is removed from the father disc resulting in the *mother disc*, which is used to create *stampers*.

Stampers are made from the mother disc, and are used to form the final polycarbonate discs. Multiple stampers are made from a single mother disc as each stamper is only good for at most 100,000 discs. The term "stamper" is inherited from the phonograph record industry; vinyl records were stamped whereas CDs and DVDs are injection molded.

Polycarbonate is taken in the form of small beads and heated in an injection molding machine with the stamper. The result is a 5.25-inch or 120mm disc that has the pits and lands impressed on one side.

This polycarbonate disc is then coated with a very thin layer of aluminum on the side with pits and lands. This is done with an electrostatic technique called *sputtering* (or *metallization*). A coating of clear lacquer or sealant is then put over the aluminum to protect it. The disc is then ready to have a label silk-screened onto it.

Recordable discs are manufactured in a similar manner, only a layer of dye is put down before the reflector and gold or silver is used instead of aluminum. Rewritable discs are made the same way, only multiple vacuum deposition steps are used to get the layers of metallic alloy.

Both write-once recordable and rewritable discs have a pre-groove, which is stamped into the polycarbonate. This pre-groove is a sine wave pattern that the writer can follow to maintain tracking on the disc when writing. In addition to providing a path for the laser to follow, this pre-groove has information encoded into it using frequency and phase modulation. The effect is changing the spacing of the curve (see Figure 1.7).

Figure 1.7 Frequency-modulated Pre-groove

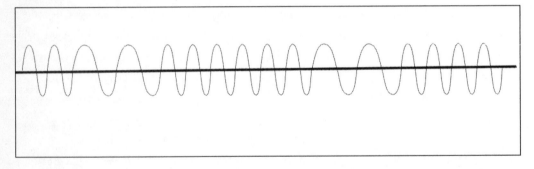

The information in the pre-groove for CD-R discs is the time coding along the spiral from 0 to 63, 74 or 80 minutes. This information is called Absolute Time in Pre-Groove (ATIP). For CD-RW discs, this was expanded on to include other information about the disc such as the laser power level that is suggested for writing and the minimum and maximum speeds for writing. For DVD media, a combination of dedicated areas on the disc as well as ATIP is used to present information about the disc to the writer.

Inside a CD-ROM Drive

Figure 1.8 illustrates how the actual mechanism in a CD-ROM drive (or other similar device) functions. It is interesting to note that the mechanism used in a 1982 audio player is very similar to that used in a current DVD+/– writer.

Figure 1.8 CD Optics

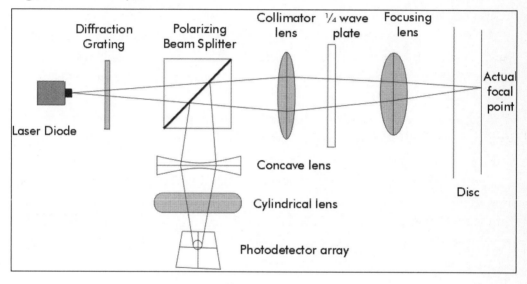

The laser diode is a small electronic part that emits a light in the IR spectrum when an electric current is passed through it. The first step is to pass this through a diffraction grating, which acts as a filter to isolate only the correct frequency. While the laser itself is brightest at the center frequency (i.e., 780 nm for CDs, 650 nm for DVDs), there are other frequencies present. The transmission diffraction grating removes all but the center frequency of the laser.

The polarizing beam splitter then divides the laser into multiple beams. One is the reference beam, which is directed towards the photodetector array. Three other beams are directed through the remaining optics and to the disc.

The main center beam is used to read the data, while two smaller beams straddle the center area and are used to maintain radial tracking.

The collimator lens, quarter-wave plate, and focusing lens are used to focus these three beams on the disc. The actual focal point is below the surface of the disc where the pits and lands that make up the data content of the disc are located. Focus is maintained by moving the focusing lens to account for minute differences in the disc shape and distance from the sled.

After being reflected by the disc, the three beams are reflected back through the lenses and towards the photodetector. The four beams (three from the disc and one reference) are then used to control tracking and focus with the use of four photodetectors in an array.

All of the optical components described above are contained on the *sled*, which is the part that is moved to access the disc. The laser diode, lenses, and beam splitter are all contained here, as well as coils for moving the focusing lens.

The same tracking technique is used when writing, where the main area is writing data and the two smaller areas are used to maintain tracking and read the pre-groove on a recordable disc.

Figure 1.9 shows a close-up of the sled assembly. As you can see, there is a large flexible cable connecting the sled to the circuit board, which has signals from the photodetector and to the laser and focusing coil. The two silver rails are the guides along which the sled moves as it accesses the full radius of the disc. It moves along the rails by the tracking motor.

Figure 1.9 Sled Assembly

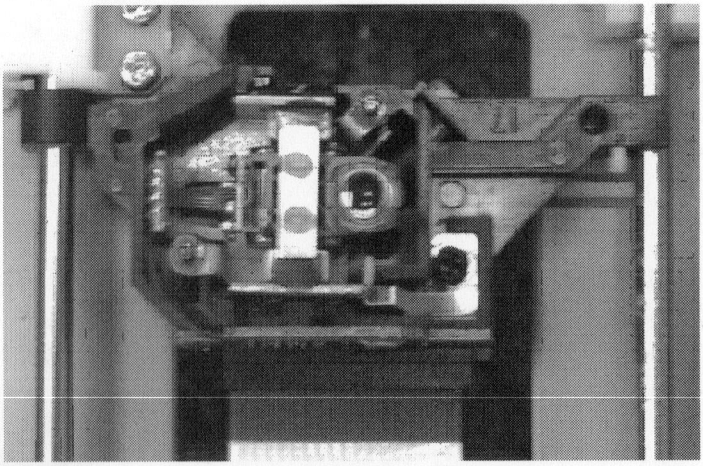

As can be seen in Figure 1.10, the sled (or laser pickup assembly) is a relatively small part of the overall device. It is moved across the surface of the disc by the tracking motor while the disc drive motor or spindle motor rotates the disc

Figure 1.10 Inside a CD-ROM Drive

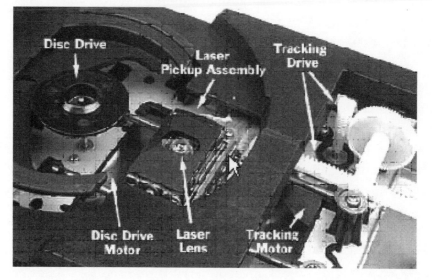

As mentioned previously, the spacing of the lands and pits remains constant across the surface of the disc. CD audio players and early CD-ROM drives were designed to maintain a constant rate of information being read from the disc, which requires the rotation of the disc to be controlled to correspond to the radius where the lens is placed. The disc rotates more slowly when the lens is positioned at the outer edge than when the lens is close to the center. This requires the spindle motor to be more closely controlled than in other devices such as floppy disks or hard drives, which rotate at a constant speed. The technique of accessing the disc in this manner is called Constant Linear Velocity (CLV). The data passing by the laser is kept at the same speed even when there is more data present at the outer edge of the disc.

When advances in technology allowed CD drive read speed exceeded 14x, a different technique for reading discs appeared called Constant Angular Velocity (CAV), where the disc is rotated at the same speed regardless of the positioning of the laser. This forces the drive electronics to adjust for the different data rates as the laser is moved across the radius of the disc. When writing to the disc, a modification of this technique called Zoned CAV is often implemented, where the disc is rotated at several different fixed speeds depending on the radius the laser is positioned at. This limits the amount of variation in the data rate that the drive electronics have to adjust for.

In modern drives there is usually one additional motor, which opens and closes the tray or otherwise moves the disc in and out of the drive. This is not available for notebook drives or for smaller CD and DVD players.

External Interfaces

All current computer CD and DVD drives have two interfaces: digital data/control bus and analog audio. Sometimes a drive has an additional digital audio interface as well. Drives also often have a front-mounted headphone jack as well as a rear-facing analog output connector. The audio interfaces are active when the drive is playing an audio track under either manual or computer control.

Today, most drives have ATA Packet Interface (ATAPI) or Serial ATA (SATA) connections only. Adapters to convert between this and other interfaces such as SATA, FireWire, Universal Serial Bus Version 2 (USB2), or Small Computer System Interface (SCSI) are common. Along with the gradual phasing out of the parallel ATA interface, it is expected that there will be more SATA drives in the future. This will lead to bridge adapters that will convert this interface to FireWire and USB2.

While the highest performing interface today is still SCSI, there are no CD or DVD drives that implement any of the high-performance SCSI interfaces. Nor is there any real need for this, because the maximum data rate for CD and DVD drives is far below the capabilities of these implementations. This could change with Blu-Ray and HD DVD drives, but it is unlikely that there will be a resurgence of SCSI in the near future. Native implementations of SATA and FireWire 800 without adapters are the choice for high-performance devices in the future.

The data interface for a drive has little effect on the data transfer rate (or speed) of the drive. This was only a problem with USB 1.1 drives where they were limited to a maximum data rate of about 6x. Today's data interfaces significantly outperform the ability of the drive to read from the media. The performance of the parallel Integrated Drive Electronics (IDE) bus is more than adequate when used with modern Direct Memory Access (DMA) implementations. Some people believe that the FireWire interface is superior for data transfer than USB2, because of higher speed and/or better negotiation on the bus. While this may be important for hard drives that can reach a significantly greater transfer rate, it is not important for CD and DVD drives with lower data transfer rates.

Drive Firmware

It is important to understand the complexity of reading CDs and DVDs. There is a significant amount of processing that is done by the drive, between reading the pits and lands from the disc and sending data to the computer. This differs significantly from how hard drive and floppy disk data is treated, where only a small amount of post-processing is required.

Floppy disk controllers in the late 1970s and early 1980s were constructed with discrete logic chips where individual gate-level integrated circuits were assembled together on a circuit board. While today a single chip accomplishes this task, the actual processing performed has not changed significantly.

The first CD-ROM drive that was sold to consumers had 4K to 8K of firmware controlling the operation of the drive. Much of the processing was accomplished by a Large Scale Integration (LSI) chip that was custom made for decoding CD data. The amount of circuitry involved was between 10 to 100 times that of a floppy disk controller.

Originally, CD writers had 64K to 128K of firmware on masked ROM (not upgradeable) chips.

Today a DVD +/- writer has as much as 8 MB or 16 MB of firmware on flash memory chips, which can be upgraded by the end user. This allows for changes and bug fixes after the drive has been released. With this much firmware, such problems occur regardless of the amount of testing done by the drive manufacturer.

The drive firmware is a specialized program to control the functioning of the drive and interacts with the LSI chip that decodes the pit and land information from the laser. There is no provision for feeding the raw information back to the computer directly—everything has to go through the drive firmware. This means that whatever limitations are built into the drive firmware are limitations as to what can be done with the disc in the drive. There is no way to bypass this.

Some people have attempted to construct mechanisms by which CDs can be read without a drive and without these limitations. To date, there has been little success in this area with CDs, and none with DVDs outside of specialized university projects.

Chapter 2

CD and DVD
Logical Structure

The logical structure of a Compact Disc (CD) or a Digital Versatile Disc (DVD) involves various writing techniques and the logical organization of data within a file system.

Writing to a CD or DVD

Writing to a CD or DVD can be done using any of the following writing strategies:

- **Track-at-once** The most common form of CD recording for user-created data discs.

- **Disc-at-once** The most common way to create audio discs and DVDs. Nearly all manufactured data discs are created this way.

- **Incremental Recording or Packet Writing** Used with drag-and-drop writing software. This is also the most common way for non-movie DVDs to be recorded.

These writing strategies are actual selections made in the writing software and sent to the writer to control it. It is important to understand that this is not connected with any particular file system—that is a different selection in the writing software that does not directly affect the writer. The writing strategy selection does impact the structure of the disc.

Incremental recording (or packet writing) is often confused with the Universal Disk Format (UDF) file system. UDF can be written using any of the writing methods listed above, and incremental recording can be used with any file system.

Track-at-once refers to writing a track and then turning off the laser, which forces a break in the sector encoding, thereby resulting in two unreadable sectors on the disc. A gap (usually 150 sectors in length) is then written, which inserts 2 seconds of silence between each track. The Table of Contents (TOC) is constructed from the track information, and is written automatically when the writing session is closed.

Disc-at-once writes the TOC first, and then writes each track. There is no gap between tracks and no unreadable sectors are created. This write strategy was originally required for discs to be manufactured properly. Today, this write strategy is very common for user-written audio discs because it eliminates the forced 2-second gap between tracks.

Incremental recording allows you to sequentially write small amounts of data to a disc without the 150-sector gap. It is commonly used for drag-and-drop writing software, which allows you to use write-once and rewritable media. There is some overhead with incremental recording on Compact Disc Recordable (CD-R) and Compact Disc - ReWriteable [CD-RW] media. This overhead consumes 7 sectors for each "packet" of information. In general these packets are the size of the file being written for CD-R media and a fixed size of 16 sectors (32KB) for CD-RW media. Most software also uses 16 sector packets on on DVD rewritable media.

Multiple sessions can be recorded with any of these recording techniques; however, it is unusual for Disc-at-once to be used for multiple sessions. Disc-at-once is called "Session-at–once" when used with multi-session recording.

All writing to optical media is done using the same laser that is used for reading, except at a higher power level. The laser changes the dye from transparent to opaque, or changes the metallic alloy in rewritable media from crystalline to amorphous or amorphous to crystalline. A change to the dye is a one-way irreversible change, whereas metallic alloy can be changed between its two states an average of 1,000 times.

When either Track-at-once or incremental writing is used, write-once media can be used multiple times. While theoretically it is possible to write over an area that was previously written to, drive firmware does not allow it, because it would result in an unreadable disc.

The primary use of rewritable media is with incremental writing; however, it can also be written using Track-at-once or Disc-at-once. With incremental writing, after the disc is formatted, you can replace a single packet anywhere on that disc. While two passes were originally required to erase and replace the original data, today a single-pass rewrite is possible, which allows existing information to be overwritten directly, fully replacing the existing data.

Recovering data from a rewriteable disc is not possible once a full erase has been performed, because there is no data written in inter-track spaces. A full erase consists of writing over the entire surface of the disc, leaving no traces of the previous data.

This is different from the quick erase operation, which leaves the data on the disc intact. An unmodified consumer drive cannot access the data on a quick-erased disc, but a modified drive can. (Instructions on how to modify a drive are located in Appendix A.) Follow all of the cautionary notes, as there are significant hazards to the user from laser exposure from such modified *drives*.

The technique for using a modified drive is to place a different disc in the drive that is as close to the subject disc as possible. In most cases, this different disc must be completely formatted for use with drag-and-drop writing software; however, you do not have to use the same software as was used for the subject disc. Place the formatted disc into the modified drive and use the magnetic spindle clamp to secure it. Press the drive tray button to open and close the tray, to inform the drive that a disc change has occurred. Wait until the disc has stopped spinning and then replace it with the subject disc. Be sure to put the magnetic spindle clamp back on the disc. The quick erased disc can then be accessed using CD/DVD Inspector (discussed in detail in Chapter 6.)

Logical File Systems

A file system is a mechanism for partitioning and allocating space to individual files, and provides the means to identify and access files. File Allocation Tables (FATs) and New Technology File Systems (NFTSes) are commonly used with PC hard drives. The purpose of a file system is to provide a generic mechanism to store files. These file systems do not define the contents of the files.

While it is possible to use FATs or NTFs for rewritable CDs and DVDs, they are not optimized for the unique characteristics of rewritable media; they are designed for hard drives and other media that does not have a penalty for repeatedly rewriting the same sectors. For manufactured and write-once discs, FAT or NTFSes are not suitable because of the read-only nature of the media.

The file systems that are used on CDs and DVDs are completely separate from those used on hard drives. When CD-ROMs were first released, there were some specialized discs that did not use any standard file system. These were mostly used in "vertical market" applications such as automobile repair and aircraft maintenance. The standard file system for CDs is called ISO9660 and was defined in 1989. The standard file system for DVD discs is called UDF, which is part of an ongoing standards process that began in 1996. Some software for writing DVD discs only writes UDF, while others write UDF and ISO9660. The actual specifications for DVD video and DVD audio discs require that you use a restricted form of UDF (version 1.01) and ISO9660 simultaneously.

Macintosh computers can use either ISO9660 discs or their own Hierarchical File System (HFS) and HFS+ format discs, which are the same file systems that are used on hard drives.

CDs were originally used for storing and playing audio. For this purpose, it was not necessary to name the songs and the technology at the same time, and did not provide reasonable ways for consumer electronics devices to display song titles. Therefore, data stored on audio CDs was not contained in a file system. There were only a collection of tracks pointed to by the TOC. This does not meet the earlier definition of a file system.

Beginning with Windows 95, Microsoft began showing tracks on audio CDs as if they were files on a disc; thus files were called *Track 1.cda*, *Track 2.cda*, and so on. These files are created by Windows and do not actually hold the audio information on the disc. Instead, they contain the control information that enables the Windows CD player application to play the track when double-clicked.

It is important to understand that there are no files or file systems on an audio disc. There is only the track data that the TOC provides pointers to. In 1997, Sony and Philips defined CD Text, which allows for storing textual information on audio CDs. However, even with this information, these audio discs do not contain a file system.

Philips CD Text information stores lyrics within the audio track information, using the same space that is used for Karaoke graphics. Sony CD Text information is stored in the lead-in area, and consists of the album, the artist, and the track names. Sony CD Text is commonly used on Sony discs and on home-created audio discs. Philips CD Text is not used today.

Another difference between hard drives and CD and DVD drives is the lack of partitions. When PC-based hard drives were first introduced and MS-DOS 2.0 was released, a partition table was defined to identify separate areas on the disk that could be used for different purposes. With CD media, a single CD contains single-purpose information.

Even without a partition table, it is possible to store multiple file systems on a single CD or DVD, because each file system has the ability to use different areas of the disc to point to the file system control information. Additionally, on a multi-session disc, each session can contain different file systems; however, incompatible structures such as Compact Disk - Read Only

Memory (CD-ROM) and Compact Disk Read-Only Memory/Extended Architecture (CD-ROM XA) cannot be present on the same disc.

The High Sierra Group (HSG) file system (defined between 1985 and 1987) was the first file system designed for CDs. The original Microsoft CD EXtension (MSCDEX) program supported both HSG and ISO9660 format discs.

ISO9660, which was adapted from HSG and adopted as a standard in 1988, was the first widely accepted CD file system intended to be used by any computer that a CD-ROM drive could attach to (e.g., all numeric data is represented in big-endian and little-endian forms that are compatible with Intel and Motorola processors). ISO9660 replaced HSG completely; no applications for creating HSG discs remain.

American Standard Code for Information Interchange (ASCII) 8-bit file names are allowed with ISO9660. However, for increased interoperability, file names are restricted to 8 characters with a 3-character extension (commonly know as "8 dot 3"), which mirrors many minicomputer and microcomputer operating systems (OSes) of the 1980s.

MSCDEX did support some non-Western languages (e.g., Japanese and Chinese), which was dependent on a technique called Multi-Byte Character Set (MBCS) and required inserting special "shift" codes into file names. This support was unique to Microsoft.

In 1995, ISO9660 was enhanced with the addition of the Joliet file system, which allows for 16-bit Unicode character file names with a maximum of 64 characters. The Joliet file system more readily supports character sets such as Japanese and Chinese, because each character is assigned a unique code. Support for Joliet and Unicode character file names is standardized and is present in different OSes other than Windows.

The process of defining the UDF file system was begun in 1996 and continues today. It supports Unicode character file names of up to 255 characters, and also supports files that are more than 4 GB in size (a limitation of ISO9660 and Joliet). Due to this limitation, UDF was the default choice for DVD media. Today, the first version of UDF is still used for DVD video and DVD audio discs.

The Macintosh platform has used the HFS file system since the inception of the Macintosh computer. During OS 8, the HFS+ file system was defined, which extends HFS by adding 255-character Unicode file names. The

Macintosh platform is unique in that the same file system is used for both hard drives and optical media. Although the HFS and HFS+ file systems are not ideal for CDs and DVDs, they make creating discs easier than PCs running Windows (see Table 5.1).

CD and DVD File Systems

...wing table indicates the types of file systems that are on

...orm	Long File Names?	Large Files (Over 4GB)	Typical Use
	N/A	N/A	Audio
	No	No	Early CD-ROM
	No	No	Data files
...lows	Yes	No	Data files, Unicode file names
Rock Ridge Linux	Yes	No	Data files
HFS Mac	No (31 chars)	Yes	Macintosh
HFS+ Mac	Yes	Yes	Macintosh, Unicode file names
UDF Windows/Mac	Yes	Yes	Windows, Macintosh, DVDs, Unicode file names

In the chart above, "All" refers to conventional PC-type computers as well as other systems, such as embedded control systems (e.g., HVAC, elevators, and so on) and UNIX- based minicomputers.

The following describes each of these file systems in more detail.

Red Book Audio

Red Book Audio is defined by the Philips/Sony "Red Book" standard (also known as IEC 908), and is the specification that all audio CDs follow. The first version of this standard appeared as part of the patent on CD technology in 1982. It does not define a file system as such, because audio CDs do not have files; they have music tracks.

In the original specification, tracks are identified by a number from 1 to 99. In 1997, Sony released an extension of this specification that defined a method by which text information could be stored on the disc to further identify tracks by name. This began to fulfill some of the requirements for a file system, but remains extremely primitive. Sony and other record labels use the Sony definition of CD Text, which is also supported by many home CD recording tools.

Each track contains subcode blocks of 588 stereo 16-bit audio samples, which are played at 44.1 KHz. Each subcode block represents 1/75th of a second of playing time.

Part of the original Red Book standard was Compact Disc + Graphics (CD+G), which was a way to display graphics on a television while playing a music CD. The graphics are low-resolution (240 × 320) and can only be drawn slowly, but are suitable for displaying Karaoke lyrics on a screen while music is playing. This information is stored in the R through W subchannels associated with the audio samples. For each subcode block of 588 samples, there is a total of 96 bytes of graphics information.

In 1997, Philips defined an extension to this specification to store textual information on the disc. This information is placed in the same R through W subchannels that are used for CD+G graphics and has the same limitations; only approximately 30 MB of information can be stored with audio.

HSG

The High Sierra Group formulated the first definition of a file system for CD-ROM discs, which was viewed as a major step for standardization, because previously there was no standard file system, which meant that CD-ROMs could not be produced for multiple computer platforms.

The original support for CD-ROMs for the Microsoft Disk Operating System (MS-DOS) included support for both HSG and ISO9660 discs. HSG is still supported by Windows 95; however, it is very difficult to find a HSG format CD-ROM today.

ISO9660

ISO9660 was adapted from the original HSG definition in 1988, and adopted as an international standard under the International Standards Organization (ISO). The principle differences between the two are the inclusion of time zone information and additional identification fields. The European Computer Manufacturer's Association (ECMA) standard 119 is an exact copy of the ISO9660 standard; however, unlike the ISO9660 standard, it can be downloaded from the ECMA Web site for free at www.ecma-international.org.

ISO9660 is currently the most widely supported file system interchange standard that is supported by most computers and other systems with CD drives (e.g., an elevator control system with a CD-ROM drive probably supports the ISO9660 file system). This is generally true even when a proprietary or real-time operating system is being used. All personal computers since 1990 support the ISO9660 file system.

The ISO9660 file system is designed for the 8-bit ASCII character set. Some attempts have been made by Microsoft and others to support the use of alternate character sets, but this is not part of the standard and has differing levels of success when used in non–Microsoft environments.

There are only three structures that define the ISO9660 file system: the *volume descriptor*, the *path table*, and the *directory entry*. The volume descriptor must be located at the 16th sector from the beginning of the track and points to all other structures. This means that for the first session on a disc starting at sector zero, the volume descriptor is located in sector 16. For a session starting at sector 40526, the volume descriptor is located at sector 40526 + 16 (or 40542).

The volume descriptor contains many important data items (e.g., the date the disc was created, and an area that can be filled in with an application identifier). If there are hex digits 01 43 44 30 30 31 01 in the contents of sector 16, there is an ISO9660 file system on the disc. If the ISO9660 file system is present, then for 17 characters at offset 814 (32E in hex) the creation date of the disc is present in the form of:

- 4-digit year

- 2-digit month

- 2-digit day of month

- 2-digit hour of day

- 2-digit minute

- 2-digit seconds

- 1-digit tenths of a second

- 1-digit hundredths of a second

- 1-byte time zone offset from Greenwich Mean Time (GMT) in 15-minute increments. This can be positive or negative.

This time is always "local," reflecting the time zone that was set on the computer when the disc was created.

Offset 575 (23F in hex) for 128 bytes is the application identifier. Many CD writing applications insert information here to indicate the software that created the disc.

The root directory consists of a list of directory entries concatenated together in one or more sectors. The beginning sector number is at offset 160 (A0 in hex) in the volume descriptor as a 4-byte integer in little-endian format. The length of the root directory is at offset 168 (A8 in hex) as a 4-byte integer in little-endian format.

By convention, the ISO9660 file names are limited to 8 characters, with a 3-character extension separated by a period. Directory names are not allowed to have extensions. Not all writing software respects these limits and can extend the file name to as many as 212 characters. File names only use upper-case letters, numbers, and a small number of special characters. Again, not all writing software respects this, so it is not unusual to find an ISO9660 file system with lower-case letters in the file names.

ISO9660 files must be less than 4 GB in size; however, this is often restricted by writing software of less than 2 GB. This limitation of ISO9660 restricts its usefulness for DVD media. This is not a factor for DVD video and DVD audio discs, because the maximum file size is limited to less than 1 GB for those formats.

The directory entries for ISO9660 contain the last time the file was modified. Because the ISO9660 file system is not intended to be updated, the creation time of the file on the disc is always equal to the last modified time and no last access time is recorded.

Until the advent of drag-and-drop recording, it was unusual to find an ISO9660 file system where all of the files were not stored in a single contiguous range of sectors. While this is provided for in the ISO9660 specification, it is rarely done. Currently, only drag-and-drop writing software creates fragmented files in ISO9660 file systems.

This is significant for forensic examiners because, even in cases where part of a disc has been destroyed, your ability to recover the contents of the remainder of the disc is excellent. Even without a directory, just examining the disc for file headers on sector boundaries is usually good enough to recover most common file types (e.g., Microsoft Office documents, digital photographs, and others). Using some type of "data carving" tool on the content of the disc should be sufficient for this.

Joliet

Joliet is an extension of ISO9660 that was defined by Microsoft for the Windows 95 operating system and uses a parallel directory structure to enable both standard ASCII file names and longer Unicode file names.

The definition of the Joliet extension specifically addresses using up to 64-character Unicode file names and removing the restriction on a maximum directory depth of eight levels. Some writing software extends this further to allow the file name to be over 100 characters in length, which appears to function correctly with current versions of Windows.

The volume descriptor for Joliet is required to be in a sector following an ISO9660 volume descriptor in sector 16; usually in sector 17, 18, or 19. This volume descriptor contains 8 bytes of the sector containing the hex values 02 43 44 30 30 31 01. The same fields that are defined for the ISO9660 volume descriptor in sector 16 are also found in this descriptor. The application identifier consisting of 64 16-bit Unicode characters is located at offset 575 (23F in hex) for 128 bytes. This content can be considerably different from that in the ISO9660 volume descriptor.

Directory entries that are used for Joliet and ISO9660 are almost identical. The only difference is that the file names are composed of 16–bit Unicode characters rather than 8–bit ASCII characters.

The number of files and the content of the files are usually identical between the ISO9660 and Joliet directory structures. Most writing software does not support having different content, only changing the content of the file names to correspond to the requirements for the different file systems. However, this is not always the case. It is easy to create a disc with different content using freely available tools such as the "mkisofs" program. The result is that it is important to treat the separate directory structures as separate file systems.

Discs using the Joliet file system have characteristics similar to the ISO9660 file system discs, in that the files are almost always contiguous. This means that even without directory information available, it is possible to recover all of the files from those areas of the disc that are readable.

Rock Ridge

In 1993, the System Use Sharing Protocol (SUSP) was defined for supporting extensions to ISO9660. A specific implementation of this protocol is "Rock Ridge," which deals specifically with extending the ISO9660 file system to support Portable Operating System Interface (POSIX) attributes (e.g., user and group ID, permissions, and symbolic links for files). Rock Ridge also supports unlimited length file names.

Rock Ridge is not commonly used today, because only Linux is considered to be a mainstream POSIX-compliant OS. Other POSIX-compliant OSes are Solaris from Sun Microsystems, Advanced IBM UNIX (AIX) from IBM, and Hewlett-Packard UNIX (HPUX) from Hewlett-Packard. Windows NT used to have a POSIX subsystem, but it has been discontinued. The mkisofs program and its derivatives are the usual source of discs used with Rock Ridge extensions. Commercial UNIX systems also use Rock Ridge extensions, and have disc-writing software specific to individual manufacturers.

SUSP extensions are identified by two-letter codes, and each file or directory can have as many extensions as needed. The most common Rock Ridge SUSP extensions are NM (NaMe) and PX (PosiX). A complete list of defined SUSP extension codes is shown below.

SUSP and Rock Ridge extensions are ignored by Windows and Macintosh OSes. The underlying Berkeley Software Distribution (BSD) core of OS X may be capable of using Rock Ridge extensions.

Discs with Rock Ridge extensions are mastered by software, which writes the files in a contiguous manner. Therefore, without a valid directory, it is possible to separate the files based on header information.

Each SUSP extension has a two-character identifier followed by the length of the extension. The extension codes and their meanings are shown below.

Table 2.2 SUSP Extensions and Their Meanings

Code	Description
AA	Apple extensions
CE	Continuation of extension data
CL	Child link
ER	Extension reference
ES	Extension selector
NM	Alternate (long) name
PD	Padding field
PL	Parent link
PN	POSIX device number
PX	POSIX file attributes
RE	Relocated directory
SF	File data in sparse format
SL	Symbolic link
SP	SUSP indicator
ST	SUSP terminator
TF	Additional POSIX time stamps

If you are manually examining an ISO9660 directory structure with Rock Ridge extensions, the most important extension types are CE, NM, and TF. CE extensions are not usually present, but should be recognized because they point to continued data in other sectors. The format of a CE extension is:

CE	28	1	Sector number	Offset	Length

The sector number, offset, and length are all expressed as combined big-endian and little-endian values with the little-endian value first. Each occupies 8 bytes; thus a value of 100 appears (in hex) as 64 00 00 00 00 00 00 64.

The format of an NM extension is:

NM	Len	1	Flags	Name characters

If bit 0 (hex 01) is present in the flags, the name is continued into the next NM extension entry. Bits 1 and 2 (hex 02 and 04) indicate that the name applies to the "." and ".." directory entries, respectively. The remainder of the flags are either reserved or not significant.

The format of a TF extension is:

TF	Len	1	Flags	Timestamp data ...

The flags specify what timestamps are present (see Table 2.3).

Table 2.3 Timestamp Types

Bit	Timestamp
0	Creation timestamp is present
1	Modification timestamp is present
2	Last access timestamp is present
3	Attribute change timestamp is present
4	Backup timestamp is present
5	Expiration timestamp is present
6	Effective timestamp is present
7	Timestamps are in long (17-byte) form

The timestamps are recorded in the extension in the order that they are listed in when multiple flags are set. If bit 7 of the flags is not set, the short 7-byte form of the timestamp is present (i.e., YMDHMSZ [Year, month, day, hour, minute, second, zone]) in binary. If bit 7 of the flags is set, the long 17-byte form of the timestamp is present, which is YYYYMMDDHH-MMSSTHZ in character form.

For forensic purposes, it can be assumed that if Apple extensions are not present, a Macintosh user program did not create the disc. An exception to this is some OS X programs that operate at the "native" BSD level. In any event, these would not be considered ordinary Macintosh user programs.

The description of the SUSP extensions is in the Institute of Electrical & Electronics Engineers (IEEE) P1281 SUSP document (see SUSP112.doc). Rock Ridge extensions are documented in the IEEE P1282 Rock Ridge Interchange Protocol (RRIP) document (see RRIP112.doc). Both of these documents can be downloaded from the InfinaDyne public File Transfer Protocol (FTP) server at ftp://ftp.cdrprod.com/pub.

UDF

The Optical Storage Technology Association manages the development of the UDF standard, which is an ongoing process that began with the release of the UDF 1.0 specification in 1995. This specification is an outgrowth of the development of ISO-13346 standard.

The only PC file system for optical media that is completely updatable is UDF. Even on write-once media, the deletion of files is supported. This is a significant difference from the other file systems previously described.

UDF is part of the definition of the DVD video and DVD audio disc formats. It is also used in digital cameras that record directly to CDs, stand-alone DVD recorders, and DVD camcorders. The first consumer exposure to UDF was in 1997 with the release of CDRW drives that could write incrementally using a technique called *packet writing*. Unfortunately, in the beginning, much of the UDF writing software did not have good error recovery, which led to a negative impression of packet writing in general. The situation has not improved much since 1997. It is common to find UDF discs that have "lost" files or directories and UDF discs with serious logical errors in the file system. Often, these discs are unreadable using the original software and Microsoft Windows.

UDF file systems can utilize either 8- or 16-bit characters for file names, thus reducing space requirements when ASCII file names are used. Multi-byte characters are not used with UDF; therefore, there can be compatibility issues with Microsoft Windows versions 95, 98, 98SE, and ME.

File names can be up to 255 characters regardless of the character set being used. There is also no limitation on the depth of the directory structure.

However, if an excessively deep directory structure is used, there are serious performance issues on optical media.

Files can have multiple timestamps under UDF (e.g., a full set of created, last modified, and last accessed times are available). For rewritable media, this shows an accurate last access time to each file. The last access time is generally not updated for write-once media, but it can be depending on the writing software.

There are many different versions of UDF and not all of them are compatible with each other (e.g., the version required for DVD video discs is 1.02, which limits files to a maximum of 1 GB in size. This limitation does not exist with other versions of UDF, which limits files to $2^{64}-1$ bytes in length. Other aspects of UDF change between versions; therefore, it is important to either use software that is independent of the specific UDF version, or to have the correct reader software installed on your computer.

Files can be fragmented for all versions other than 1.02. This means that the content of the file can be placed in more than a single range of sectors on the disc. This is important for forensic users, because nearly all CDs written using other file systems have contiguous files.

UDF uses a complicated set of descriptors to identify the volume and point to the information that defines it. The "anchor" for a UDF volume is a sector known as the Anchor Volume Descriptor Pointe (AVDP). This sector is identified by bytes 02 00 in the first 2 bytes; the last 4 bytes have a little-endian integer equal to the sector number. The AVDP can be found in any of a number of areas on a disc:

- Sector 256
- Sector 512
- Last written sector on the disc
- Last written sector on disc 256
- 256 sectors after the beginning of the track
- 512 sectors after the beginning of the track

Once the AVDP has been found, there is a sector number and length (in bytes) of the volume recognition sequence at offset 16 (10 hex). This serves the same purpose as sector 16 on an ISO9660 file system and describes the file system. There are several important values in this area that should be formatted using a forensic disc examination tool:

- The date and time when the disc was initially created. This is not the date and time when the content was written to the disc, because most UDF writing software supports incrementally adding files to the disc after it has been formatted.

- An application identifier that says which application created this UDF file system.

- The name given to the disc when it was formatted. This may be different from what is displayed by Microsoft Windows, and may reflect a different intent for the disc than the more up-to-date name shown by Windows.

For forensic examiners, it must be clarified that while files can be deleted on write-once media, the actual file is not deleted; it just drops from the directory structure. Given the potentially fragmented nature of files, it is not a simple matter to use a data-carving tool to locate deleted files on the disc. Forensic software that supports the UDF file system must be capable of searching out these deleted files and re-establishing them for the user to access.

On rewritable media, it is possible for the writing software to reuse space originally occupied by a deleted file. However, there is a very low limit as to the number of times a particular spot on rewritable media can be updated; usually an average of 1,000 times. This means that if a user keeps updating a file (i.e., writing to it, deleting it, and writing to it again) it would quickly wear out that area on the disc. The result is that it is unusual to find UDF writing software that will reuse deleted space on a disc before all of the never-used space has been used once. This serves to maximize media life, and is an important consideration for the authors of disc writing software. For forensic examiners, this is a significant advantage over hard drives, because until the user fills the entire disc, nothing will be overwritten and the entire history of content of the disc is available.

It is rare to find contiguously recorded files on UDF discs. Just examining file headers generally will not produce valid, intact files. You must use a forensic tool specifically designed to handle UDF discs, especially when there are problems with the file system. If you do not use such a tool, you are going to have a difficult time processing discs using the UDF file system.

HFS

This file system was originally incorporated into the Apple Macintosh OS version 2.1 in September 1985, and is one of the few cases where a hard drive file system was implemented for optical media directly.

The original way to create an HFS CD-ROM disc in the late 1980s and early 1990s was to copy the data to an external hard drive that was between 500 MB and 1 GB in size, being careful not to exceed the capacity of a CD (650 MB at the time.) This disk was set up with the exact content that the CD-ROM had. The hard drive content was then copied to tape for mastering the CD-ROM. This technique was replaced by Macintosh-specific CD mastering software, the first of which was Asarte Toast.

HFS supports 31-character file names using the ASCII character set. No provision for characters outside of the ASCII character set exists. HFS has been updated with HFS+, which provides for longer, non-ASCII file names.

Since this is a hard drive file system, files can be fragmented. Depending on how the disc was created, the amount of fragmentation can be considerable. In general, however, if the disc is mastered in the usual way, there will be no fragmentation on the disc.

Even though this file system was defined in 1985, it was designed to manage large files that exceed 4 GB; therefore, there is no limitation on using this file system for DVD media or larger capacity discs.

Each file has a complete set of created, last modified, and last accessed timestamps. These times are expressed as big-endian binary integers in number of seconds.

Unfortunately, HFS is not well suited for optical media. It has the fixed knowledge of 512-byte sectors built into it. This means that each CD or DVD sector contains four 512-byte HFS sectors. Additionally, file allocations are done based on allocation blocks, which can be any power-of-2 multiple of 512. CD and DVD media 2,048-byte allocation blocks are possible, but 4,096 and 8,192 are common. Due to the multiple sector and block sizes, it is difficult to examine an HFS file system with just a hex display of the sectors.

HFS has a limited amount of text information in the file system control structures. The name of the disc is contained in the Master Directory Block, which is found in sector 0. Also in sector zero are the Partition Maps, which contain the name of the software that created the disc.

It is unusual but possible to find a multi-session HFS disc. The Macintosh system does not treat multi-session discs the same way that Microsoft Windows does; therefore, the usefulness of such discs is limited. The most common HFS discs in the USA are AOL discs that contain ISO9660, Joliet, and HFS file systems. All of these are contained in track 1 of the disc.

Some forensic software can process HFS CDs and DVDs. Since the software for creating discs that have only the HFS file system on them is not common for the Microsoft Windows or Linux environments, these discs are generally restricted to users with Macintosh computers.

HFS+

The HFS file system was extended to HFS+ with the introduction of OS 8.1 in 1997. HFS+ file names extend to a maximum of 255 characters and stores them in Unicode rather than 8-bit ASCII characters.

HFS+ moves the name of the disc from the Master Directory Block to the top level of the directory tree. Unfortunately, this is not easy to find; therefore, determining this without software to interpret the HFS+ file system is not practical.

El Torito

The El Torito standard does not describe a file system but it closely interacts with file systems. El Torito was originally defined as a way for computers (not just PC-type machines) to be able to boot from CD-ROM discs. Prior to this, booting was restricted to floppy diskettes and hard drives.

What El Torito does is define a set of control structures so that it is possible to have a single CD-ROM disc bootable on many different hardware architectures. This means that a single disc can be booted on both PCs and

Macintosh computers as long as all of the required information is present for both platforms.

The El Torito standard requires the use of sector 17 to contain the boot volume descriptor, which points to the booting catalog, which in turn points to bootable images. These images can be emulated floppy diskettes, emulated hard drives, or a memory image.

Each entry in the booting catalog refers to a specific hardware platform (e.g., Intel x86, PowerPC, Macintosh, and so on). For each platform, there can be one or more bootable entries as well as additional non-bootable entries. The non-bootable entries can, in theory, be used as a primitive file system by the bootable programs.

A bootable entry then identifies the emulated media type, the starting sector of the image, and the number of sectors in the image. This is then used when booting from the emulated image in the same way a real floppy diskette or hard drive is booted. Non-emulated entries are handled differently and do not make a portion of the disc appear. Instead, the entire image is brought into memory.

The result is that it is relatively easy to take a bootable floppy diskette, transfer the files to a CD-R, and be able to boot from the copy on the CD-R. Many different writing programs assist with doing this, and provide the ability to read in a floppy diskette and place it into a disc image. Because it is common to find computers without floppy disk drives, this can be extremely helpful.

Space Allocation by CD and DVD File Systems

One of the more basic jobs of a file system is to allocate space on the media. On hard drives, this is often accomplished with a bit map or other allocation table, because the information must be updated. On CDs and DVDs, the requirements are different because the media is read-only.

For the FAT and NTFS file systems space allocation is managed on a cluster basis, a cluster being a group of sectors. This helps to minimize fragmentation. This is not necessary on read-only file systems, because there is no updating of files.

Another difference is that hard drive sectors are 512 bytes in length and CD and DVD sectors are 2,048 bytes in length. This means there is already a grouping equivalent to four hard drive sectors when allocating CD and DVD space.

ISO9660 does not define any space allocation information, because it is by definition a read-only file system. Files are stored contiguously on the disc and cannot be modified. Space for files and the file system control information are allocated on a sector-by-sector basis when the file system is created.

Joliet and Rock Ridge are extensions to ISO9660 and do not change how space is allocated.

UDF can be the same as ISO9660 when the file system is read-only, or it can require some degree of space allocation information when a rewritable disc is used. In both cases, UDF allocates space on a sector-by-sector basis. This can result in fragmentation but usually does not because of how space on rewritable media is used. In general, the entire disc is written to before any deleted space is "reclaimed" for use. The reason for this is that rewritable discs have a limited number of write/erase/write cycles for each sector. Therefore, it is optimal to spread the write/erase/write cycles over the entire surface of the disc.

It should be noted that rewritable media is not generally rewritten at the sector level but at the packet level. A packet is a group of sectors just like a cluster, but is not used for allocation purposes by any of the drag-and-drop file systems.

HFS and HFS+ use a completely different strategy for allocating space, which is to be expected because it was first defined for hard drive use. HFS knows that all sectors are 512 bytes and these are grouped into allocation blocks. Each allocation block consists of a power-of-two number of sectors (usually 2K, 4K or 8K) to accommodate the 2K CD sector size. There is an allocation block bit map that represents free and allocated allocation blocks on the media.

The most common way to construct HFS and HFS+ file systems for CDs and DVDs is to build the file system when the disc is mastered. At the beginning of CD recording, there were no CD-specific tools for creating HFS file systems; therefore, the procedure was to create the file system on a hard drive, test it completely, and then write it to a CD. It was possible then for the file system to contain fragmented files, free space, and other hard drive artifacts.

Disc Accessibility Problems

Many issues can develop that make files, subdirectories, and entire discs inaccessible to the user. This occurs frequently with UDF discs, but can happen with any file system when updating is supported. From a forensic standpoint, this is useful because, as files become inaccessible, they are left in their original state and not altered or deleted later. This can give the forensic examiner a window into the previous state of the data on the disc. CD/DVD Inspector is often able to automatically recover such files through examining alternative sources of information and through searching the disc. It is important to understand when this is and is not possible.

ISO9660/Joliet File Systems

Because of the simplicity of these file systems, it is unusual to find a disc with a damaged file system that prevents access to one or more files. However, discs such as these can have readability issues that prevent critical parts of a disc from being read, which can mean the disc is inaccessible under normal circumstances.

CD/DVD Inspector can usually bypass these types of problems through a combination of using alternative sources of information and by searching (e.g., Microsoft Windows normally uses the path table to locate directories. If the path table is not readable, Windows cannot access the disc. CD/DVD Inspector can navigate through the directory structure by using information in the directory, not referencing the path table. Therefore, the disc is completely accessible under CD/DVD Inspector.

A forensics examiner may encounter a disc with a large amount of space that is unaccounted for by the Disc Map tool. With ISO9660 and, optionally, Joliet file systems on this disc, is a clear indication that either there is another file system (such as HFS or HFS+) present on the disc that may not be readable, or possibly that the disc was created using the mkisofs tool. In the latter case, it is possible that there were files added to the disc that are not represented in the directory. Additional work is required to gain access to that data using the Copy Sectors or Sector Display tool.

UDF File Systems

UDF file systems are more complicated than ISO9660 or Joliet. Because of this complexity, these file systems are often logically corrupted or broken in such a manner as to lose one or more files or even an entire directory. This usually happens because of software errors, but can also be caused by errors when updating rewritable sectors on a disc.

Most of the software for writing discs using the UDF file system is focused on creating updatable discs on either write-once or rewritable media. The maturity of this software is approximately that of the FAT file system when the IBM PC AT was released in 1985. There were few tools for the average user to recover from errors on floppy diskettes and file system errors were common. Today, there are only a small number of tools for repairing or recovering files from damaged UDF file systems, and they have not achieved wide market penetration.

For the forensic examiner, the problems with UDF file systems are significant. When files are "lost," the user often does not realize that there is an intact copy of the file on the media that can be recovered. This can be important when other copies of the file have been deleted from the disc. There are very few tools that allow you to regain access to lost files, and only CD/DVD Inspector couples this capability with other forensic features.

Other File Systems

Logical damage to other file systems is extremely rare. Because these other file systems are less frequently encountered, it is almost certain that an examiner will never encounter problems with HFS and other file systems.

PV27

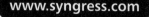

Chapter 3

Forensic Binary Images

Typically, a binary image of a hard drive is immediately created when a forensic examination begins. This is done to stem the possibility of the hard drive contents being altered during examination. As long as this binary image is an exact bit-for-bit copy of the original hard drive, it can be used as a substitute for the hard drive itself.

There are many tools that can be used to create a binary image file from a hard drive. Copying sectors from the hard drive to some other type of media (including another hard drive) is all that is required. It is common practice to perform validations on a hard drive and its image contents to make sure that they are identical. Using a hash value such as Message Digest 5 (MD5) or Secure Hashing Algorithm 1 (SHA1) can validate that this has been done.

This has also been attempted with Compact Disc (CD) and Digital Versatile Disc (DVD) media, often using the same image file format. There are those in the forensic community that believe it is possible to create a binary image file that is identical to those created with hard drives; however, this is overlooks several important aspects of how such discs are written.

Compact Disk - Read Only Memory (CD-ROM) data discs and commercially produced DVDs can be imaged easily, because they contain one type of sector that begins with sector zero and extends to an endpoint on the disc.

User-recorded music discs are commonly based on the Red Book audio and can be imaged fairly easily. User-recorded data discs are either multi-session or written with drag-and-drop software. If these types of discs involve multiple tracks, mixing the types of sectors is possible.

User-written multimedia discs can involve multiple types of sectors in a single track (e.g., it is common to mix XA Mode 2 Form 1 sectors with 2,048 bytes per sector with XA Mode 2 Form 2 sectors with 2,352 bytes per sector).

Many recording applications use multiple tracks where, unlike manufactured discs, the area between tracks is not readable. This presents a problem when treating a CD as a contiguous span of sectors. The Table of Contents (TOC) for a disc provides an index into the different tracks. There is no corresponding data for hard drives, which only contain the sector data.

The disc TOC also provides an indication of whether the track contains Red Book audio or data sectors, which is required to properly read the contents of the disc. Determining what types of sectors are present in a track can be accomplished by examining other control information for the sectors or by examining the file system.

DVDs only have a single type of sector; however, multi-session recording is possible. The index of border zones for a disc is similar to the TOC for a CD, and is required to properly process a multi-session DVD.

In order to construct a binary image of a CD or DVD, each track sector must be on the disc along with an index indicating the type of track (for CDs) and the original starting location of the track.

CD/DVD Inspector 3.0 allows you to make a binary image file of any disc, which can later be run against that image file without the disc being present. While the image file format is specific to CD/DVD Inspector, coordination with other tools is expected.

Reproducing Forensic Images

In the case of hard drives, a forensic binary image of a drive is reproducible. As long as the contents have not been altered, every image taken of a hard drive is identical as long as the scope is limited to hard drives, flash memory, and other magnetic media.

This is not always the case with CD and DVD media, where reading from a disc with different drives can produce different results. This can result from different implementations of error correction strategy in the drive firmware and the hardware controlling the laser and optics.

With some drives, it is possible to obtain non-reproducible results from successive imaging, which can be observed with some Pioneer DVD writers on packet-written Compact Disc Recordable (CD-R) discs.

Assuming that it will always be possible to create identical forensic images from reading CD or DVD media is problematic, and calls into question evidence or forensic lab procedures should the MD5 or SHA1 hash value of such images not match. It is strongly recommended that you not attempt to compare forensic images or forensic image hash values unless the examiner is fully aware that mismatches can be "normal."

A recommended procedure is to either work from the original media or to work from a single image file. When working with the original media, use proper procedures to avoid contamination by software that does not belong on a forensic computer. When working from an image file, use before and after hash values to verify that the image has not been altered. Do not attempt to re-image the media and compare images or image hash values.

Chapter 4

Collecting CD and DVD Evidence

The following sections address the number of specific considerations needed for handling and collecting Compact Disc (CD) and Digital Versatile Disc (DVD) evidence. These sections also describe how to recognize CD and DVD media, how to protect yourself while collecting this evidence, and what precautions need to be followed in order to preserve it.

Recognizing CD and DVD Media

A common belief is that it is not necessary to collect manufactured discs as evidence because such evidence can only be stored on recordable discs. If it was possible to correctly identify manufactured discs and recordable discs simply by looking at them, manufactured discs might be able to be excluded. Unfortunately, this is not the case. If it is necessary to limit the number of discs being collected and time does not permit any analysis of the discs, it may be necessary to select discs based on their appearance. This should be avoided whenever possible. Discs appearing to be manufactured that in reality have been recorded are not uncommon.

As part of the InfinaDyne CD and DVD Forensics class, students are given a disc that has been created with a clear laser-printed color label and that intentionally looks like an America Online (AOL) disc. If inserted into a computer with Windows, this disc behaves like an AOL distribution disc. Depending on the types of cases you work on, it is possible that you will encounter such a subterfuge. The question is not whether you were able to recognize the disc as recordable, but whether or not a colleague with less experience will be able to make that identification.

It is strongly recommended that you collect every disc potentially containing evidence. It is common for a case to be made on the content of a single CD or a DVD.

Collection Considerations

As mentioned previously, CDs are resistant to scratches on the data side, but the top surface can be easily damaged. If the top surface of a disc is scratched, there is no way to recover the data and the disc is rendered unreadable. Touch only the edges of the outer rim and center hole; to avoid contamination, do not touch the flat surfaces.

CDs are manufactured with a "stacking ring" near the center of the disc, which serves to keep the bottom of one disc away from the top of the disc below it when stacked on a spindle. The lacquer on the top of a disc can become sticky even under ordinary environmental conditions, and is exacerbated in humidity. Without the alignment provided by a spindle, if two discs are placed on top of each other, the lacquer may stick to the bottom of the disc placed on top of the other disc; separating the discs can also remove the reflector from the bottom disc, which can lead to a loss of evidence.

Fastening discs together with rubber bands or tape can also destroy them. Rubber bands bend the edges of discs, thus deforming them. Tape can adhere to the top surface of a disc and, when removed, also remove the reflector from the disc. Some types of plastic wrap can also adhere to the lacquer and remove the reflector. For these reasons, it is not recommended to wrap discs in plastic or tape, and they should not be secured by rubber bands.

Ideally, discs should be stacked on spindles similar to those used by manufactureres. This is the best way to package discs, but may not always be practical. If the discs cannot be stacked on a spindle, they should be arranged in a stack in a paper bag and the bag taped to hold the discs in place. Properly stacking discs and taking advantage of the stacked ring will also preserve fingerprint evidence.

NOTE

If you are given a bagful of discs or discs taped together, it is not necessarily a complete loss. Use extreme care in separating the discs. Do not try to remove tape applied to the top surface of a disc—instead, trim it. Discs that are warped can be "flattened out" with a combination of weight and time.

Marking Discs

As mentioned previously, discs are not impervious objects; both polycarbonate and the lacquer coating can absorb humidity and other chemicals. It is recommended that you use water-based markers for writing on discs because of the following:

- Ballpoint and rollerball pens will damage the data area of a disc.

- Sharpie brand markers are not rated as safe by their manufacturer because they are alcohol-based. The manufacturer says that problems have not been reported, but for evidence discs they should not be trusted, especially for writing in the data area of a disc. They may be safe for use in the clamping ring area of a disc.

- Markers that are solvent-based will dissolve the lacquer coating and destroy the reflector beneath it. Such markers can also damage the polycarbonate. While it is generally safe to use solvent-based markers in the clamping ring area of a disc, it is not recommended.

- Other markers that are not clearly identified as solvent-based or water-based can pose a substantial risk to the data area of a disc. If there is a solvent odor when the cap is removed, the marker should not be used on evidence discs.

- Labels can be applied to discs; however, if the adhesive is not the right type for CD use, a label can peel off of the disc, which will interfere with the disc when it is being used. Removing such a label would likely peel the reflector from the disc, thus destroying it. The adhesive may also interact with the lacquer and possibly destroy the reflector.

It is generally safe to write anywhere on the top surface of a disc with water-based markers (sold as water-based markers and as specially labeled "CD Markers"). Avoid writing in any area that already contains markings. Writing using a water-based marker in the clamping ring area of the disc is always safe. Using labels that are placed in the clamping ring area is also safe, and will not affect the balance of the disc. These labels are commonly available and can be laser printed.

Transporting Discs

As mentioned previously, discs are sensitive to excessive heat (over 49C/120F) and ultraviolet (UV) light. Care must be taken to keep discs out of the sun and out of a potentially hot car interior. Additionally, prevent discs from receiving excessive vibration, as it can erode the surface of a disc if it comes into contact with other objects.

Documenting and Fingerprinting Discs

At some point, it may be necessary to collect evidence (e.g., fingerprints and surface markings) from a disc. This should be done before attempting to access the data on the disc because it may be necessary to clean the disc before it can be read properly. Photographing the surface of a disc to document surface markings is recommended, because this cleaning can compromise the surface markings.

The environment inside a CD or DVD drive is not conducive to successfully processing fingerprints after the disc has spent considerable time being rotated at high speed in the hot interior of the drive. This means that fingerprints must be processed in such a manner as to not destroy the readability of the disc. Developing fingerprints with powder and photographing the results is compatible with this objective. It is possible to remove residual powder from a disc completely, even if this requires washing the disc in plain water.

We do not recommend using any cyanoacrylate (superglue) processes, which would likely leave artifacts on a disc and affect readability. Shielding the bottom of the disc can eliminate these artifacts, but excludes processing the bottom of the disc. Any use of tape-based fingerprinting processes will destroy discs. If portions of the reflector have been removed by lift tape, it is not possible to recover the information that was written on that area of the disc and may prevent the disc from being read.

How to document a disc depends on the specific procedures for your laboratory. It is not recommended that you place rectangular labels on individual discs, because they can cause serious out-of-balance conditions in modern high-speed drives. If labeling individual discs is required, we recommend using "hub labels," which are small circles that go in the center of the disc covering the clamping ring. Hub labels are specifically designed for use on CDs and DVDs, and are compatible with the high-speed drive environment. Most other label adhesives are not compatible with this environment, and can result in the label peeling off inside the drive.

Another step is to take a digital photograph of the label side of a disc; markings that are placed by the person writing the disc or the user of the disc can be useful as evidence. Some automated systems for processing discs take a photograph of each disc as it is being processed. Documenting the label of every disc can be a significant task when processing large numbers of discs, but this can be valuable especially if the markings are damaged or removed during cleaning.

After fingerprint processing and the proper documentation of any evidence on the disc, light cleaning can be done to remove residual materials and/or contaminants (e.g., powder from fingerprint processing and substances such as cocaine) from the surface of the disc. This should be done without using any cleaning solvents.

Officer Safety

CDs and DVDs are often found in areas where there are biological, chemical, and drug hazards. Polycarbonate and lacquer both absorb water and other substances, which means it is not safe to handle discs that have been exposed to hazardous substances.

It is important to note that such contamination is unlikely to affect the readability or usability of a disc. Powders and liquids can contaminate discs in ways that make it hazardous for an officer to collect that disc. However, when the source of contamination is carefully removed in the laboratory, the result is a perfectly readable disc. Be aware that when put into a drive, any contaminated disc will be spun off the disc and flung into the air.

It is not recommended that discs be cleaned in the field. While special handling considerations may apply to contaminated discs, evidence can be destroyed by improperly cleaning a disc; fingerprints and other trace evidence can also be lost.

When polycarbonate fractures, sharp fragments can be produced. Broken discs can be a significant hazard, because of sharp edges and because of tiny sharp fragments no larger than a grain of sand. Handling cracked or broken discs can result in a serious hazard if you cut yourself on broken discs and the risk is magnified by other contaminants in the collection environment.

Chapter 5

Preparing for Disc Examination

In order to conduct an examination of the digital evidence on Compact Disc (CD) or Digital Versatile Disc (DVD) media, you must have the proper hardware, software, and workstation.

Forensic Hardware

It is recommended that you have two separate devices: a reliable Compact Disc - ReWritable (CD-RW) drive and a recent DVD writer that can read both DVD+ and DVD– media. Recent writers should also be compatible with Digital Versatile Disc Plus Recordable (DVD+R) DL (dual layer) media.

While it may seem counterintuitive, you must use a writer-type device, because reader devices do not access open sessions on discs. This means that any incomplete drag-and-drop discs would not be accessible with a reader. Worse still, a multi-session disc that has been closed at least once and written to again with drag-and-drop writing software, will only show the finalized content; anything added after that would be invisible.

It is not necessary to use a write-blocker device with a CD or DVD writer, because writing software that functions without prompting is not present in Microsoft Windows. Before it will write to a disc, the CD writing capability present in Windows XP requires considerable effort on the part of the user. This writing capability also does not utilize rewritable media, such as CD-RW discs, making it difficult to write to a CD or DVD without significant user interaction.

If necessary, you can disable the Windows XP CD writing capability by opening the "My Computer" window and right-clicking the drive to be changed. Choose the properties and the select the **Recording** tab and uncheck the "Enable CD recording on this drive" option. (Microsoft has indicated that they will be incorporating the ability to use rewritable CD and DVD media into the Windows Vista program. If this happens, it may not be as easy to disable writing.) Hardware and software write-blocking tools are available to prevent modification to evidence discs. (For more information contact InfinaDyne.)

We have found that the Plextor 12x writers are the most capable for reading problematic CD-R and CD-RW discs. These drives are no longer available from Plextor, but can still be obtained on eBay. Our recommendations for reading DVD media are Plextor and Pioneer.

Using the Pioneer Axx and 1xx series of DVD writers for processing CD-R media, we saw non-reproducible Message Digest 5 (MD5) hash signatures when reading Compact Disc Recordable (CD-R) discs written with DirectCD and other Universal Disk Format (UDF) drag-and-drop writing software.

We recommend having Ivory soap (bar; not liquid) and distilled water available for cleaning discs. Using ammonia-based cleaners (e.g., glass cleaners) can "fog" polycarbonate and render a disc completely unreadable. (Read the entire Disc Triage section before using any of these products.)

Scratch filling products and disc buffing tools can help, but must be used with caution, because they can increase uncorrectable error rates or cause other types of errors.

Forensic Software

There are several alternatives for collecting evidence from CDs and DVDs. Unfortunately, most forensic software does a poor job, either because it is based strictly on Microsoft Windows capabilities and Microsoft Windows file system implementations, or because it has limited support for CD and DVD file systems.

The AccessData Forensic Tool Kit (FTK) product has an imaging component (derived from the shareware ISOBuster product) that does a good job of collecting data from CDs and DVDs with any of the commonly supported file systems.

The Guidance Software EnCase product has minimal support for CDs and DVDs, but can utilize the InfinaDyne CD/DVD Inspector product to process discs that it does not directly support.

The ILook Investigator product has some capabilities beyond EnCase in its native form, but does not support all CD and DVD file systems correctly, nor can it deal with UDF discs that have logical errors.

Other products (e.g., those from NTI) do not properly implement all of the possible CD and DVD file systems to any great extent. In general, they only support ISO 9660 and various extensions such as Joliet.

InfinaDyne's CD/DVD Inspector can be used with both EnCase and FTK to collect evidence from CDs and DVDs. It can also be used with other products, although testing and certification has not been done.

Forensic Workstation

A forensic workstation is one that is qualified for use in processing evidence, meaning it has:

- Proper Basic Input Output System (BIOS) configuration
- No conflicting software
- No contaminating data
- The time and date synchronized properly
- Properly licensed software

For the BIOS configuration, it is important to check the order of the boot devices for a forensic workstation, to ensure that you cannot inadvertently boot from an evidence CD or DVD. Doing so would seriously compromise the integrity of the workstation.

In this case, no conflicting software specifically refers to drag-and-drop writing software. Products such as DirectCD, Drag2Disc, InCD, DLA, and abCD have no place on a forensic workstation; they are all invasive and difficult to disable completely. They will potentially modify rewritable media if they are present; in some cases, they will modify write-once media. This modification is unacceptable for processing evidence.

The same conditions for contaminating data apply for CD and DVD processing as for hard drive processing. The workstation should not have any data from any other cases accessible. Exceptions to this can be made when other case files are present on a lab network server; however, care must be used to ensure that no cross-contamination is possible.

CD/DVD Inspector generally shows the timestamp information from when the disc was written, because CD and DVD file systems contain the time zone as part of the timestamp information rather than the time zone setting on the workstation. However, when copying files from a CD or DVD, the workstation time zone setting is referenced to make the file times relative to the local time on the workstation.

All software involved in processing evidence needs to be properly licensed.

Validation

The hardware, software, and workstation all need to be validated before evidence processing can be done with confidence.

The validation of a writer consists of first installing the drive either in the workstation itself or in an external case connected to the workstation, then recognition of the writer by the workstation and software, and finally the successful examination of a known disc.

Under normal circumstances, the MD5 signature value computed by CD/DVD Inspector should be compared to that determined by other software. Due to differences in how MD5 signatures are computed for multiple track discs, it is recommended that you use a single-track data disc for this purpose.

The completion of all of these steps also validates that CD/DVD Inspector software and the workstation are capable of processing discs correctly using that writer.

Disc Triage

When an examiner is given a number of discs to be processed, it is reasonable to order them in decreasing readability to get the most easily read discs processed, and then make the results available as soon as possible. Following this, the less readable discs are then processed. Using this process makes the most effective use of both the examiner's time and the workstation time.

At this point, it is assumed that all of the initial documentation gathering has been done on the collected evidence, or that it is being done as each disc is initially examined. All of the following procedures assume that the disc can be cleaned of all foreign materials and any labeling of the disc can be destroyed by the cleaning process.

The first clue to a disc being difficult to read is the degree of physical damage to the disc. This is not to say that apparently undamaged discs will always be easy to read; however, it is fairly clear that any disc that is heavily scratched, cracked, or damaged in any way is going to be more difficult to read. These should be put aside for later attention.

At this time, it is also reasonable to attempt to clean any discs that are dirty or contaminated. The first rule is that if the disc is not obviously dirty or contaminated, do not clean it. Secondly, perform light cleaning only. If stubborn dirt is present, the disc will require additional work and should be put aside for now.

Care must be taken in handling contaminated discs. Take special precautions with discs that are cracked, because they may break, leading to sharp pieces of polycarbonate that can puncture the skin. As a first step, rinse discs with distilled water to remove surface dirt, possible drug contamination, grease, and/or oils, and so forth. Dry the disc with a soft lint-free cloth.

If rinsing the disc does not remove all foreign materials, use a diluted solution of pure soap (e.g., Ivory) and distilled water and a soft lint-free cloth, preferably not woven. This specifically excludes using any detergent, dish soap, or detergent-based liquid soap; such products can react with the lacquer, label, or polycarbonate in undesirable ways. Wipe across the surface of the disc in a straight line, not a circular motion. One technique that is quite effective to protect the reflector of the disc during cleaning is to place it upside down in a jewel case, which will hold the disc securely enough while it is being cleaned, any remaining contaminants are unlikely to come off in the drive. Attempt to process the disc before proceeding with any further cleaning efforts. At this point, discs that are scratched or otherwise damaged after cleaning should be put aside.

The second phase of the triage operation is to begin examining a disc with CD/DVD Inspector while allowing it to continue for no more than five minutes. If CD/DVD Inspector has not gathered the directory information from the disc in five minutes, the disc should be put aside, because it requires more extensive work.

All of the discs that gathered the directory information within five minutes can then be processed to completion. Next, an evaluation can be done to determine if sufficient evidence has been found or if additional discs must be examined. If so, the undamaged discs that took more than five minutes with CD/DVD Inspector should be processed. It can take significant amounts of time for CD/DVD Inspector to process a disc that has readability problems.

While some or all of the files on the disc may be recovered, it can take days to do so. It can take an equal amount of time to copy the information from a disc. Therefore, it is appropriate to skip any disc that takes more than five minutes to be examined, and put it aside for later processing early in the triage process. If sufficient evidence is collected without processing such discs, this may not be necessary. Later, if such problematic discs must be processed, the examination of the disc should be left to run as long as it takes.

At this point, you are left with the discs that have stubborn dirt or physical damage. If any of these discs are partially readable and not physically damaged, you should process them with CD/DVD Inspector before continuing. It might also be helpful to attempt to make a copy of these discs. Discs that are physically damaged, especially with damage to the reflector, should not be put into a drive until these problems are addressed.

All of the techniques for working with discs from this point on can damage them. If a disc is partially readable, all of the evidence should be collected before continuing.

Removing stubborn dirt usually requires that you use some type of solvent. There are specific CD and DVD cleaning solutions that can help; try them first, as they are least likely to have damaging effects. Do not use any type of cleaner based on organic or petroleum solvents; such solvents will remove the lacquer and reflector and can "eat" the polycarbonate. Ammonia-based cleaners designed for glass or other surfaces can be used; however, first test the cleaner on non-evidence discs. Some ammonia products can fog the polycarbonate and render the disc unreadable. All of these cleaning agents can destroy any markings on the top surface of the disc.

Aside from cleaning, discs with scratches can sometimes be fixed with buffing tools, which fall into two broad categories: the consumer units for less than $50.00, and the commercial units that can range from $800.00 to $1,000.00 or more. The consumer devices are safe when used properly. Be sure to follow the directions and buff the correct side of the disc. Of primary concern is damaging the disc by removing too much material; as such, consumer devices don't remove too much and are reasonably priced.

Commercial buffing systems can remove "enough" material to eliminate scratches completely, and can also remove considerable amounts of polycarbonate from a disc. This can introduce aberrations and distortions into the shape of the disc. Use such machines with great care; it is possible to take a disc that is 50 percent readable and make it 100 percent unreadable. It is recommended that you gather all possible information from such discs before using a commercial-grade buffing system.

Scratch filling products can also be helpful when there are deep scratches. However, it must be clearly understood that CDs and DVDs are read with infrared light and not visible light. Therefore, scratch fillers can appear to have hidden scratches in visible light and be utterly opaque to infrared light. Selecting a scratch filler product that performs well can be difficult. Testing by Media Sciences (**www.mscience.com**) has found that several of these products actually make the problem worse.

Discs where portions of the reflector are missing should be handled extremely carefully to prevent further damage. One suggestion is to apply a label to the disc to "lock down" the remaining portion of the reflector and prevent further peeling. Such peeling can occur when the disc is being read in a high-speed drive. Applying a full-circle CD label can prevent this from happening.

Discs that are cracked or broken in half can be processed, but it may require the disc swap process described below. The first step is to stabilize the cracked area or to rejoin the broken halves. It is recommended that you use one of the clear discs on the end of a spindle to protect the discs. DVD end pieces are half the thickness of CD end pieces and will cause less difficultly in reading the disc. Glue the top of the cracked disc or halves onto the end piece. Many common office adhesives will work, but avoid strongly solvent-based products like rubber cement and contact cement. White glue will probably work, although the drying time may be longer than with other adhesives. After gluing, the disc will be thicker than a standard disc and may require a modified drive in order to be read.

Discs with portions of the reflector missing, with cracks, or otherwise damaged may not be able to be read in an ordinary drive, because all drives must read the Table of Contents (TOC) from the disc in order to "mount" the disc. This is how the drive determines that there is a valid disc inserted rather than a piece of cardboard. If the TOC in the lead-in cannot be read, the disc cannot be read in an ordinary drive. This is where the "disc swap" technique comes into play using a modified drive. The technique is also required for quick-erased discs. Swapping discs requires that you have a disc as close to the subject disc as possible. The type (e.g., CD-R, CD-RW, DVD-R, DVD-RW, DVD+R, DVD+RW) and color (e.g., dye formulation) are important, because the drive measures the "replacement" disc and determines how to read it. When you swap in the subject disc, these parameters are retained. If the replacement disc is not a good match, there will be problems reading the subject disc. It is not necessary that the exact dye be matched, but it is recommended that it be matched visually. This should result in a good match of reflectivity and contrast.

For write-once discs, the replacement disc should have the same track arrangement and at least as much data written to the disc as the subject disc. If you have no idea what was written onto the subject disc, you can guess; you may have a single-track data disc that is completely full (700 MB for a CD, 4.3 GB for a DVD). For rewritable media, the replacement disc should be completely formatted. The swap technique for this type of disc is as follows:

- Put the replacement disc into the modified drive and use the tray button to indicate to the drive that the disc has been changed.

- Wait until the disc stops spinning. Attempting to stop the disc before it stops spinning can result in serious cuts. Polycarbonate spinning at high speed is very sharp.

- Remove the replacement disc and put the subject disc in the drive. Replace the magnetic clamp. Do not touch the tray button; the idea is to not inform the drive that the disc has been changed.

There is a complete description of how to modify a drive for this purpose in Appendix A. Due to the hazards of exposing the drive laser, this information should only be used by qualified persons. Failure to take proper precautions can result in serious eye damage, even blindness.

If this disc swapping technique does not work with a disc, or the disc is too badly damaged to place into a drive, all is not lost. InfinaDyne has several contacts in the academic community that may be able to assist with discs that are otherwise unreadable. One system that has come to our attention can work with as little as one-eighth of a disc. Using such equipment should be a last resort and will incur significant delays and expenses.

Chapter 6

CD/DVD Inspector - The Basics

For this chapter, you will need a current copy of the CD/DVD Inspector evaluation install file. If your workstation already has CD/DVD Inspector installed, skip the "CD/DVD Inspector Installation" section.

CD/DVD Inspector Installation

Assuming that you have not installed CD/DVD Inspector on your workstation, do so now. CD/DVD Inspector is distributed as a single installation executable file; therefore, double-clicking the proper file begins the installation process.

CD/DVD Inspector does not install any drivers or files into system folders. It does install a kernel module; however, you will have to restart the computer in order to get loaded and running.

The entire installation takes approximately one minute. During the installation, you will be prompted to select either *basic* or *expert* mode. It is suggested that you leave the default at basic, which controls the degree of prompting that is done during the examination of a disc.

The evaluation version of CD/DVD Inspector has everything that is required to operate the product; however, if you are using the full version you will also need a dongle that contains the full version. Some dongles require an additional licensing file in order to operate properly. All of the required files and drivers should be present on the installation CD. If you are downloading the software over the Internet, you may need to separately download the dongle driver.

The evaluation version of CD/DVD Inspector is time-limited on each computer it is installed. Copying files from discs is only available with the full version and evaluations supplied to qualified forensic examiners. Some output is marked as being from an evaluation version of the product.

CD/DVD Inspector Facts

Some brief facts about CD/DVD Inspector:

- CD/DVD Inspector bypasses Windows to access devices directly, and uses its own file system to access the files on Compact Discs (CDs) and Digital Versatile Discs (DVDs).

- No special drivers are needed. If Windows can access the device, CD/DVD Inspector can access the device.

- CD/DVD Inspector supports any drive connected to the computer as long as it is recognized by Windows. This means all Universal Serial Bus (USB), FireWire, Serial Advanced Technology Attachment (SATA), Small Computer System Interface (SCSI), and other types of drives are immediately recognized and supported by CD/DVD Inspector.

- CD/DVD Inspector is independent of all other software. No additional software is required to access drag-and-drop discs.

- The ISO 9660, Joliet, Rock Ridge, Hierarchical File System (HFS), Hierarchical File System Extended Format (HFS+), and Universal Disk Format (UDF) file systems are all supported by CD/DVD Inspector. This means that Macintosh discs can be examined on a PC without additional software.

- All dialogs have a "Copy Text" button that copies the contents of the dialog to the clipboard where it can be pasted into a report. It is not necessary to do screen captures and insert graphics into a report.

- CD/DVD Inspector directly supports image types (i.e., *.art*, *.bmp*, *.gif*, *.jpeg*, *.png*, and *.tiff*). Additionally, over 125 digital camera (RAW) raw (camera specific) formats are supported. Right-clicking on an image file icon and choosing View Image displays the image file.

Getting Started with CD/DVD Inspector

To examine a disc with CD/DVD Inspector, you must first start the program, which then displays the Select Device dialog box of the drive to be used (see Figure 6.1).

Figure 6.1 Select Device Dialog

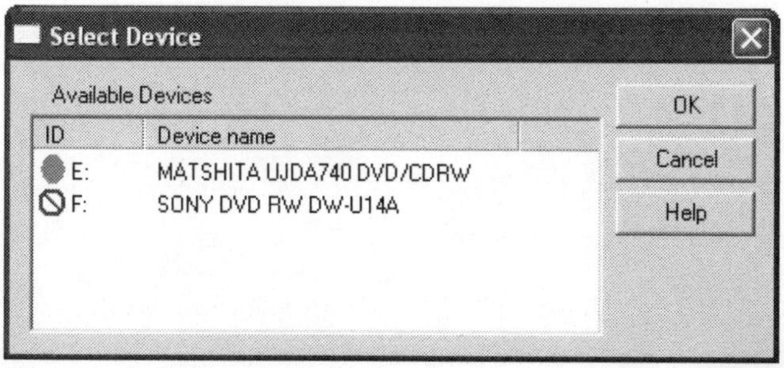

A green dot indicates that a disc is inserted and the drive is ready to be used. The red symbol indicates a drive that is not ready. Put the disc to be examined into a drive in the dialog box and wait for the red symbol to turn green. Then either double-click the drive or select the drive and click **OK** to continue.

There are no options to select and no information about the disc is required from you. CD/DVD Inspector automatically determines everything that is required.

The message shown in Figure 6.2 is displayed when the examination of the disc is complete. At this point, all of the information about the disc has been gathered, but the actual data files have not been copied.

Figure 6.2 Disc Processed Message

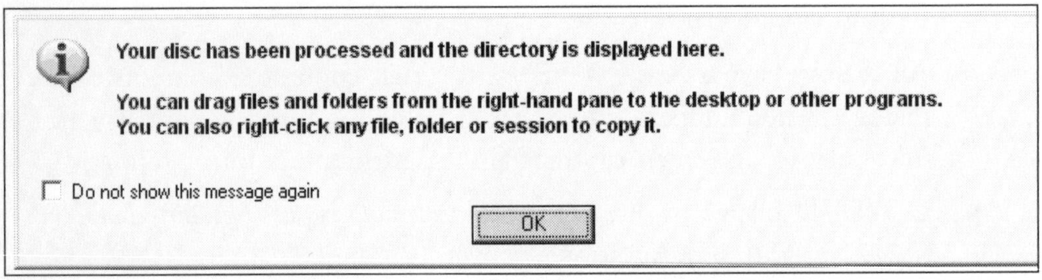

When this message is acknowledged, the CD/DVD Inspector window is displayed (see Figure 6.3).

The left window pane shows sessions, the file systems within those sessions, and directories. The right window pane shows the files contained in the selected directory. The last line in the left window pane shows "Lead out" if a proper lead-out exists on the disc. Discs that were not closed after the last session will not show a lead out. The toolbar at the top provides easy-to-reach buttons for many common functions. The toolbar buttons are:

Figure 6.3 CD/DVD Inspector Main Window

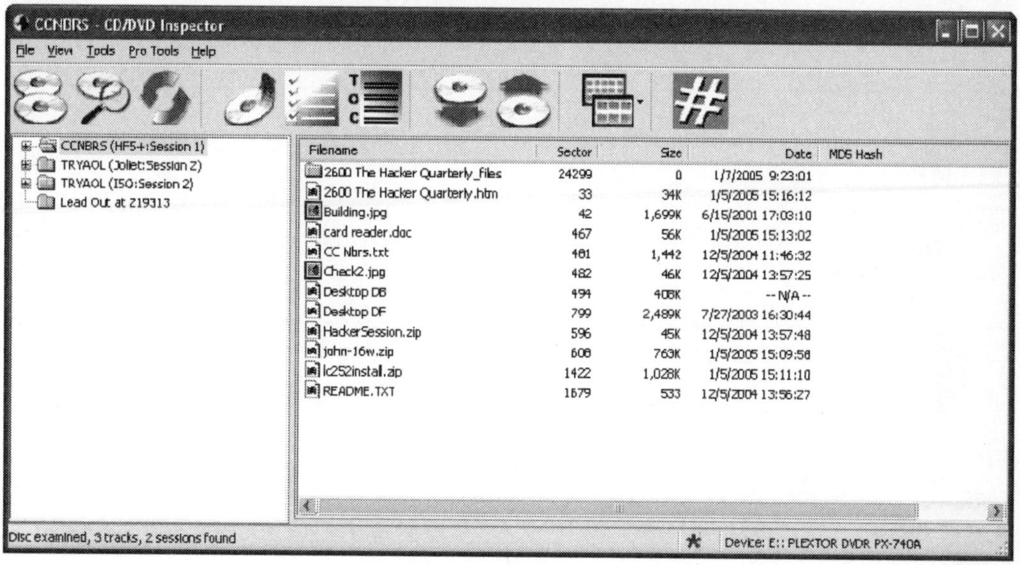

Filename	Sector	Size	Date	MD5 Hash
2600 The Hacker Quarterly_files	24299	0	1/7/2005 9:23:01	
2600 The Hacker Quarterly.htm	33	34K	1/5/2005 15:16:12	
Building.jpg	42	1,699K	6/15/2001 17:03:10	
card reader.doc	467	56K	1/5/2005 15:13:02	
CC Nbrs.txt	481	1,442	12/5/2004 11:46:32	
Check2.jpg	482	46K	12/5/2004 13:57:25	
Desktop DB	494	408K	-- N/A --	
Desktop DF	799	2,489K	7/27/2003 16:30:44	
HackerSession.zip	596	45K	12/5/2004 13:57:48	
john-16w.zip	608	763K	1/5/2005 15:09:56	
lc252instal.zip	1422	1,028K	1/5/2005 15:11:10	
README.TXT	1679	533	12/5/2004 13:56:27	

Disc examined, 3 tracks, 2 sessions found   Device: E:: PLEXTOR DVDR PX-740A

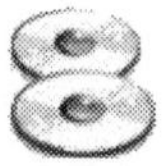

 Selects a different CD or DVD device.

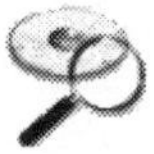

 Displays sectors from disc.

 Refreshes; rescans the disc.

Note: To rescan the disc go to **File | Preferences** and remove the disc from the disc memory. This is described in more detail below.

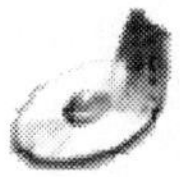

Copies all files from the disc.

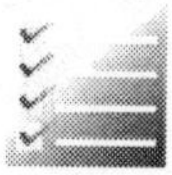

Produces an Analysis report for the disc.

Continued

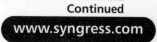

	Displays the Table of Contents (TOC) for the disc.
	Opens the tray or ejects the disc.
	Closes the tray and, if a disc is present, examines it.
	Changes the display between large icons, small icons, List, and Details.
	Changes the number of hardware and software retries performed when read errors occur.

Most toolbar functions have corresponding menu selections.

It is recommended that you use either the List view or the Details view for the right-hand window pane. The icon views are not useful for forensic purposes, but have been included for completeness. The Details view shows the starting sector for the first extent, the size of the file, the last-written timestamp, and the Message Digest 5 (MD5) hash value. To get the MD5 hash values for files, they have to be calculated using the **File | Calculate Hash Values** menu selection.

The icons used by CD/DVD Inspector are not the standard Windows icons, because, unlike the local hard drive, there is no assumption that software for particular types of files is installed on the computer that is examining the disc. Therefore, the standard Windows document icon is used for all files for which no other icon applies. Special icons are used as follows:

	The file is marked as deleted. This applies only to UDF file systems; currently, no common UDF implementations mark files in this manner.

Continued

The folder is marked as deleted. This applies only to UDF file systems; currently, no common UDF implementations mark folders in this manner.

 The file contains a viewable image. Right-clicking the file and selecting "View image" will display it. This is supported for *.art*, *.bmp*, *.gif*, *.jpeg*, *.png*, *.tiff*, and over 125 proprietary RAW camera formats.

X The file is inaccessible. There is information about the file in the file system but either no location is specified or the location is outside the bounds of the disc.

 The file overlaps another file. This is common with the UDF file system on rewritable media. One or both files are destroyed. Selecting the option "Show analysis file details" in Preferences and displaying the Analysis report will show which files overlap.

★ When a hash set is loaded into CD/DVD Inspector, this is used to mark files that have a matching hash value.

Image files are found in one of two ways: by *extension* or by *content*. It is assumed that files with the *art*, *.bmp*, *.gif*, *.jpg*, *.jpeg*, *.png*, *.tif*, or *.tiff* extensions are images and should be viewable by CD/DVD Inspector. Files with extensions other than those for images are examined to determine if the file is an image file based on the file header. If it is an image, the image icon is assigned to the file and the image viewer is enabled. This can lead to file being treated as images which are not that are not being treated as images; however, the viewer will display an error message if such files are displayed.

The image file viewer also saves files in JPEG format. This can be extremely helpful when a file is a RAW digital camera file that is supported by CD/DVD Inspector.

Inaccessible files are common with discs that are created with Roxio Easy CD Creator versions 4 and 5. A flaw in this software allows you to abort the process of creating a disc when only part of what was being written to the

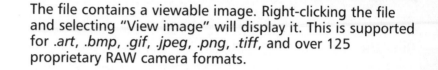

disc is actually written. However, because the directory is written first, it appears that the entire disc has been written. No message is given indicating that this has occurred.

Inaccessible files also occur with corrupted UDF file systems. You would normally see a file with the original name marked with a red X and an unnamed file found by CD/DVD Inspector in the Unattached Items folder, which holds the content of the file. Unfortunately, there is no automated way to connect the unnamed file data with the original filename.

Data Window Usage

Figure 6.4 Splitter Cursor

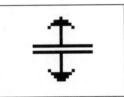

One feature of CD/DVD Inspector is the Data pane, which opens below the right-hand pane that shows the files. When you move the cursor to the bottom edge of the Files pane, it changes to a "splitter" cursor. Dragging the bottom of the File pane up opens the Data pane and automatically displays the contents of any file selected in the File pane above it.

There are three formats for the Data pane display:

- Hex and character

- Character

- Image

When the Image display is chosen and a non-image file is selected, a message appears indicating that the image cannot be displayed. The Data pane format is selected by right-clicking in the Data pane and choosing the format from the selections presented. Another choice is to close the Data pane, which removes it and restores the File pane to full size.

The Data pane can be resized any time it is open, by dragging the splitter bar between the File pane and the Data pane.

The Data pane is extremely helpful when looking at certain types of files. One suggestion is to use the Data window with JPEG files. (In most cases, the information about when a picture was taken and what camera it was taken with is in character form at the beginning of the file.) The Data pane makes this information available immediately by clicking on the JPEG file.

Disc Memory

CD/DVD Inspector can spend considerable time examining a disc, especially if the disc has problems. Because of this, one of the major features added for the transition from CD-R Inspector to CD/DVD Inspector is Disc Memory.

Disc Memory provides a "checkpoint" facility for examining discs so that a partial examination that is interrupted can be continued. Disc Memory also remembers completed examinations so that the information can be recalled quickly. Disc Memory can be extremely helpful for forensic users, because once the information from a disc is collected, the lengthy process does not have to be repeated if the disc is re-examined.

The Disc Memory feature automatically resumes examining a disc if the examination is interrupted either by termination of the CD/DVD Inspector program, or by clicking the **Cancel** button while the examination is underway.

There is also a negative aspect to Disc Memory. Because it stores the information that was gathered for a disc, it is not possible to change settings in Preferences and click **Refresh** to change how the disc was examined. The saved Disc Memory information is reread and the disc is not re-examined. It is necessary to go to the Preferences Disc Memory page to remove the entry for the disc to force re-examination. You can also completely empty the Disc Memory, but that will impact all of the discs that are currently known. A sample of the Disc Memory Preferences page is shown in Figure 6.5.

Figure 6.5 Disc Memory Controls

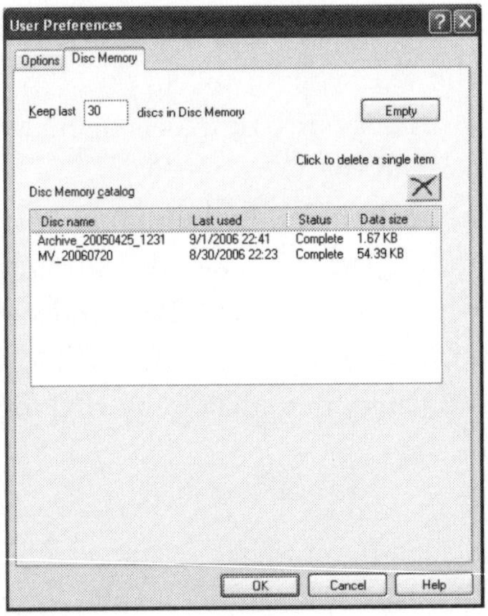

Another feature of Disc Memory is the ability to export the Disc Memory information so that it can be imported onto another computer. Right-clicking any of the disc catalog lines shown in the Disc Memory presents you with two alternatives: *Delete* or *Export*. Exporting a Disc Memory entry creates a file with the extension .dmem. This file can then be copied to a different computer and the **File | Import Disc Memory** can be used to add it to the catalog on that computer.

Exporting a Disc Memory file can be useful if you have to examine a disc on a different computer. Many user-written discs can take considerable amounts of time to initially gather file information. Once this has been done on a computer, the Disc Memory allows the disc to be re-examined quickly by saving the collected information. By exporting the disc memory file and importing it onto another computer, the second computer can use the previously collected information. This eliminates the lengthy collection process on the computer that is importing the disc memory information.

By default, the Disc Memory holds detailed information for a maximum of 30 discs. The size of the detailed information is shown in the catalog list and is generally less than 1 MB per disc.

Useful Tools

For forensic users, Figure 6.6 summarizes the important tools in CD/DVD Inspector.

Figure 6.6 Analysis Toolbar Button

Analysis

This tool can be reached from either the toolbar or from the Tools menu. It produces a report, which describes the contents of the disc, including the recording date and time and the number of files and folders found. The items of particular significance are shown in red. Clicking on a line of this report displays an explanation of the report. This report can be copied to the clipboard with the **Copy Text** button and then pasted into a document.

Compute Disc MD5

The Compute Disc Message Digest 5 (MD5) tool computes the MD5 hash value for an entire disc. The sectors that are participating in this operation are displayed and can be modified if necessary. Some users have reported that the sectors that are determined by CD/DVD Inspector are not the same as those that are used by other software; therefore, it may be necessary to make adjustments if you are trying to match information between different programs.

If the sector values are not modified, it is considered a "standard" calculation and the MD5 value is saved in Disc Memory for that disc. This value is also reported in the Analysis report.

Compute MD5 hash

This tool computes the MD5 hash values for individual files. The session or directory selected in the left window pane or the file(s) selected in the right window pane determine which files are processed.

Disc map

This tool displays a graphic map of the sector utilization on the disc. Each block represents 10 sectors and is colored in accordance to how the sectors are used. Examining this display allows you to see if there are areas of the disc that are not accounted for by the files in the directory. In addition, this is a simple graphic translation between a sector number and the file. Move the cursor to different areas in the Disc Map and the file(s) in those sectors are listed on the left-hand side of the window.

Disc report

Selecting Disc Report from the Tools men prompts you to select between different report formats. After selecting the format, the filename is requested. Reports are either in American Standard Code for Information Interchange (ASCII) text format or Hypertext Markup Language (HTML). (See the Reporting section later in this chapter for more information about reports.)

Hardware information

Selecting Hardware Information from the Tools menu displays a list of items that describe the capabilities of the selected drive.

Scan files

This Scan Files tool in the File menu searches all of the files for matching information defined by a scan specification file.

Sector display

Figure 6.7 Sector Display Toolbar Button

This tool can be located on the toolbar or on the File menu. It displays the contents of sectors in a hex and character format. Raw sector searching is done from this display.

The sector display can be opened any time after the initial examination of the disc, and as many sector display windows as needed can be opened simultaneously. However, only one Raw sector search can be performed at a time.

TOC

Figure 6.8 TOC Toolbar Button

The TOC Toolbar can be found on the toolbar or in the Tools menu. The TOC Toolbar displays the contents of the TOC for the disc, together with information about a selected file system that begins in that track.

View Image

The built-in image viewer in CD/DVD Inspector is accessed by selecting a file with the image icon and then selecting View image from the Context menu or from the File menu (see Figure 6.9).

Figure 6.9 Image Icon

The built-in image viewer supports *art, bmp, gif, jpeg, png,* and *tif* files, and over 125 proprietary digital camera RAW image file formats. Images can be saved in .jpeg format by right-clicking in the Image view window.

Write image file

The Write Image file writes to either an ISO image file or to a CD/DVD Inspector image file, to save the contents of the disc and make them available without requiring the disc.

Searching

There are three ways to search CDs and DVDs for keywords and other information using CD/DVD Inspector:

- Built-in Scan Files functionality
- Built-in Raw Sector Search functionality
- Copies all of the files from the disc and uses other external tools

There are some benefits to each of these techniques. Using Scan Files can be a fast way to determine if a disc contains important content without having to copy the content from the disc. It also isolates the search to data files while bypassing file system control information (see Figure 6.10).

The Raw Sector Search allows you to search for hex and character strings across all of the sectors of the media, including those sectors used for file system control information.

Obviously, if you have specific needs that the built-in tools do not fulfill, it is possible to copy the content of the disc and use any searching tools that you have available.

Figure 6.10 Sector Display Button

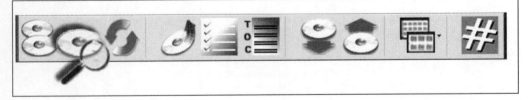

To use the Raw Sector Search tool, open the Sector Display (from the toolbar or from the File menu) and position the display to the desired starting point. Click the **Search** button and enter the search term. It will be searched for in all parts of the sector following the displayed sector, and all of the following sectors until the end of the track is reached. To resume the search, click the **Search** button and then the **OK** button.

Scan Files

The Scan Files tool is designed to quickly examine the contents of the files on a disc using multiple keywords at a single time. When Scan Files are selected from the File menu, you are presented with the dialog box shown in Figure 6.11.

Figure 6.11 Scan Files Dialog Box

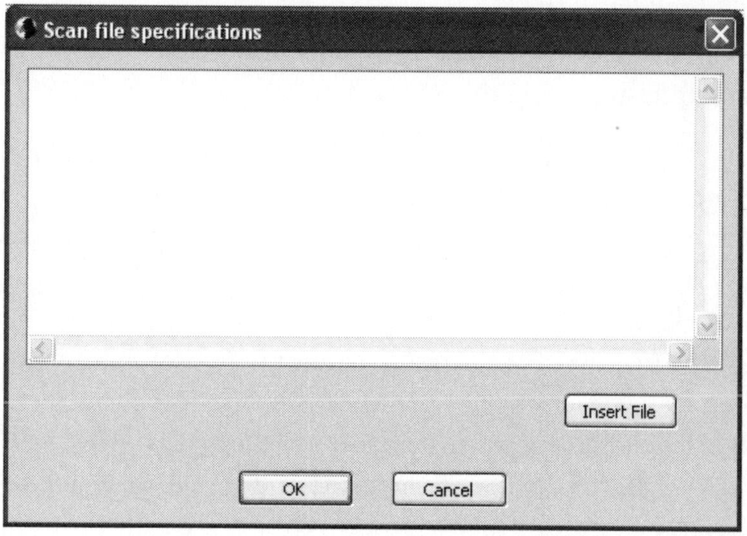

Enter the search specifications in the text area. You can also insert the contents of a file into the text area by clicking the **Insert File** button and then selecting a text file. This allows you to save common searches and bring them into CD/DVD Inspector in a simple manner.

Each line in the text area must be a valid search specification. The following are valid specifications:

- A blank line.

- A comment beginning with a sharp sign (#). Comments in this form can follow any of the search terms except regular expressions.

- A string enclosed in double quotes (" ").The following special notations are accepted within the double quotes: \r for carriage return (*0D* in hex), \n for line feed (*0A* in hex),\" for a double-quote (*22* in hex), \\ for a backslash (*5C* in hex), and \^ for a caret (*5E* in hex). Also, prefixing any letter from A to Z with a caret is treated as a single character in the range 01 to 1A hex or Ctrl-A through Ctrl-Z. All strings are considered to be case-insensitive for matching purposes.

- One or more sequences of hexadecimal digits, each consisting of an even number of digits.

- The letter R or r followed by one or more blanks followed by a regular expression using the PERL syntax.

When a character or hexadecimal specification is used, this data is searched for across the entire file and if it is found anywhere, is reported as a "hit." When a regular expression is used, various techniques to control where matches are found can be used.

The regular expression syntax that CD/DVD Inspector uses is nearly identical to that used by PERL.The maximum length of a matched expression is limited to 2,048 characters, and only the first 100 characters of any match are displayed.This means that if you use the syntax *ABC.*DEF* and there are 1,000 characters between the *ABC* and the *DEF*, it will be counted as a match and 97 characters following the ABC will be shown in the results. However, if there are 3,000 characters between the *ABC* and the DEF, this will not be counted as a match.

Using regular expressions with the Scan Files tool is a simple way to control where matches can be recognized in a file (e.g., the string *Exif* commonly occurs in digital camera image files). If you place *Exif* in quotes as a scan specification, it will match these characters anywhere they occur in a file and regardless of the file containing *EXIF*, *exif*, or *exIF*.The following regular expression can be used to narrow this down to matching only *Exif* and only at location 6 in a .jpeg file:

```
^.{6}Exif
```

This only matches the characters *Exif* that occur at offset 6 within a file. This can be expanded to match all .jpeg headers with the regular expression below:

```
^.{6}(JFIF|Exif)
```

This will match the characters *JFIF* or Exif at offset 6 in a file.

This is not a complete reference of regular expressions, but rather a guide to the escape sequences that can be specified for CD/DVD Inspector. It is recommended that you refer to a PERL tutorial for information about constructing regular expressions and how to use them.

Char	Description	Char	Description
\	General escape character	i	Start subpattern
^	Assert start of string (or line, in multiline mode)	)	End subpattern
$	Assert end of string (or line, in multiline mode)	?	Extends the meaning of (, also 0 or 1 quantifier, also quantifier minimizer
.	Match any character except newline (by default)	*	0 or more quantifiers
[	Start character class definition	+	1 or more quantifiers or "possessive quantifiers"
|	Start of alternative branch	{	Start minimum/maximum quantifier

An alternative branch allows for different alternatives; a logical OR condition. The pattern *(abc|def)* matches the characters *abc* or *def*.

The minimum/maximum quantifier controls how many occurrences are required or can optionally be present. $A\{6\}$ means that at least six occurrences of A must be present, and $A\{6.9\}$ means that there must be at least six, but not more than nine, occurrences.

The part of a pattern enclosed in square brackets ([]) is called a *character class*. The only metacharacters in a character class are:

Char	Description	Char	Description
\	General escape character	[	Start of Portable Operating System Interface (POSIX) character class, if followed by POSIX syntax
^	Negates the class, but only if used as the first character	]	Ends character class
-	Indicates character range		

A character class consists of characters, character ranges, and POSIX character classes. A character range such as A–Z matches all characters from A through Z.

The escape character (or backslash) has several uses. If a non-alphanumeric character follows the escape character, any special meaning that character has is taken away. Using a backslash as an escape character applies to both inside and outside of the character classes.

For example, if you want to match a * character, you write * in the pattern. This escaping action applies whether or not the following character would otherwise be interpreted as a metacharacter. Therefore, it is always safe to precede a non-alphanumeric with a backslash to specify that it stands for itself. In particular, if you want to match a backslash, write \\.

The backslash also provides a way of encoding non-printing characters into patterns in a visible manner. It is difficult to input these characters correctly into the text area for the Scan Files tool, so the following must be used.

Char	Description	Char	Description
\a	BEL character (hex 07)	\r	Carriage return (hex 0D)
\cx	"Control-x," where x is any character	\t	Tab (hex 09)
\e	Escape (hex 1B)	\ddd	Character with octal code ddd (digits 0–7)
\f	Form feed (hex 0C)	\xhh	Character with hex code hh (character 0–9, a–f, and A–F)
\n	New line (hex 0A)		

The effect of \cx is to convert lowercase letters to uppercase and then invert bit 6 (hex 40) of the character. Thus, \cz becomes hex 1A and \cd becomes hex 04. Using non-alpha characters is possible, but the results are not usually desirable. This has the same effect as the caret character when using a quoted string specification as described above.

After \x, from zero to two hexadecimal digits are read (letters can be in upper- or lowercase).

Octal coding of characters is not common and is not recommended. The only practical use of octal coding would be to match a string like *ABC\0* where \0 represents a trailing byte of binary zero.

The third use of a backslash is for specifying generic character types. The following are always recognized:

Char	Description	Char	Description
\d	Any decimal digit	\S	Any character that is not a whitespace character
\D	Any character that is not a decimal digit	\w	Any "word" character
\s	Any whitespace character (space, tab, newline)	\W	Any "non-word" character

The fourth use of backslash is for certain simple assertions. An assertion specifies a condition that has to be met at a particular point in a match, without consuming any characters from the subject string. The use of subpatterns for more complicated assertions is described below. The backslashed assertions are:

Char	Description
\b	Matches at a word boundary
\B	Matches when not at a word boundary

These assertions may not appear in character classes; however, note that \b has a different meaning (namely the backspace character) inside a character class.

POSIX Character Classes

POSIX character classes are used to define entire ranges or types of characters, such as uppercase letters or numeric digits. A character class is specified by a square bracket ([), a colon (:), the name of the character class, a closing colon, and a closing square bracket (e.g., the regular expression *"01[:alpha:]"* matches the characters *0, 1* and any alpha character. The following names are supported for specifying POSIX character classes:

Name	Description	Name	Description
alnum	Letters and digits	lower	Lowercase letters
alpha	Letters excluding space	print	Printing characters,
ascii	Character codes 0–127	punct	Printing characters, excluding letters and digits
blank	Space or tab only	space	White space (not quite the same as \s)
cntrl	Control characters (0–31)	upper	Upper case letters
digit	Decimal digits (same as \d)	word	"Word" characters (same as \w)
graph	Printing characters, excluding space	xdigit	Hexadecimal digits

The space characters are *HT (9), LF (10), VT (11), FF (12), CR (13),* and space *(32).* Notice that this list includes the VT character (code 11.) This makes space different than \s, which does not include VT (for PERL compatibility.)

Producing a Forensic Image

CD/DVD Inspector has two techniques for producing what is commonly referred to as a "forensic image," which is a binary image that contains all of the content from the media as a close to its original form as possible.

This is easy for hard drives, because they contain only data sectors, which are numbered from 0 to the end of the drive; each is 512 bytes in size. There is no other user-controlled data on a hard drive; therefore, copying only these data sectors is sufficient.

The same principles apply to flash media, such as thumb drives, camera cards, and floppy diskettes. Unfortunately, there is considerably more data on CDs and DVDs, which creates significant problems when creating a "forensic image" in the same manner. As previously described, the TOC provides a significant amount of information that is required to access multiple sessions. There can also be multiple track formats on CD media that require additional information. There can also be information in the R–W subchannel. Simply copying you data portion of the sectors is not sufficient to collect all of the information from CD and DVD evidence.

There are two methods of collecting the data on a CD or DVD using CD/DVD Inspector. There are also significant differences in the portability of the information that is collected. These methods are described below.

Creating an Image Zip File

Selecting the "Create image ZIP file" function in the Pro Tools menu copies all of the data files from the disc to one or more .zip files. These files can then be imported into various forensic tools, such as EnCase and FTK.

If the "Use 64-bit ZIP extensions" option is not selected, the standard 32-bit representation is used, which is more compatible with other software (e.g., EnCase version 5 does not support 64-bit *ZIP* files). However, it does restrict the total size of a *ZIP* archive to less than 2 GB, and cannot contain any file 2 GB or larger. When the archive reaches the point where adding the next member would reach or exceed 2 GB in size, it is split and a numeric suffix is applied to the filename. If the filename specified by you is *image.zip*, the first split will result in a filenamed *image (2).zip* and the second split will create *image (3).zip*.

Splitting and restricting files that are 2GB or larger, is removed when the "Use 64-bit ZIP extensions" option is checked. Until the archive exceeds 2 GB in size, it continues using only 32-bit offsets and is compatible with all ZIP software. Once the archive size reaches 2 GB, all further members are added using 64-bit extensions that are not compatible with many software packages. The advantage is that it is possible to encounter 2 GB or larger files on DVD media, which will be included in a *ZIP64* archive. In addition, regardless of size, only a single image file will result from any media.

Prior to version 3.0 of CD/DVD Inspector, there was an issue with multi-session discs, where a copy of a file that was carried in each session would appear in the *ZIP* archive. It took considerable time to copy the same file over again, and also made the archive file very large. With version 3.0, a new feature has been added that uses hard links within the *ZIP* archive. This allows the same member to be referenced by multiple names within the archive. Prior to the version 3.0 release, if the same file appeared in both ISO 9660 and Joliet file systems and there were 10 sessions on the disc, the same file content would appear in the *ZIP* archive 20 times. With hard linking present in version 3.0, only a single copy of the file content will be present in the archive, although it will be referenced in each session and file system where it is found. This significantly reduces the processing time and the archive size.

Creating a Binary Image File

With the introduction of CD/DVD Inspector 3.0, it is possible to create a binary image file that captures all of the content on any CD or DVD. It is also possible to allow CD/DVD Inspector to be used against the image file without using the original media. The image file format that is used preserves all of the content, regardless of the type of CD track or DVD border zone that is encountered. This means that Video Compact Discs (VCDs) or Super Video Compact Discs (SVCDs) can be preserved as image files and as Compact Disc + Graphics (CD+G) Karaoke discs. Many copy-protected discs can also be imaged in their original form, with full preservation of the original content.

Content Scrambling System (CSS)-protected DVD movies can be imaged in this manner, but require the addition of an optional component of CD/DVD Inspector. Distribution of this component is restricted. Contact InfinaDyne sales if you believe you need to have this.

To create a binary image file, select the "Create Disc Image" item from the Pro Tools menu. You will be prompted for a filename and the type of image file to be created. If the disc can be represented as an ISO image file, it will appear as an option, but will not preserve all of the possible contents of the disc. Selecting the "InfinaDyne image file" type will preserve all of the contents of the disc. An InfinaDyne image file consists of two files: a *track image* file and an *eXtensible Markup Language (XML) information* file.

InfinaDyne is committed to working with all forensic software publishers to support this image format as widely as possible.

Copying Files from the Media

The toolbar button copies the entire contents of the disc (all file systems and all sessions) automatically (see Figure 6.12). You are prompted to select the location that the files are stored in; the entire directory structure of the disc is then reproduced from that point.

Clicking the toolbar button does not prompt you if an error occurs. Depending on the setting of the "Accept read errors during copy" option, any file with an unrecoverable error will either be skipped or, whatever is returned by the drive will be stored in the file and the copy processing continued.

Figure 6.12 Copy All Button

For more control over the copy process, you can right-click any file, folder, or session displayed by CD/DVD Inspector and select the copy item (Copy File or Copy Directory) that will copy that item. If an error occurs, the user is prompted to select an action (e.g., skipping the file, retrying the read operation, or accepting bad data). Clicking **Shift Accept** results in no further prompting or accepting of bad data for all errors during the remainder of the copy operation.

Even when accepting errors, CD/DVD Inspector has a requirement that 90 percent of the file must be intact to keep the file contents. If more than 10 percent of a file cannot be successfully read, it is considered destroyed and is deleted. This can be overridden by selecting the "Show all files, no matter what" option in (for CD/DVD Inspector 2.x) or the "Enable special features" option (for CD/DVD Inspector 3.x) Preferences, which allows a completely unreadable file to be copied.

After copying files, you are given the option of obtaining a Copy report. This report is written as a text file and is automatically opened in the default text file application after is has been written.

An alternative to copying the individual files from the disc is to use the "Create image ZIP File" function in the Pro Tools menu.

Audio discs can be copied using any of the above techniques. Audio tracks are copied by creating either a *.wav* or a *.cda* file from the audio samples in the track. A *.wav* file is easily played and can be compressed, or other operations can be performed on it for analysis. A *.cda* file is an exact raw representation of the 16-bit samples in the audio track without any additional header. Such files can be used to produce a new audio track. Both formats are uncompressed 16-bit PCM audio samples and result in approximately 10 MB per minute of playing time.

User Preferences

CD/DVD Inspector has a number of options and controls spread out over a number of pages. There are several different types of options available. The following describes each of the various settings that can be changed on each of the pages.

One option on the first page is called "Forensic use" and controls a significant part of the operation and presentation of CD/DVD Inspector. This option is set by default when CD/DVD Inspector is installed. When this option is not checked, additional pages appear in the User Preferences dialog box (see Figure 6.13).

Options Settings

This page contains the bulk of the simple yes or no settings for CD/DVD Inspector.

Figure 6.13 User Preferences

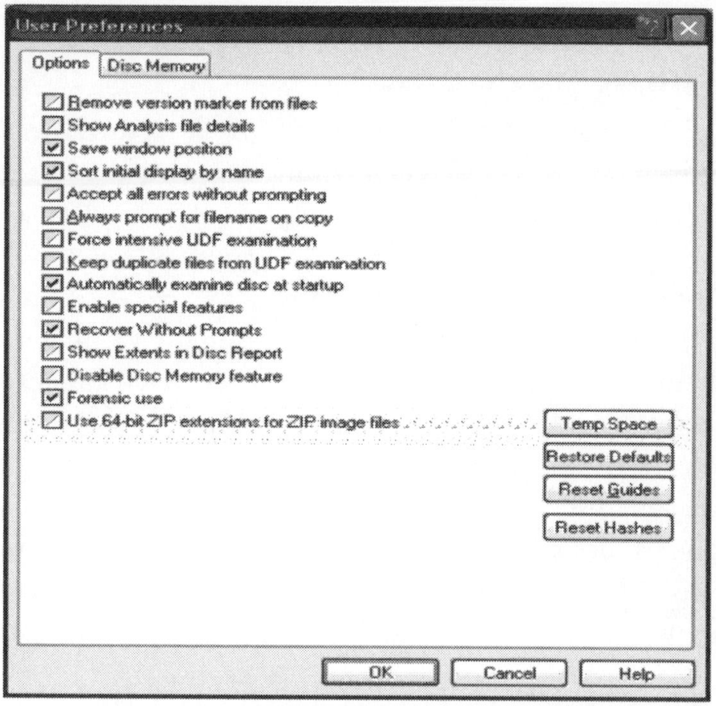

Remove version marker from files

For ISO 9660 file systems, removing version markers from files causes the filenames to be displayed without the *;1* version marker that is normally present. The default is to display the version marker when it is present. Because the version marker is part of the ISO 9660 standard, it is included in most writing software, even though it is not used today.

Because the version marker has no function today, there is no reason to set this option.

Show Analysis file details

Selecting this option causes the Analysis report to include information about specific files rather than just a summary count. This can significantly increase the size of the Analysis report, often by including hundreds if not thousands of files.

It is not recommended that this option be set all of the time; only when it is required.

Save window position

When this option is selected, the position and size of the main window for CD/DVD Inspector is saved and the next time it is used, the window appears in the same place and is the same size. This option is set by default.

Sort initial display by name

Disc directories are not necessarily sorted (e.g., it is not a requirement for UDF file systems). This means the directory can be shown either "as is" or sorted by name. When this option is selected, the list of files is initially sorted by name so that it always appears in name order regardless of how the directory is arranged on disc.

If this option is not selected, the files in a directory appear in the order in which they are stored in the directory itself. Clicking on any of the headings in the Details display will sort the files into the requested order.

Accept all errors without prompting

Selecting this option turns off most error messages while copying files from the media, and treats all errors as if they have been accepted. If no data is returned from the drive, a sector of binary 0 is inserted into the file.

There is a limit on how many unreadable sectors can be in a file. If more than 10 percent of a file is not readable, the file is deleted after it is copied. There are a few cases where a file that is less than 90 percent intact is still usable.

Setting this option when you don't need it is a bad idea, because you will not be warned about errors that occur during copy operations. A better solution to having too many prompts for file copy errors is to hold down the shift key and click **Accept** when no further error notifications are desired. Then, check the report produced at the end of the copy process for the files that have been copied correctly.

Often, large files are found to be mostly usable even when errors occur and are accepted. Compressed files do not fair as well, because the compression cannot be restarted after the first block of data is lost. Video and audio that is block-compressed (e.g., MPEG-type compression) can survive with the loss of only a few frames.

Always prompt for filename on copy

Selecting this option forces a prompt for every file that is copied, giving you the option to rename every file individually. This is not practical for most discs, but under certain controlled circumstances, this option can be very useful.

Force intensive UDF examination

Under normal circumstances, if an error is detected in a UDF file system, an intensive examination is done automatically. If no errors are detected, the lengthy process of examining the disc sector-by-sector is skipped.

In cases where deleted files are suspected of being on a disc and are not being shown, this option together with a complete re-examination of the disc will force a full, intensive examination that will find all disconnected files including those that have been deleted.

This option is not saved from session to session; it must be set explicitly every time it is used.

Keep duplicate diles from UDF examination

Normally, after an intensive examination of a UDF file system, the results are processed to remove duplicated files from the directory that CD/DVD Inspector builds into memory. These duplicates come from a variety of sources, but are mostly the result of the same directory information being found multiple times on the disc. This option prevents the deletion of duplicate files.

Significant effort is made to only delete files that are true duplicates, and to retain "named" files. This option is provided when retaining files is not working properly and it is necessary to keep the duplicates in order to be able to access all of the files.

This option should only be set after consulting with InfinaDyne Technical Support.

Automatically examine disc at startup

This option is set by default. When the CD/DVD Inspector is started, the last drive used is examined. If a disc is present, that drive is automatically selected and the disc is examined. If there is no disc in the last drive used, CD/DVD Inspector prompts you to select the drive to be used.

If your computer has multiple drives that are all used for examining discs, this option should be turned off so that time is not wasted starting an examination that will be terminated. This also eliminates the possibility of the wrong disc being examined.

If your computer only has a single drive attached, it is a good idea to leave it selected so that mounted discs are examined without needlessly prompting you.

Enable special features

This option is somewhat of a catch-all. It bypasses some of the checks made to prevent files from being treated as accessible when they appear not to be, and it enables some special handling features for processing discs with certain types of defects.

It also turns off the 90 percent intact restriction for copying files, which means that when this option is set and the "Accept all errors without prompting" option is selected, it is possible to copy a file and have 0 percent of the original content.

In general, this option should not be set for normal use except for copying files when any fragment of usable data from a file is needed.

Recover without prompts

This option selects between basic or expert mode of operation. In basic mode, you are prompted less for decisions, and various file system analyzing is automated. If this option is not set, there will be more prompts when errors occur and you will be given greater control over skipping various aspects of recovery operations. Deselecting this option makes using CD/DVD Inspector in an unattended mode almost impossible.

Show extents in disc reports

When this option is selected, additional lines are added to the various disc content reports to include extents after the first line of each file when the files are fragmented. This is not useful except in cases where the actual location for each fragment of file data is significant. Selecting this option can significantly increase the size of disc reports.

Disable disc memory feature

Normally the Disable Disc Memory option provides substantial benefit towards preventing the re-examination of discs (see Figure 6.13). Once a disc has been examined and the Disc Memory information has been stored, it takes as little as 10 seconds to recognize the disc again.

However, Disc Memory can also interfere with the examination of duplicated discs, which are unlikely to have significant errors. Having the Disc Memory feature turned on can hide the differences between discs in some cases. It is recommended that the Disc Memory be cleared between cases.

Forensic use

This option separates the two primary uses of CD/DVD Inspector. With this option set, the features and functions that are not forensically relevant are hidden or disabled, and the functionality designed to assist the forensic examiner is enhanced. This option is set by default, and should not be turned off when using in a forensic setting.

If this option is turned off, the primary focus is on disc recovery and error checking. This makes the Readability Test and its preference settings visible and changes the way files are copied.

Use 64-bit *ZIP* extensions for *ZIP* image files

Setting this option ensures that only a single *ZIP* image file is created. The *ZIP* image file uses the *ZIP64* extensions to the *ZIP* standard and is therefore compatible only with those tools that implement the *ZIP64* extensions.

EnCase does not support *ZIP64* extensions; therefore, image files created in this manner are not compatible. Image files can be reprocessed and broken into smaller *ZIP* files that do not use the extensions. These broken-apart files are compatible with EnCase. It is not known if FTK supports importing *ZIP64* extended *ZIP* files.

Disc Memory Settings

Figure 6.14 Disc Memory Settings

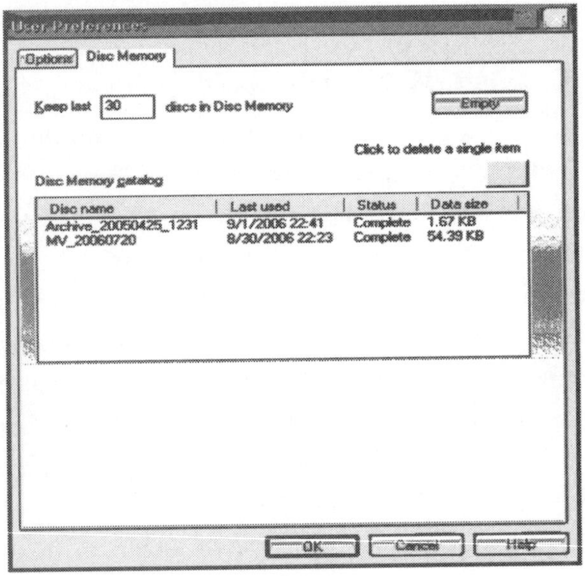

The Disc Memory page shows the contents of the Disc Memory catalog and the controls for it. The controls are described below.

Keep Last nnn discs in disc memory

This setting controls how many discs are maintained in the catalog; the default is 30. If you are working on a case where you frequently refer more than 30 discs, change this value to be significantly larger.

Empty button

This button clears the entire Disc Memory catalog at one time. This should be done between cases.

Click to delete a single item

Selecting any line in the Disc Memory catalog and clicking the button with the red X will delete that disc from the Disc Memory.

Disc Memory catalog

This displays each entry in the Disc Memory catalog in order by date and time of last use, with the most recently used disc entries appearing first. Each disc contains the disc name, the date and time it was last used, the status, and the data size shown.

Clicking any heading in the catalog (e.g., Data Size) will result in the list being sorted by that column. Clicking the same heading again will reverse the sort order.

Right-clicking on any disc entry causes a Context menu to be displayed. The Context menu has two options: *Export* and *Delete*. Export allows the disc entry to be saved into an external file that can then be taken to a different computer and imported. Delete causes the selected disc entry to be removed from the catalog.

Exporting a disc memory entry is faster than creating a disc image and bringing the disc image to a different computer.

The Analysis Tool

The Analysis tool is accessed from the Tools menu or the Analysis toolbar. This tool produces a report that can be copied to the clipboard for insertion into a report document. This report is a summary of all of the information found on the disc.

In each of the message descriptions below, italics are used to represent substitutions in the message. By convention, one or more *ns*' represent numeric digits and one or more *s*'s represent a string that is inserted in the message. All of the messages appear in alphabetical order, with alternatives listed with the primary message (see Figure 6.15).

Figure 6.15 Analysis Results Dialog

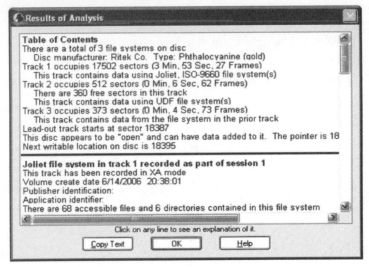

name file system in track *nn* recorded as part of session *nn*

The track is a data track that belongs to the recording session shown. The name is the name of the file system, and is shown as HFS, HFS+, High Sierra, ISO 9660, Joliet, or UDF. This line is displayed in bold at the beginning of the detailed information about a data track.

nnnnn sectors are used out of *nnnnn* available sectors

This message indicates the difference between how many sectors were written and how many sectors the file system occupies. If this number is large, it should be a warning that something may have been added to the end of the file system. This can legitimately occur when a combination of file systems is present in a single track, such as ISO 9660 and HFS.

type (media) load *nnnn* at *0xnnnn* from sector *nnnn*

This message describes an El Torito bootable entry. It follows the message "Bootable media from *company*, platform=*platform*" and further describes the bootable program entry found.

- *type* is shown as either "Bootable" or "Not bootable." Not bootable entries are placeholders in the El Torito standard, and can be used as a primitive type of file system by the software being booted.

- *media* shows the type of media that is being described. This can be an emulated floppy diskette, an emulated hard drive, or no emulation at all. No emulation simply loads the data into memory.

- *nnnn* is the amount of sectors to be loaded.

- "0x*nnnn* is the hexadecimal load address for the bootable data.

- *nnnn* is the sector number that begins the bootable data or emulated image.

A properly written post-gap was found for this track

A post-gap consists of 150 sectors of Mode 1 data sectors containing all binary 0s. Some programs and operating systems require that this be present for replicated discs. It is not required for DVDs.

CD/DVD Inspector checks for a minimum of 130 sectors to qualify for a post-gap. While it is unlikely that a mastering program will write a short post-gap, there can be difficulties in determining the exact end of the track. Therefore, this program allows for some tolerance in this determination. This can be significant in matching a disc up with a particular writing program.

All linked files (*nnnn*) in this session came from session *nn*

All of the files that appear in this directory come from the session indicated.

Application identification

This message documents the string set in the Application field for ISO 9660 and Joliet file systems. The identification often contains information about the writing software (e.g., the name and version of the program).

ATIP Reference Power = *nn*, Reference Speed = *nn*

This message is displayed for Compact Disc - ReWritable (CD-RW) discs, to indicate how the disc's various writing information laser power was determined. It gives the drive a starting point for performing running Optimal Power Calibration (OPC) determinations. This information can be useful when comparing discs. The program does not indicate a maximum or minimum speed for writing a disc.

Blank disc with *nnnnn* free sectors

This message is displayed when the disc is determined to be blank and the number of available sectors is shown.

Bootable disc information found, boot catalog at sector *nnn*

This message is displayed when bootable information is found for this disc. Care must be exercised when handling this disc, because if your computer boots from CDs or DVDs, it may boot this disc.

Bootable media from *company*, platform=*platform*

This message is displayed when the El Torito boot catalog and bootable information have been examined and an entry has been found for the platform indicated. The company name is generally the publisher of the booting software. Platform refers to the hardware environment and is either Intel x86, PowerPC, Macintosh, or is not defined.

CDDB key for this CD is *xxxxxxx*

The CDDB key is a well-defined non-unique coding system for audio discs. It was originally developed to allow access to a common database of album and track names. Today, there are several databases that can be accessed using the CDDB key.

The CDDB key is based on the number of tracks and the length of the individual tracks. While this is a reasonable hash value for identifying a disc, it is not unique. There are many discs with the same number of tracks and within the same resolution of the track length.

Data Preparer identification: *sssssss*

This message documents the string set in the Data Preparer field for ISO 9660 and Joliet file systems. It often contains useful information that can assist in determining the writing software.

Disc is a DVD-*kind* type is *type*

The disc is a DVD *kind*, which is either –R, –RW, +R or +RW. *type* indicates the book specification that the disc used when writing, which is usually Digital Versatile Disc - Read Only Memory (DVD-ROM), but can also be Digital Versatile Disc Recordable (DVD-R), Digital Versatile Disc - Rewriteable (DVD-RW), Digital Versatile Disc Plus Recordable (DVD+R), Digital Versatile Disc - Rewriteable (DVD+RW), or Digital Versatile Disc - Random Access Memory (DVD-RAM).

Disc manufacturer: *sssss* Type: *sssss*

This message is displayed if the device used to read the disc supports returning disc manufacturer information. There are also cases where new manufacturer codes are found and, instead of text messages, only the codes are shown.

The disc type is displayed as either "Cynanine (green) or Azo (blue)" or as "Phthalocynanine (gold)." The table of manufacturer codes is updated periodically. If you receive a message about an unknown code, the software may need to be updated.

DVD manufacturer is *sssss*

This message displays the DVD manufacturer code when it is present. This is commonly available for DVD-R and DVD-RW discs only.

Error *nnn* in manufacturer determination, manufacturer information not available

This message is displayed when an error has occurred while determining the manufacturer of a disc and the manufacturer cannot be displayed. The codes refer to specific syntax errors in the manufacturer information database. Manufacturer information is found in the *Inspector.mandb* file, and should not be modified. Reinstalling the product or extracting the manufacturer database file may resolve this problem.

Error reading boot catalog, sense=0x*nn* 0x*nn*

While reading the El Torito boot catalog, an error was returned by the drive. The sense code for this error is displayed. No further analysis of El Torito bootable disc information is possible.

Error reading file system data from disc, no further information available

An error occurred while reading the volume descriptor from the Analysis tool disc; therefore, it is not possible to display further information about this track.

Error reading sector *nnnnn* in track *nn*, analysis of track skipped

This message indicates that an error prevented the reading of file system information for that track. This is normal for discs where data tracks can only be read in raw mode (e.g., VCDs and SVCDs); however, in most cases, the video tracks are recognized as part of the ISO 9660 file system. If this occurs for a normal data CD, it may indicate that there is a problem reading a sector of the disc or a problem with the drive being used to read the disc.

The first response to this error is to try again. If the error persists, try a different device with better performance with reading marginal discs.

Error returned obtaining ISRC code, sense = *ss ss*

This message is displayed when the drive returns an error in response to requesting the Information International Standard Recording (ISRC) code for an audio track. No ISRC information is available for this track, which is usually due to difficulties in reading audio data from the disc.

Audio tracks can optionally use an ISRC code to identify the track. This code comprises the country (2 characters), the owner (3 characters), the year (2 digits), and a 5-digit serial number. This code is present on commercially produced audio discs, but is usually not present on home-recorded audio discs. This is not the same as a Uniform Product Code (UPC) or Media Catalog Number (MCN), and does not uniquely identify tracks.

File *sssss* is linked to track *nnn*, session *nn*

The file indicated in this message is not recorded in the current track; instead, it is referenced by the directory in a prior track. This is normal for multi-session discs when earlier tracks are linked with later tracks. This message is displayed only when the "Show Analysis file details" option is selected.

HFS volume name *sssss*

This message displays the name given to the HFS or HFS+ (Macintosh) volume. It serves the same purpose as the volume name for other disc formats.

Image file in *type* format: *sssss*

This message is displayed when an image file is being analyzed to show the type of image file (i.e., ISO 9660 or InfinaDyne) and the name of the image file.

Invalid boot catalog found, key values = 0x*nn* 0x*nn*

This message means that the El Torito boot catalog has an invalid key, which means that the disc was intended to be bootable, but is not.

Lead-out track starts at sector *nnnnn*

The lead-out track serves as a marker for the end of the disc. The sector number indicates the last sector used on the disc. The rest of the disc is blank.

If the disc is open, additional tracks can be added after this point. The second number indicates approximately how much space is left on the disc. The last sector available on standard 80-minute CDs is approximately 359800. The last sector available on a standard DVD-R is approximately 2298400.

Little-endian block size (*nnnn*) not equal to big-endian block size (*nnnn*)

This message is the result of a mastering program that ignored the big-endian or Motorola format values in the ISO 9660 or Joliet volume descriptor.

Although this has no effect on the disc in the Windows operating system, the disc may not work on Macintosh machines or other big-endian systems such as Sun. Check the Volume information display for more details about this message.

Little-endian volume size (*nnnnn*) not equal to big-endian volume size (*nnnnn*)

This message is the result of a mastering program that ignored the big-endian or Motorola format values in the ISO 9660 or Joliet volume descriptor. Although this has no effect on the disc under the Windows operating system, the disc may not work on Macintosh machines or other big-endian systems such as Solaris. Check the volume information for more details about this message.

Media catalog number for this disc is *sssss*

This message displays the MCN for a disc. The information is recorded in the lead-in for the disc with the TOC. Historically, the MCN was called the UPC number; however, this number ignored several important aspects of UPC coding, such as when one physical item has multiple UPC codes because of discount programs and different distributions. Additionally, because most companies only have a limited number of UPC codes, they are frequently reused. Consequently, when a CD is removed from current sales, that UPC is reassigned to a different title. The result of this is that the UPC code is not a unique identifier for a disc.

Due to the lack of a unique identifier on audio discs, the CDDB code is created, because it can be calculated for every audio disc. However, the CDDB code is also not unique.

Minimum recording speed = *nn*X, Maximum recording speed = *nn*X

This message identifies the minimum and maximum recording speeds for the disc from the Absolute Time in Pregroove (ATIP) information for a CD-RW disc. Most drives respect these limits.

Mismatched file counts between this file system and the *sssss* file system

This message is displayed in red when there are different numbers of files between the ISO 9660 and Joliet versions of a file system. In general, these file systems are exact copies of each other as far as the number and content of the files are concerned; only the filenames are different. If the counts are different, it is worth comparing the file directories to determine what the differences are.

Next writable location on disc is *nnnnn*

The next writable location is where additional information can be added to an open disc. This message displays the sector number where additional information can be added.

No directory was found for this file system

This message is only displayed (in red) under unusual circumstances. It indicates that the directory could not be found, which is normal with certain packet-written discs where the directory structure is created but not filled in.

When this message is displayed, no further examination of the disc is possible.

No ISRC/RID code present for this track

This audio track does not have an ISRC code or a recorder identification code, which is normal for audio tracks that are produced by consumer tools that make Red Book audio discs.

No manufacturer information was returned for this disc

The manufacturer information is only available for CD-R and CD-RW discs, and requires you to use hardware that is capable of returning it.

None of the files in this session are linked to prior sessions

This message indicates that the files in prior sessions are not linked to the session being described. These files are hidden from most disc users. Any prior files are not reflected in this directory, which means they are not accessible.

Note: directory depth of *nn* may cause problems on some MSCDEX versions

This message is displayed when a disc that does not meet other ISO 9660 restrictions has a directory depth in excess of eight levels.

ISO 9660 has a limit of a total depth of eight directories. Exceeding this limit can cause problems with some systems (e.g., Microsoft Disk Operating System (MS-DOS) with Microsoft CD-ROM Extension (MSCDEX); however, Windows 2000 and Windows XP do not have a limit. If compatibility with MS-DOS and other systems is important, this restriction should not be exceeded. Joliet file systems do not have this limit.

Note: directory depth of *nn* violates ISO 9660 limit of eight

ISO 9660 is limited to a total depth of eight directories. Exceeding this limit can cause problems with some systems (e.g., MS-DOS); however, Windows 2000 and Windows XP do not have a limit. If compatibility with other systems is important, this restriction should not be exceeded. This limit does not exist for Joliet file systems.

One or more files are using characters which MS-DOS cannot access

This message indicates that lowercase letters or MS-DOS separator characters appear in one or more filenames. While this is acceptable for Windows 95 and later versions of Windows, you may not be able to access these files under MS-DOS or other systems.

One or more files do not have a trailing version identifier (";1")

This message indicates that some files have a version identifier, and some do not. Generally, this indicates a problem with the writing software; either all of the files have the version identifier, or none of them do. A mixture of the two alternatives should not occur.

The version identifier should be present for full ISO 9660 compatibility. Although no current operating system uses this information, it is part of the standard. Commercial discs should have a version identifier; however, it is optional for user written discs, and it is suggested that it be left out.

Partition name: *sssss*

This message indicates the name of the partition for an HFS or HFS+ file system.

Publisher identification

This message documents the string set in the Publisher field for ISO 9660 and Joliet file systems. This string often contains useful information about the writing software. Microsoft Windows XA uses this field to identify the version of Image Mastering API (IMAPI) when it is used through the CD Writing Wizard and other IMAPI applications.

Rock ridge extension information is present

This message is displayed when Rock Ridge extension information is found in a file system. Rock Ridge allows for POSIX attributes for files such as long ASCII filenames, symbolic and hard links, user and group ownership, and permissions. This information is typically used by Linux and other UNIX systems. It is not used by Microsoft Windows or Macintosh operating systems.

When present for a disc, Rock Ridge information can yield useful information such as the user and group names that originally owned the files.

Table of Contents

This is a heading in the display for the TOC portion of the analysis report.

The "." directory entry is missing from one or more directories

This message indicates an error (displayed in red) in how the disc was mastered, and can be an indication that the disc was modified by hand. The "." directory entry is required and describes the current directory. It is required to be the first directory entry in any directory.

The ".." directory entry is missing from one or more directories

This message indicates an error (displayed in red) in how the disc was mastered, and can be an indication that the disc was modified by hand. The ".." directory entry is required and points to the previous directory in the hierarchy. In the root directory, this entry also points to the root directory itself. This directory entry is required to be the second directory entry in any directory. This message is.

The *tttttt* code for this track is *cccccc*

This audio track includes the indicated ISRC or Recorder Identification (RID). An ISRC code is composed of the country (2 characters,) the owner (3 characters,) the year (2 digits,) and a 5-digit serial number. A RID code is composed of a manufacturer and model followed by a 5-digit serial number.

The block size is *nnnn*, not 2048 as would be expected

This message (displayed in red) means that the block size specified for an ISO 9660 or Joliet volume should always be 2048. Some systems (e.g., Sun in the early 1990s) use other block sizes (e.g., 512), which are generally not usable on Windows. If the content of a disc is displayed normally, it means that the block size in the volume descriptor is wrong and the disc was written with a 2048-byte block size.

The directory in this file system qualifies as using the *setname* character set

This message means that the *setname* is replaced with ISO 9660 or MS-DOS, depending on how the disc was mastered. If the characters used are not acceptable to MS-DOS, a different message is displayed:

"In order to qualify as using the ISO 9660 character set, the disc must use only 'd' characters in directory and filenames. These are the upper case letters, numbers, and the underscore."

If other lower case letters are used, a different message is displayed, because the disc cannot be accessed by MS-DOS. Windows 95 and later versions have no problem accessing these types of discs.

If there are illegal characters in MS-DOS or Windows 95 filenames, the files may not be accessible. Different versions of Windows will exhibit different error messages.

The disc *Is Not* recorded in XA mode, but this file system is marked for XA mode

The disc *Is* recorded in XA mode, but this file system is not marked for XA mode

These messages indicate that there may be a mixture of Extended Architecture (XA) and non-XA tracks on the disc, which means that a disc image was constructed for an XA-mode track and then written in non-XA mode, or vice-versa. ISO 9660 and Joliet have a specific marker at offset 1024 in the Volume Descriptor, that says the file system was created in XA mode. If the characters CD-XA001 do not appear in the Volume Descriptor at this offset, the file system was not created for XA mode.

This is important, because you cannot mix XA mode tracks and non-XA mode tracks on the same disc. It is also important, because file systems created for XA mode contain XA directory extensions that identify files as being recorded in Mode 2 Form 2. VCD and SVCD discs utilize XA mode 2 Form 2 files and must be recorded in XA mode.

If you encounter a disc with mixed XA and non-XA tracks, it is important that you use the proper drive. Many drivves will refuse to mount such discs. Plextor CD-RW drives can read discs written in this manner.

The file "*ssssss*" appears in the directory but is not present

This message is displayed (in red) only when the "Show Analysis file details" option is selected, which is often the result of an aborted recording session with ISO 9660 or Joliet format disc. The directory information is recorded on the disc first, followed by writing the files. If something happens (e.g., a buffer under-run), the actual file is not recorded on the disc, but the directory still points to it. Roxio Easy CD Creator versions 4 and 5 have this problem. Attempting to access such files by software that is not aware that the file is not physically present on the disc, can lead to unpredictable results.

The files *ssssss* and *ssssss* overlap and one or both are destroyed

While writing to a rewritable CD or DVD, the files indicated were allocated to the same physical location on the disc. They now overlap, and one or both of them may be unusable. The files can be fragmented and only partially overlapping.

These files are displayed (in red) with a question mark icon in front of them to warn you of this situation. You can copy both of the files from the disc; however, they may not be usable. This is fairly common with rewritable media that has been used for working storage rather than archival purposes.

The last track in the table of contents is not the lead-out

The TOC does not have a lead-out track, which can have an adverse effect on the ability of some programs to read the disc. This is usually the result of the disc not being finalized properly, but can also occur because of problems in the writing software or cable problems with SCSI drives.

The mastering program for this disc did not Place version numbers (";1") after the filenames

This message indicates that the mastering program consistently did not place version identifiers in filenames. No current operating system uses these version identifiers. Discs created this way are acceptable to all systems, but do not meet the ISO 9660 standard.

The post-gap for this disc is either missing or invalid. *nnn* trailing sectors found

This message indicates that the post-gap could not be found for this track. It is possible that it may not be present or it may not be possible to determine the correct end of the track. Generally, it is difficult to determine the end of the track on a CD-ROM drive; it is much easier using a CD-RW drive, a DVD-ROM drive, or a DVD writer.

Due to this uncertainty, this error message should be taken as a warning rather than as an absolute indication of a problem.

A post-gap consists of 150 sectors of Mode 1 data sectors containing all binary 0s. Some programs and operating systems require replicated discs; they are not required for DVDs.

The system identifier in the ISO 9660 volume descriptor contains other than "a" characters

This message indicates that the disc was not created following the ISO 9660 standard; therefore, there may be problems using the disc on non-Windows computers.

The volume identifier in the ISO 9660 volume descriptor contains other than "d" characters

This message indicates that the disc was not created following the ISO 9660 standard; therefore, there may be problems using the disc on non-Windows computers. This is fairly common, because Windows accepts discs with lower-case letters in the Volume Identifier.

The volume identifier is blank. This may cause problems

This message (displayed in red) indicates that no name for the disc was provided by the user and no default name was used by the mastering software. The usability of the disc can be affected and can lead to strange errors when trying to use the disc. When using Windows, a primary technique of determining if a disc has changed is by inspecting the Volume Identifier.

There appear to be additional Boot definitions present

The El Torito standard allows for multiple boot definitions for a single company and platform; however, this is not generally supported by any PC Basic Input Output System (BIOS). CD/DVD Inspector does not display these additional boot definitions.

There are *nnn* files in the directory which are not recorded in this file system

This message indicates that a partially written disc has been recovered. The directory points to files that were not recorded. Attempting to access these files with software that does not recognize the situation (e.g., Microsoft Windows) can cause unpredictable results. You can look for files that are not written by displaying the file list in the Details format and looking for N/A in the sector number column. If you turn on the "Show Analysis file details" option, a complete list of the files is displayed by the Analysis tool.

> **NOTE**
>
> The files that are marked N/A are not physically recorded on the disc and, therefore, cannot be recovered.

There are *nnn* accessible files and *nnn* directories contained in this file system

This message documents how many files and directories are contained in the entire file system. Files included in this session that are contained in previous sessions, are not included.

There are *nnn* directories in this file system

This message displays the overall count of directories found in an HFS or HFS+ file system.

There are *nnn* files in this file system

This message displays the overall count of files found in an HFS or HFS+ file system.

There are *nnn* files linked from session *nn*

This message identifies the number of files that have been obtained from earlier sessions. If the "Show Analysis file details" option is selected, this message is followed by the message, "File *sssss* is linked to track *nnn*, session *nn*."

There are *nnn* files that could not be connected to a filename

When unconnected file entries are found, unnamed files occur in UDF file systems. These items are placed into the "Unattached items" folder and given names in the form of "Unnamed_*nnnn*."
This message is displayed in red.

There are *nnnn* free sectors in this track

This message is displayed for several reasons. The most common is for write-once media, where the disc has been written to with some type of drag-and-drop writing software and is not finalized. The remaining space on the disc is considered to be free sectors. This also occurs with partially completed discs, when a track has been reserved but not completely filled in.

When files are deleted, it does not mean that there is available space on rewritable media (such as a CD-RW). This space is the unused space at the end of a track, and has no relationship with sectors that are considered free on rewritable media.

There is a total of *nnn* file systems on disc

This message describes the number of file systems found on the disc. Each file system is ISO 9660, HFS, HFS+, High Sierra, Joliet, or UDF, and occupies one or more tracks on the disc. Some tracks contain multiple file systems.

This disc appears to be "open" and can have data added to it. The pointer is *nnnnn*

The last write operation to the disc did not close the disc; therefore, additional sessions may be added. The pointer refers to the location where additional sessions can be added.

This disc has *nn* layers

This message shows the number of layers present on the disc (always 1 or 2). This message is displayed only for DVD discs.

This disc is still "open" and can have data added to it

This message indicates that the disc has not been closed (or finalized) and that it can still be written to. This is very helpful, especially if the disc appears to be a commercially created.

Note that discs that are closed become much faster when inserted in a CD or DVD drive.

This file system contains compressed data

The file system recorded contains data compressed in a manner recognized by CD/DVD Inspector. DirectCD and Drag2Disc from Adaptec/Roxio/Sonic use one system of compression, and PacketCD from CeQuadrat uses a different system. Both systems are supported by CD/DVD Inspector.

Normally, it is required that you install the proper version of the software to access such discs when the file system contains compressed data. Such software can compromise the integrity of a forensic workstation; it is not recommended that you install this.

This File system was written by *sssss*

This message identifies the software that created the UDF file system. The information can be forensically significant for identifying the computer where the disc was originated.

This file system was written by packet-writing software

This message is displayed when a UDF file system is found. It is a warning that the disc is not suitable for replication, because it was created with packet writing. The specific program that created the track data is displayed in the details portion of the Analysis output.

This track contains audio with pre-emphasis

This track contains audio without pre-emphasis

These messages are displayed when the track contains Red Book audio with or without the standard CD pre-emphasis. It is unusual to find an audio track without pre-emphasis for music.

This track contains data and contains *sssss* file system(s)

This message identifies the contents of a data track. The various types that appear in this message are Compact Disk Interactive (CD-I), High Sierra, HFS (Macintosh), HFS+, ISO 9660, and UDF.

This track contains data from the file system in the prior track

This message is displayed when a file system started in a previous track continues into this track. This occurs for a number of reasons, but mostly because of the way the disc is constructed. VCD and SVCD discs use multiple tracks for the file system, as do packet-written write-once discs (e.g., CD-R, DVD-R and DVD+R).

This track has been recorded in XA mode

This message is displayed when a disc has been recorded in XA mode. This should be compatible with nearly all CD-ROM drives manufactured since 1992; however, if the disc is for some non-PC usage, it may be a problem.

Mastering software should not allow for mixing XA and non-XA sessions on the same disc. Some drives read discs that have been written with mixed XA and non-XA sessions. We strongly recommend that you use Plextor drives that support reading such discs.

This track is marked as being blank

This message is displayed when a track is marked as blank on the disc, even though it may not actually be blank. If the track was not recorded completely, this flag may be left as "blank" even though data is present. This is a warning that the track was not completed properly.

CD/DVD Inspector will attempt to inspect the track further to determine if the data is accessible. This can be dependent on the capabilities of the device being used.

Track *nn* has been added to represent an open session

An unfinished track has been found that does not appear in the TOC. This is a common occurrence with packet-written discs, and indicates that the disc has not been finalized.

Track *nn* is an audio track

This message precedes the detail information for an audio track.

Track *nn* Occupies *nnn* sectors (*nn* Min, *nn* Sec, *nn* frames)

This is the message for a track on the disc. For Audio tracks, the length is described in minutes, seconds, and frames. The information that follows describes the track and the file systems found in it.

Track contains MCN of *nnnnnn*

This message is displayed when a MCN entry is found within the first 1,000 sectors of an audio track. This generally does not occur, because the MCN should only be placed in the lead-in. If it is present, it should match the MCN in the lead-in.

Track image written with *nnnn* byte sectors

This message is displayed when an image file is being analyzed, to show the size of the sector data in the image file. The optimal number of sectors is 2,448, which indicates that the image contains the full subchannel data.

Track was written with fixed-length packets *nnnn* bytes in length

This message is displayed when a track is written with fixed-length packets on the disc. Discs written with fixed-length packets can only be read on CD-RW, Multi-Read compliant, and DVD devices. Most Compact Disk - Read Only Memory (CD-ROM) drives manufactured before 1997 cannot be used to read discs with fixed-length packets.

Track was written with variable-length packets

This message is displayed when a track is written with variable-length packets on the disc. Discs with variable-length packets can be read on any compatible device, including CD-ROM drives manufactured before 1997.

UDF examination error: *sssss*

This message is displayed when an error is encountered while processing a UDF file system. It can indicate that one or more files were found, but could not be processed successfully.

UDF partition exceeds
Size of track according to disc information

This message warns you that the UDF file system is not complete; the size of the UDF data is reported to be larger than the data that is written to the disc.

If there are other error messages regarding the disc, they are probably significant. If all of the files on the disc are accessible, this is a warning about the construction of the UDF file system.

Volume create date *date*

This message indicates that the file system was created.

Volume size appears suspicious; header says *nnnnn* while track is *nnnnn* sectors

This message (displayed in red) is usually the result of a "recovered" disc, where a track was partly written to but not completed. This message may be accompanied by the message, "There are *nnn* files in the directory that are not recorded in this track," which confirms that the track was partially written.

If this occurs on a manufactured CD or a CD that is known to not have been partially written to and recovered, it indicates a problem with how it was mastered, because the volume size is inaccurate. The volume size can be displayed by selecting the proper file system and Volume item under the Tools menu.

Warning: one or more checksum errors were detected in the UDF structures

This message indicates that there are problems in the UDF file system. From a forensic standpoint, this can indicate that the file system has been modified by hand in order to hide information or mislead you.

Warning: root directory length is specified as zero

The root directory information in the volume descriptor for an ISO 9660 or Joliet file system indicates a 0-length root directory. This is ignored on Windows but not on other platforms; it is clearly a violation of the ISO 9660 standard. An attempt is made to process the root directory using the length in the "." directory entry.

Warning: this disc is marked as having a sparable partition, but no sparing information table is present

Sparable partitions are used for rewritable discs, where unusable sectors can be avoided using "sparing." This indicates that the information for the sparing table (which is required) was not found on the disc.

This can also be an indication of poor implementation of the UDF file system, and can be used to uniquely identify the writing software.

Warning: virtual allocation table missing

This message is displayed when the Virtual Allocation Table (VAT) for the UDF file system cannot be found on write-once media. The result of this is that filenames are not associated with the content of the files, even though the filenames appear in the directory display. All such files have a red X icon displayed.

The data content of the files is in the "Unattached Items" folder with assigned names. If a determination of the file type is made, the proper extension is assigned.

Warning: VAT not found in conventional place

This warning is displayed when the VAT for the UDF file system in not found in the usual place, which indicates that the UDF file system cannot be normally accessed, even by the software used to write it.

In many cases, this is an older version of the VAT, and may not include all files that have been written to the disc. Check the "Unattached Items" folder for additional files that may have generated filenames.

Whole Disc MD5 Hash Value *xxxxxxxxxxxxxxxxxx*

This message shows the whole disc MD5 hash value when it has been calculated before using the Analysis tool. It is only shown when the defaults are taken while calculating the MD5 value for the disc.

The hardware information display

The hardware information display shows the various capabilities of the current CD or DVD device (see Figure 6.16). While much of this information simply identifies the device and what it can do, several of the items are of significant interest for a forensic examiner.

The Hardware Information Display dialog box is shown below.

Figure 6.16 Hardware Information Display Dialog

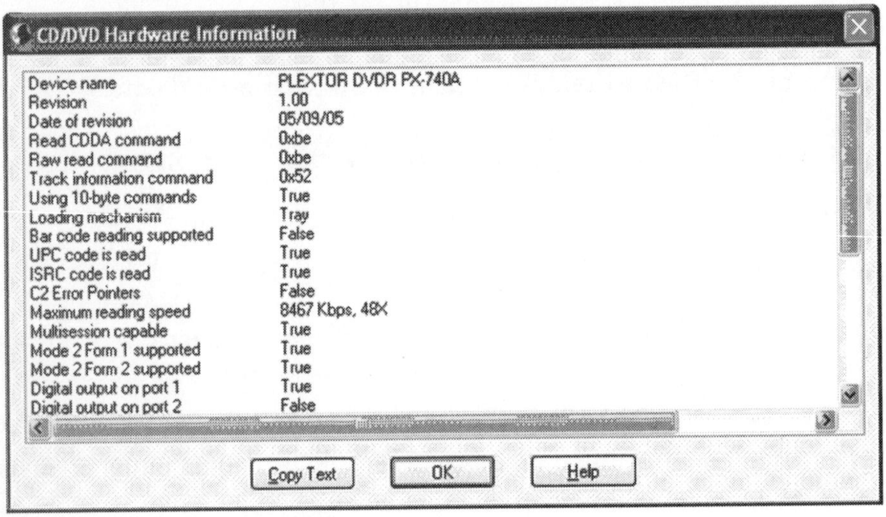

Device name

The "device name" shows the name of the device as reported by the device itself. It can differ considerably from the name on the outside of the device.

Revision

The "revision" shows the revision level of the drive firmware, which is usually in the form *M.mm* for the major and minor version levels. This can be significant for forensic purposes, because some drives behave differently at different firmware revision levels.

Date of revision

The "date of revision" shows the date of the revision release, which is the date that it was released by the drive manufacturer; not the date the revision was applied to the drive.

Read CDDA command

The "Read CDDA" command shows the command code that is used to read audio track data from the drive. The most common command code is 190 (or hex BE), which is used with current standards-compliant drives. This command code is in the device database entry for the drive.

"Raw read" command

The "raw read" command shows the command code used to read RAW data sectors from the drive. The most common command code is 190 (or hex BE), which is used with current standards-compliant drives. This command code is in the device database entry for the drive.

Track information command

The Track Information command shows the command code used to read track information from the drive. It is almost always 82 (or hex 52), except for very old drives. The command code is in the device database entry for the drive.

Using 10 byte commands

10 byte commands are used when necessary by CD/DVD Inspector. This message is informational and can be helpful in resolving drive issues.

Readability Test reason code

The "Readability Test reason code" is reported only when an error code has been set by the Readability Test. This information is presented to assist in resolving drive issues.

Loading Mechanism

The "Loading Mechanism" describes the mechanism that the drive uses to load discs. This can be any of the following items: caddy, tray, pop-up, changer (individual discs), changer (cartridge), or reserved. The standard does not address notebook or slot-loading drives; therefore, these drives are generally reported as having a tray loading mechanism.

Bar code reading supported

The "Bar Code Reading Supported" item is reported as true or false, based on the capabilities of the drive. This capability is a holdover from the early 1990s; no current drives support this.

UPC code is read

The "UPC Code is Read" item is reported as true or false, based on the ability of the drive to return the MCN from audio discs. Originally, this was intended to be the UPC code of a retail audio CD; however, it was soon realized that the UPC code was not constant or unique. The data stored on the disc was renamed MCN in the late 1990s. Nearly all drives today report this as true.

ISRC code is read

The ISRC Code is Read" item is reported as true or false, based on the ability of the drive to return the ISRC for audio tracks. Nearly all drives report this as true.

C2 Error Pointers

The C2 Error Pointers" item is reported as true or false, based on the ability of the drive to return C2 error pointers to indicate that correctable read errors have occurred. C2 Error Pointers are used with the Readability Test to obtain information about correctable errors when testing a disc. If this is reported as true, the results from the Readability Test are more accurate.

Maximum reading speed

The "Maximum Reading Speed" item reports the maximum reading speed of the drive in kilobytes (KB) per second, and as an x factor. For CDs, $1x$ is equal to 150 KB per second. For DVDs, $1x$ is equal to 676 KB per second.

Multi-session capable

The "Multi-session Capable" item is reported as true or false, based on the ability of the drive to read multi-session discs. This has been a standard feature on all drives since 1994.

Mode 2 form 1 supported

The "Mode 2 Form 1 Supported" item is reported as true or false, based on the ability of the drive to read XA Mode 2 Form 1 sectors. This has been a standard feature on all drives since 1994.

Mode 2 form 2 supported

The "Mode 2 Form 2 Supported" item is reported as true or false, based on the ability of the drive to read XA Mode 2 Form 2 sectors. These sectors are used for multimedia discs such as VCD or SVCD. This is a standard capability of nearly all drives.

Digital output on port 1

The Digital Output on Port 1" item is reported as true or false, based on the existence of a digital output connector on the rear of the drive. This is fairly common with modern drives, but is seldom used.

Digital output on port 2

The "Digital Output on Port 2" item is reported as true or false, based on the existence of a second digital output connector on the drive. This is not a common feature on recent drives.

Audio play supported

The "Audio Play Supported" item is reported as true when the drive supports commands that begin playing an audio track through the analog and/or digital audio ports. It has been a requirement for compatibility with Microsoft Windows since Microsoft Windows 95.

Reading CDDA supported

The "Reading CDDA Supported" item is reported as true when the drive supports reading audio track data, and is common for all drives manufactured since 1998. If it is not supported, you cannot collect audio track information in a disc image file. For forensic purposes, it is recommended that you check to ensure that this is reported as true.

CD-Text/CD+G supported

The "CD-Text/CD+G CDDA Supported" item is reported as true when the drive can access R–W subchannel data where Philips-style CD text information and CD+G graphics information are stored. For forensic purposes, it is recommended that you check to ensure that this is reported as true.

CD-Text/CD+G Decoded

The "CD-Text/CD+G Decoded" item is reported as true when the drive decodes and de-interleaves R–W subchannel data. Both higher accuracy and better error correction are provided when CD/DVD Inspector does the de-interleaving for displaying CD+G graphics. This is not required for forensic purposes; however, many high-quality drives support this.

Accurate CDDA positioning

This is reported as true when the drive supports accurate positioning within an audio track. Such accurate positioning requires additional work by the drive because audio sectors are only required to have position information every 15 sectors. Some software is affected but CD/DVD Inspector is not.

Transfer Block supported

The "Transfer Block Supported" item is reported true when the drive supports transferring sector data with errors. It is not common with lower cost drives. For forensic purposes, this item should be checked and only those drives that support Transfer Block should be used for collecting evidence.

Inactivity spin-down

The "Inactivity Spin-down" item reports the amount of time a drive waits before turning the spindle motor off.

Device capabilities

The "Device Capabilities" item reports the types of discs that the drive supports for reading and writing.

Device buffer size (in K)

The "Device Buffer Size (in K)" item reports the size of the drive buffer, which is used for buffering during read and writing operations.

Drive serial number

The "Drive Serial Number" item reports the drive serial number when it is available.

The Volume Information Display

The volume information display is accessed by clicking the Volume Information item in the Tools menu (see Figure 6.17). The file system information display is chosen by selecting one of the file systems and/or sessions in the left-hand side of the Volume Information window. Each file system type (e.g.,ISO 9660 Joliet, HFS, HFS+, HSG, and UDF) has a different display. Other file system types (e.g., Red Book Audio), do not have volume information available.

Figure 6.17 Volume Information Display Dialog

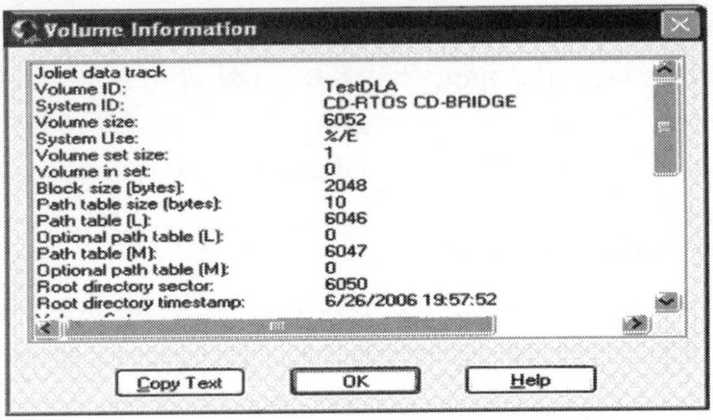

The following describes the information that is displayed for each of the file system types.

ISO 9660 Volume Information

For ISO 9660 file systems, all of the fields from the Primary Volume Descriptor are formatted and displayed.

Volume ID

The name of the file system can be up to 32 characters. Correctly constructed ISO 9660 file system names use only uppercase letters, numbers, and the underscore (_) characters.

System ID

The "System ID" field contains information that is designed to be used by the operating system reading the disc. Common values for this field are "APPLE COMPUTER INC," which indicates that the disc has Apple Macintosh extensions, and "CD-RTOS CD-BRIDGE," which indicates that the disc is written in XA mode.

Other information can also appear in this field (e.g., the software and/or operating system that created the disc). Windows ignores this field completely; therefore, many writing programs use this for their own purposes.

Volume size

The "Volume Size" field indicates the size of the volume declared by the file system. It can differ from the actual space taken by the track. Some writing software terminates writing without writing the entire file system. In this case, the value is reflected in the intended size of the volume, whereas the actual track size will be considerably smaller.

It is not necessarily a bad situation when the volume size is smaller than the space occupied by the track. However, when the volume size is larger than the track, it indicates a serious problem; files are probably missing from the disc that is represented in the directory.

This value is shown from the little-endian or Intel format) value. The big-endian or Motorola format value is displayed later in the list of values.

System use

The "System Use" field contains information on how to use the operating system. It does not have any defined use for ISO 9660 file systems.

Volume set size

The original use of the "Volume Set Size" field was to indicate how many discs made up the entire volume of data. There were very few multi-disc volumes created. Today, this field always contains the value 1. This value is shown from the little-endian or Intel) format value. The big-endian or Motorola format value is displayed later in the list of values.

Volume in set

When the volume set size is larger than 1, it indicates the volume that is within the set. No current operating system examines this field; however, it should be set to a value between 1 and the number of discs in the volume set. This value is shown from the little-endian ªor Intel° format value. The big-endian or Motorola format value is displayed later in the list of values.

Block size (bytes)

This field indicates the number of bytes for each "block" of data used in this volume. It is possible to see values of either 512 or 2,048 in this field; however, discs with the value of 512 may be difficult to read under existing operating systems. A value of 512 bytes was common in discs created for Sun workstations in the early 1990s.

The value is shown from the little-endian or Intel format value. The big-endian or Motorola format value is displayed later in the list of values.

Path table size (bytes)

The "Path Table Size (Bytes) field contains the number of bytes used in the path table for the file system. The path table contains the names of subdirectories and the starting sector of the subdirectory, which is used to quickly navigate through directories.

This value is shown from the little-endian or Intel) format value. The big-endian or Motorola format value is displayed later in the list of values.

Path table (L)

The "Path Table (L) field contains the sector number on the disc of the L-format path table. If the path table size is greater than 2,048, there are multiple sequential sectors beginning with the sector number in this field. This version of the path table has little-endian or Intel format integers.

Path tables contain one entry for each subdirectory in the file system. Each entry consists of the following data items:

Length	Type	Description
1	Binary	The length of the path table entry
1	Binary	The length of the extended attributes
4	Integer	The starting sector number for a subdirectory
2	Integer	The path entry of a parent directory
???	Character	The name of a subdirectory

In the L path table, the fields identified as integers are in little-endian or Intel form. In the M path table, these fields are in big-endian or Motorola form. Clicking on the path table line will result in a new window showing the contents of the path table.

Optional path table (L)

The "Optional Path Table (L) field specifies the starting sector number of the optional second L format path table. This is not commonly used.

Path table (M)

The "Path Table (M)" field contains the sector number of the M format path table on the disc. If the path table size is greater than 2048, there are multiple sequential sectors beginning with the sector number in this field. This version of the path table has either big-endian or Motorola format integers.

Optional path table (M)

The "Optional Path Table (M)" field specifies the starting sector number of the optional second M format path table. This is not commonly used.

Root directory sector

The "Root Directory Sector" field contains the sector number of the beginning of the root directory. The first entry in the root directory contains the information about the directory itself. This value is shown from the little-endian or Intel format value. The big-endian or Motorola format value is displayed later in the list of values.

Root directory timestamp

This field contains the timestamp from the root directory "." entry. This usually matches the volume create date and time (described below). If it does not match, it is a clear indication that the person creating the disc is attempting to mislead people about the creation date and time of the disc, thus, there is no way to be certain which date and time is actually correct.

Volume set

The "Volume Set" field describes the volume set. This can be used to describe the disc; however, it is not commonly used.

Publisher

The "Publisher" field contains a message that describes the publisher of the disc. It can be set by most mastering software; however, it is not done often.

If the first character of this field is a vertical bar ("|," [hex 5F]), the remainder of the field is a filename in the root directory containing the publisher information.

Data preparer

The "Data Preparer" field contains a message describing the data preparer of the disc. It can be set by most mastering software; however, it is not done often. The Microsoft Windows XP disc writing tool inserts a message in this field about the IMAPI interface licensed from Roxio by Microsoft. This makes identifying discs written by the Windows XP disc writing tool simple.

If the first character of this field is a vertical bar ("|," [hex 5F]), the remainder of the field is a filename in the root directory containing data preparer information.

Application

The "Application" field contains a message describing the application that created the disc. It can be set by some mastering software; others insert their own text in this field (e.g., Roxio Easy CD Creator inserts information describing the application into this field).

If the first character of this field is a vertical bar ("|," [hex 5F]) the remainder of the field is a filename in the root directory containing application information.

Copyright file

The "Copyright File" field contains the name of a file in the root directory containing the copyright information for the disc. It is usually blank or binary 0.

Some writing software provides an easy way to set this information, while others make it extremely difficult. It is unusual to find this set on commercial discs where copyright information is important. No current operating system uses this information or makes it available in any manner.

Abstract file

The "Abstract File" field contains the name of a file in the root directory containing information about the contents of the disc. It is usually blank or binary 0.

Some writing software provides an easy way to set this information, while others make it extremely difficult. No current operating system uses this information or makes it available in any manner.

Bibliography file

The "Bibliography" field contains the name of a file in the root directory containing bibliographic information about the disc. Because this field is rarely used, it is usually blank or binary 0.

Volume created

The "Volume Created" field is the date and time the volume was created. The date is a string of numeric digits with the following meanings:

- 4-digit year
- 2-digit month
- 2-digit day
- 2-digit hour
- 2-digit minute
- 2-digit second
- 1- digit tenths of seconds
- 1-digit hundredths of seconds
- 1-byte binary time zone

The binary time zone is a signed 8-bit value with positive values representing time zones that are east of GMT, and negative values representing time zones that are west of GMT. The value is in 15-minute increments, therefore, a value of 4 bits is 1 hour east of GMT, and a value of −24 (hex E8) is 6 hours west of GMT.

Volume modified

The "Volume Modified" field is the date and time that the contents of the volume were last updated. While this field might have originally had some meaning, today it is either equal to the volume-created timestamp, blank, or all 0s. If a time is present, it has the same format as the volume created time.

Volume expires

The "Volume Expires" field is the date and time that the contents of the volume are considered obsolete or expired. There is no other meaning for this field other than descriptive and, because it is never displayed, it has no real use. It is sometimes set to 10 or 100 years after the volume created date by the writing software, but it also commonly contains 0s or is left blank. If a time is present, it has the same format as the volume created time.

Volume effective

The "Volume Effective" field is the date and time the contents of the volume are considered effective. There is no other meaning for this field other than descriptive and, because it is never displayed, it has no real use. The usual values for this field are the same date and time as the volume created date, all 0s, or blank. If a time is present, it has the same format as the volume create time.

Volume size

"The Volume Size" field is the big-endian or Motorola-format volume size.

Volume set size

The "Volume Set Size" field is the big-endian or Motorola-format volume size. It should be equal to the previous volume set size.

Volume in set

The "Volume in Set" field is the big-endian or Motorola-format volume size. It should be equal to the previous volume in set.

Block size (bytes)

The "Block Size (Bytes)" field is the big-endian or Motorola-format volume size. It should be equal to the previous block size.

Path table size (bytes)

The "Path Table Size (Bytes)" field is the big-endian or Motorola format volume size. It should be equal to the previous path table size.

Root directory sector

The "Root Directory Sector" field is the big-endian or Motorola format volume size. It should be equal to the previous root directory sector.

Joliet volume information

For Joliet file systems, all of the fields in the Supplementary Volume Descriptor are formatted and displayed. In most cases, the fields for a Joliet file system are identical to those for an ISO 9660 file system. However, all character strings are Unicode rather than ASCII, and some of the fields have special meaning. All Unicode characters are stored in big-endian or Motorola format.

Volume ID

The name of the file system can be up to 16 UCS-2 16-bit Unicode characters. Unlike ISO 9660, there are no character restrictions.

System ID

The System ID contains information that is designed to be used by the operating system reading the disc. Most commonly, this contains the string "CD-RTOS CD-BRIDGE," indicating the disc is written in XA mode. This string should be in UCS-2 16-bit Unicode characters, but is often ASCII. The System ID should be considered an identifying characteristic of writing software.

Volume size

The "Volume Size" field indicates the size of the volume that is declared by the file system. It can differ from the actual space taken by the track. Some writing software terminates writing early without finishing the entire file system. In this case, the value reflects the intended size of the volume, whereas the actual track size will be considerably smaller.

When the volume size is smaller than the space occupied by the track, it indicates an unusual, but not necessarily bad, situation. However, when the volume size is larger than the track, it indicates a serious problem and there are probably files missing from the disc that may be represented in the directory.

For Joliet file systems, this is almost always the same as the value for the corresponding ISO 9660 file system.

This value is shown from the little-endian or Intel-format value. The big-endian or Motorola format value is displayed later in the list of values.

System use

The "System Use" field contains information about operating system use. The field is used to indicate the type of character set that is present in a Joliet file system. The following coding is used for this:

ASCII Characters	Hex Coding	Description
%/@	25 2F 40	UCS-2 level 1
%/C	25 2F 43	UCS-2 level 2
%/E	25 2F 45	UCS-2 level 3

The definitions of various UCS levels are found in ISO–10646 and the Unicode standard. For forensic purpose, the specific meanings are not important.

Volume set size

The original use of the Volume Set Size was to indicate how many discs made up the entire volume of data. There were very few such multi-disc volumes created. Today this field always contains 1.

This value is shown from the little-endian or Intel format value. The big-endian or Motorola format value is displayed later in the list of values.

Volume in set

When the Volume in Set size is larger than 1, it indicates the volume within the set. No current operating system examines this field; however, it should be set to a value between 1 and the number of discs in the volume set.

This value is shown from the little-endian or Intel-format value. The big-endian or Motorola format value is displayed later in the list of values.

Block size (bytes)

The number of bytes for each "block" of data used in this volume, is indicated in the "Block Size (Bytes) field. For Joliet volumes, this is always 2048 bytes.

This value is shown from the little-endian or Intel format value. The big-endian or Motorola format value is displayed later in the list of values.

Path table size (bytes)

The "Path Table Size (Bytes): field contains the number of bytes used in the path table for the file system. The path table contains the names of the subdirectories and the starting sector of each subdirectory. This is used to quickly navigate through directories.

This value is shown from the little-endian or Intel format value. The big-endian or Motorola format value is displayed later in the list of values.

Path table (L)

The "Path Table (L)" field contains the sector number on the disc of the L-format path table. If the path table size is greater than 2048, there are multiple sequential sectors beginning with the sector number in this field. This version of the path table has little-endian or Intel format integers.

The path table contains one entry for each subdirectory in the file system. Each entry consists of the following data items:

Length	Type	Description
1	Binary	The length of the path table entry
1	Binary	The length of the extended attributes
4	Integer	The starting sector number for the subdirectory
2	Integer	The path entry of the parent directory
???	Character	The name of the subdirectory (UCS-2 characters)

In the L path table, the fields identified as integers are in little-endian or Intel form. In the M path table, these fields are in big-endian or Motorola form.

The path table contains UCS-2 16-bit Unicode characters, and is always an even number of bytes.

Optional path table (L)

The "Optional Path Table (L)" field specifies the starting sector number of the optional second L format path table. This is not commonly used.

Path table (M)

The "Path Table (M)" field contains the sector number on the disc of the M format path table. If the path table size is greater than 2048, there are multiple sequential sectors beginning with the sector number in this field. This version of the path table has big-endian or Motorola format integers. A complete description of the path table contents are above. Clicking on the path table line will open a new window displaying the contents of the path table.

Optional path table (M)

The "Optional Path Table (M)" field specifies the starting sector number of the optional second M format path table. This is not commonly used.

Root directory sector

The "Root Directory Sector" field contains the sector number of the beginning of the root directory. The first entry in the root directory contains the information about the directory itself.

This value is shown from the little-endian or Intel format value. The big-endian or Motorola format value is displayed later in the list of values.

Root directory timestamp

"The "Root Directory Timestamp" field contains the timestamp from the root directory "." directory entry. This usually matches the volume create date and time. If it does not, it is a clear indication that the person creating the disc is attempting to mislead people about the creation date and time of the disc. There is no way to be certain which date and time is correct.

Volume set

A message describing the volume set. This can be used to describe the disc but it is not commonly used.

Publisher

The "Publisher" field contains a message describing the publisher of the disc. This field is available to be set by most mastering software; however, it is not done often.

For a Joliet file system, this field should contain UCS-2 characters; however, some incorrect writing software will put ASCII characters in this field, which is considered an identifying characteristic of the writing software.

If the first character of this field is a vertical bar ("|," [hex 5F]), the remainder of the field is considered to be a filename in the root directory containing the publisher information.

Data preparer

The "Date Preparer" field contains a message describing the data preparer of the disc. It is available to be set by most mastering software, but is not done often. The Microsoft Windows XP disc writing tool inserts a message in this field about the IMAPI interface licensed from Roxio by Microsoft. This makes identifying discs written by the Windows XP disc writing tool simple.

For a Joliet file system, this field contains UCS-2 characters; however, some incorrect writing software will put ASCII characters in this field. This is considered an identifying characteristic of the writing software.

If the first character of this field is a vertical bar ("|," [hex 5F]), the remainder of the field is a filename in the root directory containing data preparer information.

Application

The "Application" field contains a message describing the application that created the disc. It is available to be set by some mastering software; however, others insert their own text in this field (e.g., Roxio Easy CD Creator inserts information into this field that describes the application).

For a Joliet file system, this field contains UCS-2 characters; however, some incorrect writing software will put ASCII characters in this field. This is considered an identifying characteristic of the writing software.

If the first character of this field is a vertical bar ("|," [hex 5F]), the remainder of the field is considered to be a filename in the root directory containing application information.

Copyright file

The "Copyright File" field contains the name of a file in the root directory containing the copyright information for the disc. It is usually blank or binary 0.

Some writing software provides an easy way to set this information, while others make it extremely difficult. It is unusual to find this set on commercial discs where copyright information may be important. No current operating system uses this information or makes it available in any manner.

For a Joliet file system, this field contains UCS-2 characters; however, some incorrect writing software will put ASCII characters in this field. This is considered an identifying characteristic of the writing software.

Abstract file

The "Abstract File" field contains the name of a file in the root directory containing information about the contents of the disc. It is usually blank or binary 0.

Some writing software provides an easy way to set this information, while others make it extremely difficult. No current operating system uses this information or makes it available in any manner.

For a Joliet file system, this field contains UCS-2 characters; however, some incorrect writing software will put ASCII characters in this field. This is considered an identifying characteristic of the writing software.

Bibliography file

The "Bibliography File" field contains the name of a file in the root directory containing bibliographic information about the disc. It is usually blank or binary 0, because it is rarely used.

For a Joliet file system, this field contains UCS-2 characters; however, some incorrect writing software will put ASCII characters in this field. This is considered an identifying characteristic of the writing software.

Volume created

The "Volume Created" field is the date and time the volume was created. The date is a string of numeric digits with the following meanings:

- 4–digit year
- 2-digit month
- 2-digit day
- 2-digit hour
- 2-digit minute
- 2-digit second
- 1-digit tenths of seconds
- 1-digit hundredths of seconds
- 1-byte binary time zone

The binary time zone is a signed 8-bit value with positive values representing time zones that are east of GMT, and negative values representing time zones that are west of GMT. The value is in 15-minute increments; therefore, a value of 4 is 1 hour east of GMT, and a value of -24 (hex E8) is 6 hours west of GMT.

Volume modified

The "Volume Modified" field is the date and time the contents of the volume were last updated. While this field might have originally had some meaning , it is either equal to the volume created timestamp, blank, or all 0. If there is a time present, it has the same format as the volume created time.

Volume expires

The "Volume Expires" field is the date and time the contents of the volume are to be considered obsolete or expired. This field is only descriptive and, because it is never displayed, it has no real use. It is sometimes set to 10 or 100 years after the volume created date by the writing software, but it also commonly contains 0s or is left blank. If there is a time present, it has the same format as the volume created time.

Volume effective

The "Volume Effective" field is the date and time the contents of the volume are to be considered effective. This field is only descriptive and, because it is never displayed, it has no real use. In this field, you will find the values to be the same date and time as the volume create date, all 0s, or blank. If there is a time present, it has the same format as the volume created time.

Volume size

The "Volume Size" field is the big-endian or Motorola format volume size. It should be equal to the previous volume size.

Volume set size

The "Volume Set Size" field is the big-endian or Motorola format volume size. It should be equal to the previous volume set size.

Volume in set

The "Volume in Set" field is the big-endian or Motorola format volume size. It should be equal to the previous volume in set.

Block size (bytes)

The "Block Size (Bytes)" field is the big-endian or Motorola format volume size. It should be equal to the previous block size.

Path table size (bytes)

The "Path Table Size (Bytes)" field is the big-endian or Motorola-format volume size. It should be equal to the previous path table size.

Root directory sector

The "Root Directory Sector" field is the big-endian or Motorola format volume size. It should be equal to the previous root directory sector.

HFS and HFS+ Volume Information

Volume ID

The "Volume ID" field shows the volume identifier or name of the disc. For HFS discs, this can be up to 31 ASCII characters. For HFS+ discs, this can be up to 255 Unicode characters.

Files

The "Files" field shows the number of files declared in the file system. This can differ from the number of files shown by the Analysis tool, which counts the files that are present.

Directories

The "Directories" field shows the number of directories declared in the file system. It can differ from the number of directories shown by the Analysis tool, which counts the directories that are present.

Allocation size (bytes)

The "Allocation Size (Bytes)" field shows the size of an allocation block for the HFS or HFS+ volume. Allocation blocks are similar to clusters for File Allocation Table (FAT) or New Technology File System (NTFS) file systems on a hard drive. Due to the construction of HFS and HFS+ CDs and DVDs, it is unusual to find anything other binary 0s in the trailing part of an allocation block.

Allocation blocks

The "Allocation Block" field shows the number of allocation blocks that are present on the media.

Free blocks

The "Free Blocks" field shows the number of free allocation blocks present on the media. This is usually 0 for all CDs and DVDs.

Volume created

The "Volume Created" field shows the date and time the volume was created. No time zone information is present.

Volume modified

The "Volume Modified" field shows the date and time of the last modification to the volume. In general, this is equal to the volume create date and time. No time zone information is present.

HSG Volume Information

High Sierra Group (HSG) volumes are not commonly used, but they are supported by CD/DVD Inspector. The fields have the same meanings as those for ISO 9660 volumes.

UDF Volume Information

The UDF volume information display summarizes information from several of the data structures in the UDF file system.

Volume descriptor sequence

The "Volume Descriptor Sequence" field shows the sequence number in the Primary Volume Descriptor for the UDF file system. It indicates the order of the volume descriptors in the volume recognition sequence, and in some cases, can identify the writing application.

Volume ID

The "Volume ID" field shows the name of the file system and/or disc from the volume descriptors. The name of the disc can be changed after the disc has been written to, but the changes are made to the File Set Descriptor.

Interchange level

The "Interchange Level" field shows the interchange level declared for the volume. It is generally 1 or 2. A value of 1 indicates the volume is intended only for reading by other applications.

Volume set name

The "Volume Set Name" field shows the name of the volume set if this has been set. Some applications set this equal to the volume name.

Implementation identifier

The "Implementation Identifier" field shows the name that the writing application has placed into the volume recognition sequence, in order for the UDF file system to identify the application that produced the volume. Many of these identifiers are registered with the Optical Storage Technology Association (OSTA) and in most cases, is correct.

The Implementation identifier corresponds to the Application identifier in other file systems, and serves to identify the writing software.

Application

The "Application" field is similar to the Implementation Identifier. Some writing software will set both of these identifiers; some will only set one or the other.

Recording time

The "Recording Time" field shows the date and time the file system was created, which is generally when the disc was formatted initially or when the disc was mastered, depending on the type of media. For rewritable media, this is when the disc was initially formatted, not when it was written to last. The time zone for this is shown as an offset from GMT.

Disc Reports

CD/DVD Inspector can produce a number of different reports regarding the content of the disc being examined (see Figure 6.18). These reports fall into two basic groups: text reports listing the all files on the disc, and image reports showing graphics found on the disc. The following dialog box is presented when the Disc Report menu item is chosen from the Tools menu:

Figure 6.18 Disc Report Selection Dialog

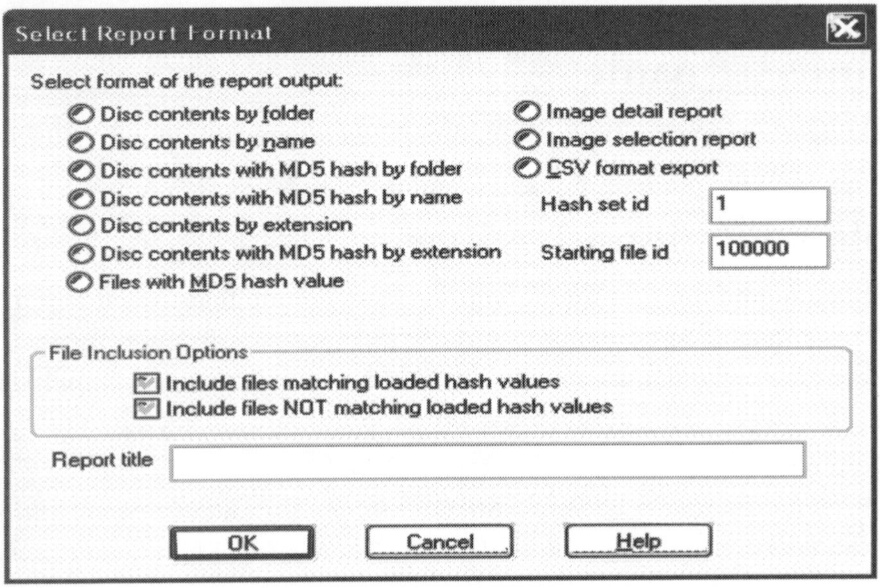

The report choices are divided into two columns, the first for text-format reports that include the full content of the disc, and the second for other formats.

If MD5 hash information is requested it has not yet been calculated for every file, you are prompted to calculate the MD5 hash value for all remaining files. This is a simple way of computing the hash value for every file on the disc all at the same time.

All reports can have their content selected by hash matching. In order to take advantage of this, it is first necessary to load a hash set (e.g., Hashkeeper-style CSV format) into CD/DVD Inspector. This is done via the "Load Hash Set" selection in the Pro Tools menu. Then files that either match or do not match the loaded hash values can be selected for inclusion in the report.

For the Image Detail report and the Image Selection report, the report title can be specified in the text field near the bottom of the dialog. This title does not apply to the text format reports.

The following sections describe the various reports that are available.

Disc Contents by Folder

The "Disc Contents by Folder" report breaks down the content of the disc with a separate group of files in each folder, file system, and session on the disc. This is not the most compact report, but it does present the basic details of each file found.

This report can also be requested to include the MD5 hash information for each file. It is inserted after the time and before the filename.

If the "Show Extents in Disc Report" option is selected, additional lines are displayed below the filename that show each extent of the file when the file is fragmented.

```
Directory information for data track 1 beginning at sector 0 ---------------
------------------


Contents of folder CCNBRS (HFS+:Session 1)

  Sector        Size       Date/Time          Filename
------- -------------- ------------------- --------------------
  24299              0   1/7/2005  9:23:01 2600 The Hacker Quarterly_files\
     33         34,043   1/5/2005 15:16:12 2600 The Hacker Quarterly.htm
     42      1,738,755   6/15/2001 17:03:10 Building.jpg
    467         57,344   1/5/2005 15:13:02 card reader.doc
    481          1,442  12/5/2004 11:46:32 CC Nbrs.txt
    482         46,867  12/5/2004 13:57:25 Check2.jpg
    494        417,792          -- N/A -- Desktop DB
    799      2,548,098   7/27/2003 16:30:44 Desktop DF
    596         45,645  12/5/2004 13:57:48 HackerSession.zip
    608        781,010   1/5/2005 15:09:58 john-16w.zip
   1422      1,051,998   1/5/2005 15:11:10 lc252install.zip
   1679            533  12/5/2004 13:56:27 README.TXT


Contents of folder CCNBRS (HFS+:Session 1)\2600 The Hacker Quarterly_files

  Sector        Size       Date/Time          Filename
------- -------------- ------------------- --------------------
   1680             43   1/5/2005 15:15:48 1.gif
```

Disc Contents by Name

The "Disc Contents by Name" report shows the complete path to every file with the sector, size, and last-modified date and time. This is an easy report to sort by sector number, size, or date and time. The output of this report can also be imported into a spreadsheet for further analysis.

This report can be requested with MD5 hash information, which is inserted after the time and before the filename.

If the option "Show Extents in Disc Report" is selected, additional lines are included below each file to indicate the extents for fragmented files. This makes the report output less usable for sorting or importing into a spreadsheet.

```
Files from disc CCNBRS


  Sector       Size          Date/Time        Filename
------- --------------- -------------------- --------------------

   1680              43   1/5/2005 15:15:48  \2600 The Hacker
                                             Quarterly_files\1.gif

     33          34,043   1/5/2005 15:16:12  \2600 The Hacker Quarterly.htm

   1681           1,568   1/5/2005 15:15:50  \2600 The Hacker
                                             Quarterly_files\725274831586.gif

 119741          35,218   3/11/2004  5:03:53 \AOL90\COMPS\COACH\
                                             AFIXES\92001ADC.GDP;1

 119741          35,218   3/11/2004  5:03:53 \AOL90\COMPS\COACH\AFIXES\
                                             92001ADC.GDP;1

 119759          35,958   3/11/2004  5:03:53 \AOL90\COMPS\COACH\AFIXES\
                                             92002CCA.GDP;1

 119759          35,958   3/11/2004  5:03:53 \AOL90\COMPS\COACH\AFIXES\
                                             92002CCA.GDP;1

 119777          25,633   2/9/2004   8:28:33 \AOL90\COMPS\COACH\AFIXES\
                                             92003GPF.GDP;1

 119777          25,633   2/9/2004   8:28:33 \AOL90\COMPS\COACH\AFIXES\
                                             92003GPF.GDP;1

 119790          25,629   2/9/2004   8:28:33 \AOL90\COMPS\COACH\AFIXES\
                                             92004BRW.GDP;1

 119790          25,629   2/9/2004   8:28:33 \AOL90\COMPS\COACH\AFIXES\
                                             92004BRW.GDP;1

 119803          15,206   12/9/2003  9:42:55 \AOL90\COMPS\COACH\AFIXES\
                                             92005ASA.GDP;1
```

119803	15,206	12/9/2003	9:42:55	\AOL90\COMPS\COACH\AFIXES\92005ASA.GDP;1
119811	36,038	3/11/2004	5:03:54	\AOL90\COMPS\COACH\AFIXES\92006ARS.GDP;1
119811	36,038	3/11/2004	5:03:54	\AOL90\COMPS\COACH\AFIXES\92006ARS.GDP;1
119829	16,300	12/9/2003	9:42:56	\AOL90\COMPS\COACH\AFIXES\92010CAA.GDP;1
119829	16,300	12/9/2003	9:42:56	\AOL90\COMPS\COACH\AFIXES\92010CAA.GDP;1
168856	35,916	3/11/2004	5:09:15	\AOLTECH\AOL90E\COMPS\COACH\AFIXES\93001ADC.GDP;1
168856	35,916	3/11/2004	5:09:15	\AOLTECH\AOL90E\COMPS\COACH\AFIXES\93001ADC.GDP;1
168874	35,416	3/11/2004	5:09:15	\AOLTECH\AOL90E\COMPS\COACH\AFIXES\93002CCA.GDP;1

Disc Contents by Extension

The "Disc Contents by Extension" report format is identical to the "Disc Contents by Folder" format, with the exception that the files are ordered by their extension.

This report can be requested with MD5 hash information, which is inserted after the time and before the filename.

If the "Show Extents in Disc Report" option is selected, additional lines are included below each file to indicate the extents for fragmented files.

```
Files from disc CCNBRS


  Sector      Size         Date/Time         Filename
  -------  --------------  -------------------  --------------------
     494       417,792        -- N/A --  \Desktop DB
     799     2,548,098   7/27/2003 16:30:44  \Desktop DF
  129905    14,076,719    5/7/2004 11:10:42  \AOL90\COMP01.000;1
  179151    12,785,587   5/10/2004  9:38:46  \AOLTECH\AOL90E\COMP01.000;1
  129905    14,076,719    5/7/2004 11:10:42  \AOL90\COMP01.000;1
  179151    12,785,587   5/10/2004  9:38:46  \AOLTECH\AOL90E\COMP01.000;1
  136779    27,907,843    5/7/2004 11:10:18  \AOL90\COMP02.000;1
  185394    34,507,624   5/10/2004  9:38:18  \AOLTECH\AOL90E\COMP02.000;1
  136779    27,907,843    5/7/2004 11:10:18  \AOL90\COMP02.000;1
  185394    34,507,624   5/10/2004  9:38:18  \AOLTECH\AOL90E\COMP02.000;1
```

101748	104	7/12/2004	6:30:43	\AOL90\ADDONS\FSCOMMAND\ COPYSHORTCUT.BAT;1
101748	104	7/12/2004	6:30:43	\AOL90\ADDONS\FSCOM~H0\ COPYS~_N.BAT;1
218015	23	11/4/2003	7:41:28	\AOLTECH\NOMEDIA.BAT;1
218015	23	11/4/2003	7:41:28	\AOLTECH\NOMEDIA.BAT;1
203675	53,580	2/8/2004	11:15:10	\AOLTECH\Tools\ InspectorInstall.bmp;1
203675	53,580	2/8/2004	11:15:10	\AOLTECH\TOOLS\INSPE~0G.BMP;1
16276	548	7/12/2004	6:47:50	\SETUP.DAT;1
16276	548	7/12/2004	6:47:50	\SETUP.DAT;1
168953	57,344	3/11/2004	5:09:07	\AOLTECH\AOL90E\COMPS\COACH\ ACPVER.DLL;1
119837	57,344	3/11/2004	5:03:44	\AOL90\COMPS\COACH\ACPVER.DLL;1
168953	57,344	3/11/2004	5:09:07	\AOLTECH\AOL90E\COMPS\COACH\ ACPVER.DLL;1
119837	57,344	3/11/2004	5:03:44	\AOL90\COMPS\COACH\ACPVER.DLL;1

Files with MD5 Hash Value

The "Files with MD5 Hash Value" report is similar to the "Disc Contents by Name" report, except that the path to the file is not included. Instead, the matching hash set and file identifier for a loaded hash set are included.

This report is only valuable if you are using hash matching within CD/DVD Inspector.

```
Files from disc TRYAOL
```

Sector Match	Size Filename	Date/Time	MD5 Hash Value
75	6,148	7/29/2004 12:26:49	D6FEAFDC921BBADF7ED2DD2C6BA3E15D .DS_Store
735	12,292	6/23/2004 15:25:08	44CA679E62CBE8A127E49477CAB4A766 .DS_Store
4757	6,148	6/23/2004 15:25:08	B3871914B7A756B64C12B7CD250EA118 .DS_Store
787	6,148	4/25/2003 13:58:20	14D546093A8CB18BF66A9AEFBCB97C38 .DS_Store
686	6,148	6/23/2004 15:25:08	6E6015108B890E20F08EDFA06379FF32 .DS_Store

79	48,797	4/25/2003	12:11:31	1E8BF6FB5D90E300ED53F9BE07E77FBF .VolumeIcon.icns
139449	35,218	3/11/2004	11:03:53	C433B4A0ED5AFF65452FDC1264667DF4 92001ADC.GDP
139449	35,218	3/11/2004	11:03:53	C433B4A0ED5AFF65452FDC1264667DF4 92001ADC.GDP
139467	35,958	3/11/2004	11:03:53	8F69FC0058D880E1BF8F3D6E36A06889 92002CCA.GDP
139467	35,958	3/11/2004	11:03:53	8F69FC0058D880E1BF8F3D6E36A06889 92002CCA.GDP
139485	25,633	2/9/2004	14:28:33	2B48A55FE1587178EBA3D8B352B95079 92003GPF.GDP
139485	25,633	2/9/2004	14:28:33	2B48A55FE1587178EBA3D8B352B95079 92003GPF.GDP
139498	25,629	2/9/2004	14:28:33	739A85C4718D8FBE1A82C6CFF7325939 92004BRW.GDP
139498	25,629	2/9/2004	14:28:33	739A85C4718D8FBE1A82C6CFF7325939 92004BRW.GDP

CSV Format Export

The "CSV Format Export" report is listed on the selection of reports; however, it is not truly a report. This exports the hash information about files in the same format as can be loaded by the "Load Hash Set" menu selection. The output is a file with the extension *.hsh* or *.csv* and has the following fields:

- File identifier (numeric)
- Hash set identifier (numeric)
- Filename
- Directory path
- Hash value
- File size
- Date modified (mm/dd/yy)
- Time modified

This file can then be loaded as a hash set using the Load Hash Set menu selection in the Pro Tools menu. It is also compatible with other tools that can import Hashkeeper format hash sets.

Image Reports

Users can choose between the two image reports that are written as HTML files, with the images present as thumbnails linked to the full size image (see Figure 6.19). These reports should be saved to an empty or new folder, because they will copy the image file thumbnails and image files over to that folder. Placing two image reports in the same folder will result in naming conflicts.

The Image Detail report shows the picture thumbnail, filename, file size, starting sector for the first contiguous portion of the file, last modified date, MD5 hash value, and a link to session information. Clicking the thumbnail image opens the full-size image. All full-size images are saved as a *.jpeg* files regardless of the original picture format.

Figure 6.19 Image Detail Report Example

Picture	Filename	Size	Sector	Modified	MD5 Hash Value	Creation Information
	100_1754.JPG	196.41 KB	34	9/9/2004 9:47:50	66266DA7C98BD75481E27FEDD2157566	Joliet:Session 1

The image selection report presents a selection dialog box to choose what images are to be included in the report (see Figure 6.20). This dialog box shows the filename of each image, with a preview of the selected image. Selections are saved in the Disc Memory information for the disc. The report appears as a two–up list of images with the filename, file size, and last modified date beneath each image. Clicking an image brings up the full-size image. All full-size images are saved as a *JPEG* regardless of the original picture format.

Figure 6.20 Image Selection Report Example

Chapter 7

Using CD/DVD Inspector

This chapter discusses using the various capabilities of CD/DVD Inspector in the course of a forensic examination.

Examining a Disc— A Step-by-step Guide

For this chapter, we assume that you have the multi-session disc image file named "Exercise1Image.iso" (see Appendix B). If you are using CD/DVD Inspector version 3.0 or later, you can directly access this image file. For previous versions, you will have to burn the image to a disc first.

Also for the purpose of this example, we assume that you are looking for images or documents relating to the keyword "Bullfrog," which is the codename assigned to a new anti-tank weapons system; however, pictures of frogs can also be significant, possibly containing information hidden using stegonography.

The first step of any CD/DVD Inspector analysis is to create a folder where information about the disc or discs can be stored. It is recommended that you also open Notepad or another text editor, where you can paste information from CD/DVD Inspector during the course of examining a disc.

The following steps describe the process of examining this disc and performing additional keyword searches.

Starting CD/DVD Inspector

Start the CD/DVD Inspector program. When prompted to select a device, insert the disc into any of the devices displayed, wait for the display to change to a green dot in front of that device, and double-click that line. This will start the process of examining the disc and should take less than a minute to complete.

If you have a single CD or DVD device attached to your computer, the default behavior of CD/DVD Inspector is such that if there is a disc in that drive it will automatically be examined when the program is started. However, if you have multiple CD or DVD devices connected, the default behavior may result in unintended discs being examined automatically, in which case it is recommended that you turn off the "Automatically examine a disc at startup" option.

Dismiss any messages that appear during the examination or after the examination has completed. When the program is first installed, a message is displayed each time the examination of a disc is completed. This can be turned off; doing so will reduce the number of interactions during the course of examining a disc.

Initial Observations

There are two file systems shown for each of the two sessions on the disc, and each system is labeled either ISO or Joliet. Clicking on file systems/sessions in the window allows users to navigate between these file systems and sessions. Users can also navigate through the different folders in each file system by expanding each session.

When displaying a folder for the first time, there can be a delay while the files are checked for images. Any files with supported image file extensions (i.e., *.art, .bmp, .gif, .jpg, .jpeg, .png, .tif,* or *.tiff*) are assumed to be images. Other files are checked to determine if they contain image content. This checking can take time to perform if there are a large number of files in the folder.

Analysis Tool

The first information you should gather from any disc is the output from the Analysis tool. This can be displayed by clicking the **Analysis** toolbar button. When the display is presented, click the **Copy Text** button and paste the information into the text editor that you previously opened (See Figure 7.1).

Figure 7.1 Analysis Toolbar Button

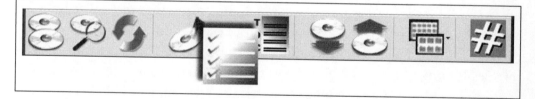

For the disc image in this example, there is a warning about mismatched file counts between the ISO-9660 and Joliet file systems. This warning is intended to call your attention to the different counts of files between these two file systems. This difference is unusual; most writing software does not provide for these file systems to have different content. When this warning is displayed, it is a clear indication that something unusual is happening with the disc. The examiner should closely examine the source of these differences.

Disc Map

Select the Disc Map item from the Tools menu to display the space utilization map for the disc. The examiner should see a small amount of control information and a large amount of space being used for data files. There should not be any space marked as not being accounted for, except perhaps at the very beginning and very end of the disc. There should not be any areas marked as "Data – unknown type" on the disc.

If any space is marked as unaccounted for or unknown, click on those areas to display the sector numbers and use the Sector Display toolbar button to display the contents of the sectors not accounted for. At this point, all you are doing is looking for anomalous data.

A raw sector search (described below) can be useful for locating items of interest on a disc, especially when such information is contained in space outside of any files. The Scan Files tool does not work for data contained outside of files.

Quick Image Examination

Many different tools are available for displaying image thumbnails and information about these images. However, if there are problems accessing a CD or DVD, CD/DVD Inspector can often gain access to the files that other tools cannot. It is important to understand the available options.

The first and most obvious option is to use CD/DVD Inspector to copy the files from the disc to a different location and then process those files using conventional means. The examiner then has the advantage of being able to use whatever tools he or she is familiar with to examine the images. However, this can take considerable time.

The second option is to use the CD/DVD Inspector image reporting capabilities to create a Hypertext Markup Language (HTML) file showing thumbnails of all of the images on the media. Either the Image Detail or Image Selection report can be used for this purpose; however, the Image Selection report uses a larger thumbnail size, which is more suitable for examining images.

Unless the examiner has additional reasons to copy all of the content of the disc, using the reporting capabilities of CD/DVD Inspector is much faster.

Within the scenario of this example, you should run the Image Selection report by clicking the Select All button and then the Ok button. This will produce an HTML report with thumbnails of all of the images found in the disc image. The examiner should look over this report to see if there are any images related to Bullfrog.

Scan Files for Keywords

Search the contents of the files on the disc for the keyword "bullfrog" using the Scan Files tool in the File menu. There are two ways to do this search: using a string search or using a regular expression. Since we are searching for any mix of upper- and lowercase letters, using the string search specification is easiest.

To search using the string search specification, enter the keyword "bull-frog" surrounded by double quotes (" "). To search using a regular expression, explicitly indicate that either upper- or lowercase is acceptable. The format of this specification is shown below:

```
R [Bb] [Uu] [Ll] [Ll] [Ff] [Rr] [Oo] [Gg]
```

Regardless of the format chosen, click **OK** in the Scan Files dialog box and begin the search. The results dialog box will be displayed after the scan finishes. This can be copied to the clipboard using the **Copy Text** button and the results saved in the report file for the disc. There are three files that contain various forms of the keyword for this example.

Other Examination Tasks

The following topics address features and capabilities of CD/DVD Inspector which may not be required for all examinations.

Create an ISO Image File

CD/DVD Inspector can be used to copy the contents of a track to an ISO-formatted binary image file. Unfortunately, this is only valid for the first session and first track of a disc, and automatically disqualifies discs used with drag-and-drop writing software or multi-session discs. Discs with this type of file can be used with other tools to reproduce the contents of a disc.

If the disc does not have an ISO-9660 file system or if the file system is divided across multiple tracks, it is possible to copy the tracks; however, the result is not useful. Unfortunately, there is no standard for an image file for a Universal Disk Format (UDF) file system, and no software that currently understands a UDF file system in such a file.

Beginning with version 3.0 of CD/DVD Inspector, the examiner can select the "Create Disc Image" selection from the Pro Tools menu to write an image file. If you want to create an ISO-format image file, you must make that selection under the image file type. The extension .ISO will automatically be applied to the file name you enter. This selection is not available if the disc cannot be fully represented by an ISO-format image file. In such cases, only an InfinaDyne format image file can be written using this tool.

For versions of CD/DVD Inspector prior to 3.0, or in cases where only the first track is required, the Copy Sectors tool can be used. To copy the first track of any disc, click on any of the "session 1" file system lines shown in the left pane of the window, and then select the Copy Sectors item from the File menu. Do not enter any value for the starting and ending sector; however, enter the output file name. An extension of ".ISO" is suggested.

Create an InfinaDyne Image File

A complete binary image file for any type of disc can be collected using the Create Image File selection from the Pro Tools menu. This image file works with CD/DVD Inspector to allow access to the contents of the disc at a later time, without requiring that the physical disc be present.

At the time of this writing, no other applications support this image format. It is expected that tools for importing this type of image file into various forensic applications such as EnCase, FTK, and ILook will be available in the future. InfinaDyne plans on releasing a tool for creating a duplicate disc from an image file.

Determining the Writing Application

The Volume information display (from the Tools menu) and the Analysis report both show the application name written in the file system volume definition, if any. This can be an important clue to what application and what computer created the disc.

Determining the platform that created the disc may be possible even when identifying the specific writing application is not. The following are some guidelines:

- If Apple extensions are present, it is reasonable to guess that either a hybrid writing application was used or the disc was created on a Macintosh computer. The most common hybrid writing application is the combination of the mkisofs and cdrecord programs for Linux. Apple extensions are indicated by a directory extension with the .AA identifier.

- If Rock Ridge extensions are present, the file system was probably created by the mkisofs tool. If Rock Ridge extensions are present, this is noted in the Analysis report.

- If a Joliet file system is present, it usually indicates that the disc was created on a Windows computer. While it is possible for this to be created on other systems, Joliet is used on Windows only. Macintosh support for Joliet is very limited.

- UDF file systems are created by all platforms, but read-write access mode UDF file systems are almost completely unique to Windows.

Date Correspondence

There are a number of different dates on any user-written recordable disc. The most basic is the timestamp of the recording itself, which is contained in the volume definition information of all of the different file systems. It is displayed by either the Analysis report or the individual Volume information displays under the Tools menu. Another significant date is that of the root directory and, if present, the "." directory entry in the root directory.

On read-only file systems (except UDF) these timestamps should always be the latest on the disc. If an individual file has a later time, it is clear that something happened to the timestamps on the disc. There is no definitive indication of how the dates have been modified, but all timestamps on the disc should be treated with suspicion.

Similarly, UDF and Hierarchical File System (HFS)/HFS+ file systems have created last-access timestamps in addition to last-modified, which provides an additional check on the last modified date that is the easiest to modify. It is a clear sign of tampering if the last-modified date is earlier than the last access or created date.

Missing Files

When multiple file systems are present, it is possible that there is a significant difference in the files contained within them. Typically, ISO-9660 and Joliet have the same files, whereas ISO-9660 and HFS will have some differences if there is any correspondence at all. Examine any America Online (AOL) distribution disc to see an example of a disc with ISO-9660, Joliet, and HFS. You will see complete correspondence between the ISO-9660 and Joliet file systems and no files in common in the HFS file system.

This correspondence can be useful if the number of files is different between the two file systems. A simple way to "hide" a file is to not have it represented in the Joliet directory. This can be easily accomplished using the mkisofs program, which was originally developed for Linux but has been ported to Microsoft Windows. With the "hidejoliet" option, it is possible to remove files from the Joliet directory while they remain in the ISO-9660 directory. Because Windows 95 and later exclusively use the Joliet directory, any such deletion will prevent the file from being shown by Windows.

The Analysis tool makes it easy to detect this, by showing the counts of files for each file system and then comparing them by using any of the full-content report selections from the Disc Report tool. With version 3.0 of CD/DVD Inspector, a specific warning is displayed in red if this condition is found.

Multi-Session Hiding

When a multi-session disc is created, most tools will allow files to be deleted from later sessions that appear in earlier sessions. This effectively hides files from being seen by Windows. By selecting the "Show analysis file details" option, the Analysis report will show a complete list of how files are linked between sessions on the disc. In addition, the full-content disc reports can be used to show what files have been dropped from earlier sessions.

Chapter 8

Advanced Tasks with CD/DVD Inspector

This section describes some advanced uses of CD/DVD Inspector which may be required in some cases.

Using Hash Matching and MD5 Hashes

CD/DVD Inspector can compute MD5 hash values for either selected files or all files in a session by selecting any file, folder, or session and selecting the menu item "Calculate MD5 Hash" in the File menu. This will populate the MD5 Hash value column in the file Details display.

CD/DVD Inspector has the capability of loading hash sets and using them to match against files on the media being examined. If you have a set of known files being checked for, this can make the process significantly faster and more productive.

A hash set is a comma-separated-value (CSV) format file with following fields:

- File identifier (numeric)
- Hash set identifier (numeric)
- File name (ignored by CD/DVD Inspector)
- Directory path (ignored by CD/DVD Inspector)
- Hash value
- File size (ignored by CD/DVD Inspector)
- Date modified (mm/dd/yy) (ignored by CD/DVD Inspector)
- Time modified (ignored by CD/DVD Inspector)
- Time zone (ignored by CD/DVD Inspector)
- Date accessed (mm/dd/yy) (ignored by CD/DVD Inspector)
- Time accessed (ignored by CD/DVD Inspector)

Any of the fields following the hash value can be omitted.

The menu selection Load Hash Set in the Pro Tools menu is used to load a hash set into memory for comparison. This is done after the initial examination of a disc and the comparison is done immediately. If hash values have not been computed for the files on the disc being examined yet, the user will be prompted to do this before proceeding.

After hash values have been computed, a blue star is shown as the icon (see Figure 8.1) for all files for which a matching hash value has been found.

This icon overrides any other icon that CD/DVD Inspector would normally apply to the file. Files that have a blue star icon can be selected or excluded from reports easily. The HTML image reports can also be selected to include or exclude hash matches.

Figure 8.1 Blue Star Icon

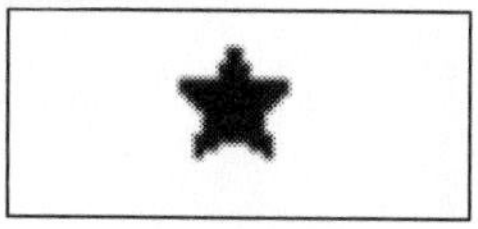

The report called "Files with MD5 Hash Value" will show the hash matches to the hash set and file identifiers. This report is suggested to have the option to included unmatched files unchecked.

Space Utilization Analysis

The Disc Map tool (in the Tools menu) displays a graphic representation of the space utilization on the media. It is designed to combine only 10 sectors into a single point in the chart, to allow a maximum of visibility and resolution. With larger and larger media (dual-layer, HD, and Blu-Ray) this will likely have to change, but there will always be an attempt to make this is high resolution as possible.

Each point in the chart is assigned a color based on either the most significant utilization, with "unused" being the default if no use can be found of the sector. This discussion is focused on examining either of those areas that are marked as "Unused" (black) or "Not accounted for" (Red). All of the other assignments indicate there is content there, which is significant and part of the file system in one way or another.

You may want to download the ISO image file for this disc so that you can perform the same examination. This disc is called Exercise2Image.iso and is available by following the instructions in Appendix B.

Figure 8.2 Disc Space Utilitization Display

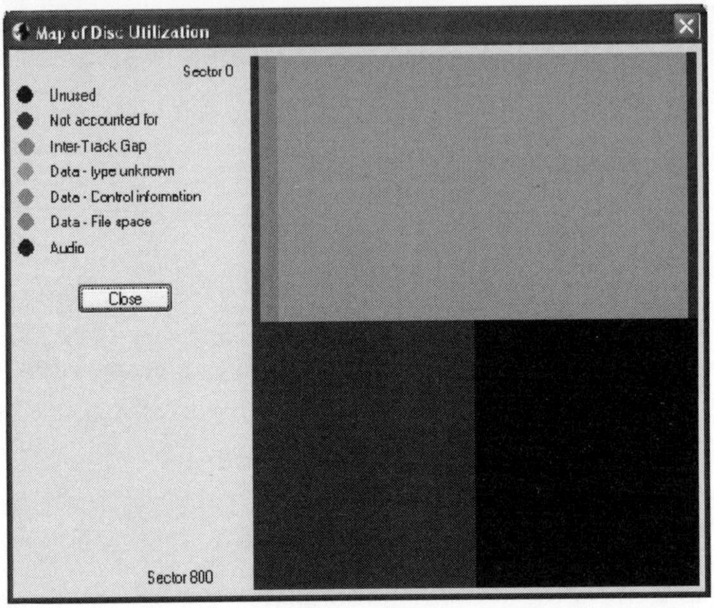

Referring to the example at the right, we have a disc where a significant part of it is categorized as "Not accounted for" and "Data – type unknown." It is common for there to be some "Not accounted for" space on a disc but because of the relatively large area that is unknown data as well, we will investigate this disc further. When an area is marked as "Data – type unknown" it is a clear indication that there is data on the disc that CD/DVD Inspector could not connect to any file system. Such data is not difficult to access, but it is beyond the scope of most users.

For example, with even nothing more sophisticated than Linux and the standard command-line tools, the data beginning at sector 30 (the beginning of the large "Data – type unknown" section) could be copied from the disc easily. It is relatively easy to create a disc with real data but not part of the file system. This would be an excellent way to hide documents, photographs, or any other digital material. This would especially be true if the disc was to be sent through the mail or by courier to another party. If the disc was intercepted, it is highly unlikely that anyone would consider the possibilities of such data existing.

The first step in determining if there is real content in the space marked "Unused" is to identify the sectors involved. By clicking on points on the chart the sectors represented by that point are displayed on the dialog. Doing so with this disc shows the following areas of interest:

- 0 to 9 marked as Not accounted for

- 30 to 489 marked as Data – type unknown

- 490 to 749 marked as Not accounted for

It is often the case that sectors below 512 are not used with the UDF file system. Sectors below 16 are generally not used with the ISO9660 and Joliet file systems. This disc was written using the ISO9660 file system, so while we can probably ignore the first 10 sectors, the remainder is of interest. Additionally, while the trailing "Not accounted for" space will often occur on a disc, being combined with the area marked "Data – type unknown" makes this area suspicious as well.

With the sector numbers in hand, the next step is to determine if there is any non-zero content in these sectors. While it is possible that simply a long string of binary zero bytes could be significant in some situations, it seems safe to say that such cases are very unusual. For our purposes with this disc, we are going to ignore any sector containing only binary zeros.

You can close the Disc Map dialog now, having obtained the relevant sector numbers. Remember that the resolution is 10 sectors – this is important.

Using the Sector Display tool, display the first potentially unused sector on this disc. It can clearly be seen that this sector does not contain binary zeros – the first few lines of the sector display appear as shown below.

```
0000  1A935E1C 70EF1334 A5EE7A25 2A44352D  ..^.p..4 ..z%*D5-
0010  D21455A4 DB852410 6B6AF24B E03C12B1  ..U...$. kj.K.<..
0020  6CFE18A6 17D4AFA2 C0DBC496 6CF2AAC4  l....... ....l...
0030  0776AB7B A91B6BFF D32A3CCF 303C161E  .v.{..k. .*<.0<..
0040  93CE3530 1D7699C9 0917549D C5C78D60  ..50.v.. ..T....`
```

There does not appear to be any immediate significance to this data. Because of the resolution of the Disc Map, it is probably a good idea to scan backward looking for where this begins. In sector 22 a message is present indicating that this disc was written by AccuBurn-R and the write operation apparently failed. This may be interesting, but for now all we can do is note that the data follows this text message and continues to sector 30. Scanning forward it can be seen that this continues to sector 31. We will return to this data later.

Sector 32 is all binary zero. The question is if there is any other data present between sector 32 and sector 489. While it would be possible to move through the sectors one at a time manually checking each one, there is a simpler approach. Back up to sector 31 first and then click the Search button and enter "!00" (without the quotes) in the search text and select Hex. This will search for any byte in any of the following sectors, which is not binary zero. This is an extremely fast search and precludes the possibility that you might miss some non-zero bytes at the end of a sector. Note that the search ignores the sector currently being displayed.

The sector search will stop at sector 307 in the example image file and show the following data with the first character ("T") highlighted. The first two lines of this sector are shown below.

```
0000 54444901 50010202 0280FFFF FF000000 TDI.P... ........
0010 00000000 00000000 00000000 00000000 ........ ........
```

If you scroll down through the rest of the sector, it is clear that only the first line has any information in it – the rest is binary zero. This is a track information block that is written by the writer in the 150 sector inter-track gap area. This clearly means that this image file was constructed from a disc with multiple tracks and not all of the information about the disc was preserved. This is a common problem when attempting to use the limited ISO image file format to represent anything but the simplest disc.

Because of the position of this and the data contained in it, there should be exactly 145 of these track information block sectors before the beginning of the data in the next track. We can check this by looking at sector 450 and 451 – they should look identical to sector 307 in all respects. In this case they do, and sector 452 is completely different. To further verify that these are 145 track information block sectors quickly scan through the sectors looking for any indication that something is different. This is done with the up and down arrows to the right of the sector number. You should see nothing to indicate there is any change from sector 307 to sector 451.

Sector 452 is interesting in that it is not referenced by any file in the file system but yet obviously contains data.

```
0000 0000001C 66747970 33677034 00000300 ....ftyp 3gp4....
0010 33677034 33677035 33673261 0000003F 3gp43gp5 3g2a...?
0020 6D646174 54686973 2066696C 65207761 mdatThis file wa
0030 73206765 6E657261 74656420 6279206F s genera ted by o
0040 6E65206F 66204E65 78656E63 6F646572 ne of Ne xencoder
0050 28544D29 2046616D 696C7900 00001A6D (TM) Fam ily....m
0060 64617401 10110602 9F0F0200 01010605 dat..... ........
0070 1F0F0200 02000000 206D6461 74C01012 ........ mdat...
0080 819302A0 57260428 22829D04 1FC00000 ....W&.( ".......
0090 1FC00000 780001F7 086D6461 743CAD31 ....x... .mdat<.1
```

This continues on until sector 524, where we find another sector of all binary zero. We need to determine if there is anything else on the disc from this point forward, so once again back up to sector 523 and enter the "!00" hex search term. CD/DVD Inspector responds with there was nothing further found in the track.

We have found some unknown data following a text message (sectors 22-31) and a "hidden" file (sectors 452–523) on this disc that are not represented by the file system. The data in sectors 22 to 31 is pretty short and has no apparent header information. It could just be a fragment of a file and without further information there isn't much that can be done with this.

To evaluate the content in sectors 452 through 523 simply all that is required is to write the content to a separate file where it can be examined. Using the Copy Sectors tool, enter the sector numbers 452 and 523 for the start and end sectors and a file name such as sector452. The extension is not significant. Using the FileIdentify tool (supplied with CD/DVD Inspector) the file can be evaluated and it will be shown as a .3gp MMS video file. This is the sort of video clip that can be sent from a cell phone.

Renaming the file (using FileIdentify) and playing it will show the video clip that was taken with the cell phone.

ISO9660 Directory Analysis

There are a number of important characteristics of an ISO9660 directory that can provide additional information about a disc. The following describes the directory structure, how to find it, and how to examine it. Usually all of the information that can be derived from examining the directory in detail can be found in the root directory but there may be some cases where it is useful to examine a different directory.

The first step is to locate the directory to be viewed. For the root directory click on the ISO9660 session line in the left pane and then pick the Volume Information item in the Tools menu. This will display the sector number for the root directory. Close this dialog, open the sector display, and enter the sector number for the root directory. For a non-root directory right click the folder entry in the directory above and choose "Display sectors." This will immediately display the correct sector.

ISO9660 directory entries are constructed of three parts: the base, the file name, and the extension. The following describes how these are arranged.

Offset	Length (in bytes)	Description	Type
0	1	Length of the entire entry	Binary
1	1	Length of extended attribute data	Binary
2	4	Starting sector of data	Integer (I)
6	4	Starting sector of data	Integer (M)
10	4	Length of file	Integer (I)
14	4	Length of file	Integer (M)
18	7	Timestamp (YMDHMSZ)	Binary
25	1	Flags	Binary
26	1	Unit size	Binary
27	1	Gap size	Binary
28	2	Volume sequence	Integer (I)
30	2	Volume sequence	Integer (M)
32	1	File name length	Binary
33	?	File name	Character

The offsets are byte positions with the first byte of a directory entry 0 (not 1.) All values for offsets and lengths are in decimal. Integers can be either Intel byte order indicated by "(I)" or Motorola byte order indicated by "(M.)"

The timestamp field consists of individual binary fields each one byte in length. The first byte is the year minus 1900. The next five bytes are month, day, hour, minute, and second. The last byte is the time zone, which a signed byte representing the offset from GMT time in 15-minute increments. Central Standard Time USA (GMT –6 hours) is represented as –6 * 4 or –24 which is E8 in hex.

The file name is 8-bit characters for ISO9660 or 16-bit characters for Joliet.

If the length of the entry is greater than the length of the base (33) and the length of the file name then one or more extensions are present. There are three types of extensions: Apple, XA and SUSP (System Use Sharing Protocol). Apple and SUSP extensions allow multiple extensions to be present. Rock Ridge is a particular use of SUSP to include POSIX information in an ISO9660 file system. Linux is a POSIX-compliant operating system.

Some mastering software, notably Nero Burning ROM®, puts in invalid data following a directory entry which is not a valid extension. Every disc examined with this shows that this extension is a directory entry for a file. The file doesn't appear in the directory because it is hidden as an extension.

Apple extensions are written by Macintosh computers or for discs that are specifically intended for use on Macintosh computers. The first two bytes are the letters AA and the third byte is the length of the extension. Apple extensions are 14 bytes in length and contain information for processing the disc on a Macintosh computer, such as the 4-character code of the application that created the file and some information for Finder about positioning the file icon.

XA extensions are also 14 bytes in length with the letters XA in positions 6 and 7. The only meaningful item in an XA extension is byte 4 that has bit 4 (0x10) set if the data is recorded in Mode 2 Form 2 (2352 bytes per sector) format. This is the case for VCD discs and some other multimedia formats.

SUSP extensions are written by programs like mkisofs and enable storing POSIX attributes in an ISO9660 file system. This is used specifically with UNIX and UNIX-like operating systems, such as Linux, to store file permissions, ownership, symbolic links and other information. Each SUSP extension has a two-character identifier followed by the length of the extension. The extension codes and their meanings are shown below.

Code	Description
AA	Apple extensions
CE	Continuation of extension data
CL	Child link
ER	Extension reference
ES	Extension selector
NM	Alternate (long) name
PD	Padding field
PL	Parent link
PN	POSIX device number
PX	POSIX file attributes
RE	Relocated directory
SF	File data in sparse format
SL	Symbolic link
SP	System use sharing protocol indicator
ST	System use sharing protocol terminator
TF	Additional POSIX time stamps

The format of some of the more important extensions is described on in the Rock Ridge section in Chapter 2.

For forensic purposes it can be assumed that if Apple extensions are not present that a Macintosh user program did not create the disc. An exception to this would be some OS X programs that operate at the "native" BSD level. These would not be considered to be ordinary Macintosh user programs in any event.

If SUSP extensions are present this will generally indicate the disc was created on Linux as the SUSP information is not available on Windows. It is possible to create a disc with some SUSP information but this is unusual at the very least.

The description of the SUSP extensions is in the IEEE P1281 System Use Sharing Protocol document. Search for the file name SUSP112.DOC. Rock Ridge extensions are documented in the IEEE P1282 Rock Ridge Interchange Protocol document. Search for the file name RRIP112.DOC. Both of these documents can be downloaded from the InfinaDyne public FTP server at ftp://ftp.cdrprod.com/pub.

Unknown Data Track Issues

Let us assume that the examiner is given a stack of discs to examine and one of them is shown by CD/DVD Inspector to simply have a track that says "Unknown data track, 64536 sectors." What can he/she do with this disc?

The reason that CD/DVD Inspector displays "Unknown data track" is because no distinguishing features were found which identify a file system. It does not mean the disc is blank it just does not have sufficient information to determine what file system it has. This can be due to a number of factors but usually it is just because critical parts of the disc are not readable.

If the disc is a rewritable CD or DVD it is likely the original file system was UDF. In order to determine that there is a UDF file system on the disc a very small number of sectors are referenced and if they cannot be read it is not really possible to access the disc through the file system. This is not a small problem because rewritable media will often have fragmented files on it. Thus, it is not certain that the examiner can simply cut the files apart using header information as he/she could if the files were contiguous.

However, if the disc is a CD-R, DVD-R or DVD+R it is likely it was "mastered" and all of the files are contiguous. In this case, the Copy Sectors tool can be used to create a single binary file, which can then be cut apart based on file header information. If the user has such a disc but no tools for performing this cutting operation contact InfinaDyne for further assistance.

It is also worth exploring such a disc with the Sector Display tool just to see if there is anything meaningful on the disc at all. If the user finds a large number of sectors of binary zero there is a trick that can be used with the Raw Sector Search to help the examiner determine if there is anything meaningful on the disc at all.

To do this "is there *anything* here?" search position the sector display to a low sector where user data is expected. For ISO9660/Joliet discs this would be anything after sector 20 but for UDF 512 is a better starting point. Click the Search button, select hex and enter "!00" (Exclamation point, zero, zero) as the search text. Click OK. If there is any byte found in a sector other than binary zero the search will stop.

This form of the search can also be used with other byte values but in general only 00 is useful.

Chapter 9

Reporting
Your Findings

The last step of any examination is assembling the data into a report. There are a number of items to consider when doing this with CD/DVD Inspector. If you import the data into a case management system such as EnCase, a lot of the necessary information can be taken from that environment. However, the problem with this approach is that it obscures the origin of the data, whether from a Compact Disc (CD) or Digital Versatile Discs (DVDs). This may or may not be important, depending on the specific case and any additional data obtained from other sources.

You should be familiar with the informational dialogs presented by CD/DVD Inspector, as well as the reports that are produced directly from it. The informational dialogs are specific to the media and provide information unique to CDs and DVDs, whereas the reports are focused on the files found on the media.

If one or more discs are the sole source of evidence in a case, documenting the specifics about the disc(s) is important; information from CD/DVD Inspector should be used to fulfill this requirement.

When gathering information from CD/DVD Inspector, it is recommended that you create a folder to hold all of the reports. If an image report is generated, it should be saved to individual folders within the common reporting folder.

The following sections discuss each of the data items that are recommended to be collected from CD/DVD Inspector. Whether or not a particular data item applies to a particular case is up to the individual examiner; however, you should be aware of all of these items and how to obtain them.

Full List of All Files on the Media

The "Disc Contents by Folder" report is recommended for listing all of the files on the media. It is suggested that the Message Digest 5 (MD5) version of the report be used, especially if the identity of specific files is questioned later. This implies that the MD5 hash value for all of the files must be computed. When the report is selected, it can be done automatically.

This report is obtained by selecting the Disc Report item from the Tools menu and then choosing either the " Disc Contents by Folder" or the "Disc Contents by Folder with MD5" report. Ensure that both inclusion checkboxes are checked to obtain the full contents of the disc. The report name is not used for this report; when you click **OK** you will be prompted for a file name for the report. The report is displayed in the default text editor when it has completed.

Image Report(s)

If a case involves images, the reporting capabilities in CD/DVD Inspector may be helpful for documenting them directly from disc. These reports produce Hypertext Markup Language (HTML) files that reference the images from the disc. Each report should be saved in its own folder to prevent file conflicts. The report title is used , and should be set to the appropriate value.

Analysis Report

The Analysis report examines the disc and reports on all of the file systems and all of the sessions. This includes any anomalies and items of importance such as the recording date and time for each file system in each session.

It is recommended that you calculate the MD5 value for the entire disc before running the Analysis report. The standard MD5 value for a disc is defined by the values that are displayed by the entire disc MD5 calculation tool. If these values change, the result is not saved or displayed in the Analysis report.

To include details about file linking between sessions and other file level details, you may want to select the option "Show analysis file details" in Preferences before displaying the Analysis report. However, this can significantly increase the size of the Analysis report, and the information may not be useful in all cases.

Access this report by clicking either the fifth toolbar button or by selecting **Analysis** from the Tools menu. Then click the **Copy Text** button and paste the report into a document.

Figure 9.1 Analysis Toolbar Button

Scan Files Results

If you find meaningful results using the Scan Files tool, you should include those results in your report. This can be done using the Copy Text button displayed on the Results dialog box.

Raw Search Results

If you use raw sector searching and find meaningful results, you should include those results in your report. Highlighting one or more lines in the sector display window causes only the highlighted lines to be copied to the clipboard when the Copy Text button is pressed. If no lines are highlighted, the entire sector is copied to the clipboard, which eliminates the need to use a screen capture for sector contents.

Chapter 10

Things to Keep In Mind

1. Discs come in a wide variety of shapes and colors; however, recordable discs are limited to two standard sizes: 120mm and 80mm. Business card-size discs are not part of the CD standard; they are either manufactured or recordable. Do not attempt to sort between recordable/rewritable and manufactured discs.

2. Discs are sensitive to heat and ultraviolet (UV) light, and can stick together, especially in a high humidity environment. Discs are not sensitive to magnetic fields; scratches on the bottom of a disc are not a problem, whereas scratches on the top of a CD can be fatal.

3. Discs are incredibly tolerant of contaminants; the range of materials that can be found on a disc is astonishing. Be careful when handling discs.

4. There are a number of different file systems that can be put on Compact Discs (CDs) and Digital Versatile Discs (DVDs). Each has their own unique properties and limitations, as well as unique information that helps identify the source of the disc.

5. Accessing data on a disc that appears to be blank may require advanced techniques.

6. Collecting "hidden" information from volume descriptors and other areas of a disc helps determine information about the source of the disc. Use all of the tools available to collect as much information as possible.

7. You need tools that are capable of examining multi-session discs with any of the file systems commonly found on CDs and DVDs. If you don't use such a tool you will not be able to examine some discs.

Disc Swap Modifications

The requirements for disc swap modifications are:

- A small straight-blade screwdriver

- A #1 Phillips head screwdriver

- A tray-opening tool or an unbent paperclip

- A Compact Disc - ReWritable (CD-RW) or Digital Versatile Disc (DVD writer to be modified; the drive should have an Advanced Technology Attachment Packet Interface (ATAPI) interface.

- A Universal Serial Bus (USB) 2.0 or FireWire enclosure to use with the drive after modification

It is possible to use a Small Computer System Interface (SCSI) drive and a SCSI enclosure; however, this can increase the hazards of operating the drive, because most SCSI enclosures have larger, more exposed power supplies that increase the risk of coming into contact with 120–240 voltage.

Figure A.1 Drive and Tools

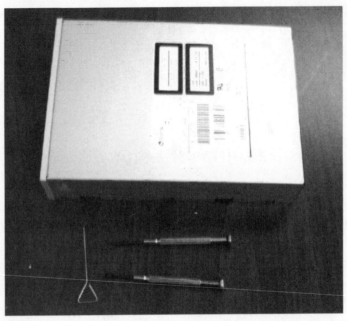

It is recommended that the drive be dedicated for this purpose and disassembled fully to remove the tray. This makes reassembling the drive nearly impossible, but is more convenient. If you cannot dedicate a drive for this purpose, do not remove the tray, because it will be easy to reassemble the drive into its original form with all of the original safety features.

Start by opening the tray on the drive; pull it about halfway out of the drive. If there is a disc in the drive, remove it. With the tray open, push in the tabs that hold the front cover on the drive and pry the tray out. Note that the tabs are usually on the sides and bottom of the drive. Be gentle.

Figure A.2 Drive with Tray Out and Front Removed

Figure A.3 Bottom of Drive Detail

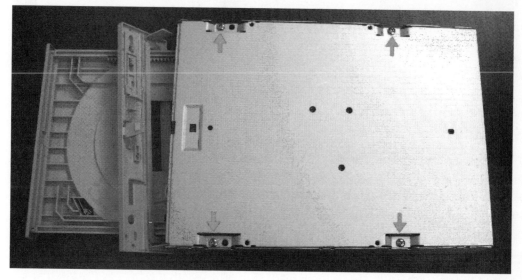

The next step is to turn the drive upside down and carefully remove the four screws that hold the outer casing on; put them with the front cover. These should be saved if you want to put the drive back together. Pull the top cover off of the drive very carefully. Do not bend the cover, which can damage the drive. Prying around the base of the drive with the straight-blade screwdriver can help.

Do not remove the bottom cover, because it protects the circuit board. You may want to fasten the bottom cover to the drive frame with small screws and nuts.

An optional step is to remove the tray, which can make using the drive easier; however, it is nearly impossible to reinstall the tray in a drive and have it work properly. If the drive is "scrap," remove the tray; otherwise, leave it in to enable the drive to be reassembled. In general, the tray is driven by a single gear and slides on both sides of the drive. A limit stop is present to prevent the tray from coming out of the drive (usually a bendable tab on the tray itself). Pressing this tab in will make the tray come out of the drive easily.

Figure A.4 Spindle Clamp Detail

If you choose not to remove the tray from the drive, inspect the front of the tray to determine if the front panel can be removed. The front panel snaps onto the tray and can be easily removed. Remove the front of the tray and then slide the front panel off of the tray. The tray will still function and the difficult-to-reassemble tray mechanism will still be intact; however, moving the tray will no longer be obstructed by the loose front panel of the drive. This is important, because otherwise it will be very difficult to insert and remove discs.

You should now be looking at a drive similar to that in Figure A.5. There may be a metal bar across the spindle with the spindle clamp, or this part may be attached to the top cover. If there is a crossbar, remove it.

Figure A.5 Drive without Top Cover

Regardless of the location of the spindle clamp, you must remove it. For the drive being disassembled in Figures A.4 and A.5 (i.e., a Plextor 12-4-32), the spindle clamp is held in place by the top cover, and only falls out of when the crossbar is removed. It may be necessary to disassemble the spindle clamp to detach it from the crossbar or the top cover of the drive. It can generally be disassembled by pushing the tabs and prying it apart. After removing it, snap it back together to keep the magnet from falling out.

It is necessary to use the spindle clamp when placing a disc on the spindle. Without the clamp, the disc will either not rotate properly or will fly off of the spindle.

This completes the disassembly process for the drive. The photo below shows the drive ready to be connected to the USB external case.

Figure A.6 Final Appearance of Modified Drive

Connecting the Modified Drive

In order to operate the drive, it is necessary to connect the power and data paths. While it is possible to do this directly with a computer, it is strongly recommended that you use a USB 2.0 or FireWire enclosure, which will allow the drive to be connected externally. This will also facilitate turning the power on and off for the drive if necessary. InfinaDyne uses ME-320U2 enclosures exclusively, which include the power supply and the USB bridge in a case only slightly larger than a drive, which is available from a variety of vendors.

Using the Modified Drive

WARNING

Using this modified drive is contrary to the way the drive was manufactured. By removing the top cover, direct laser radiation is exposed. While the laser appears to be red visually, nearly all of the laser energy is concentrated in the infrared part of the spectrum and is invisible. Looking down at the drive while it is operating (especially without a disc) can seriously damage your eyes to the point of causing blindness. Everyone that is using this modified drive should be aware of the hazards of using this device.

WARNING

While the drive is in use, there is a rapidly rotating piece of thin polycarbonate exposed, which can cause serious cuts and/or burns to the fingers or other body parts that come into contact with it. Do not attempt to operate the drive without a properly functioning spindle clamp. Do not touch the disc while it is spinning. Touching the disc may cause it to fly off the drive at high speed.

WARNING

Now that you have modified the drive, it no longer conforms to government regulations concerning safety for lasers. Unauthorized personnel should not be allowed near the drive when it is operating in this configuration. Under no circumstances should a modified drive be sold or exchanged.

To read a disc with a modified drive, a replacement disc must first be examined by the drive, which is a disc that is the same type, color, and speed rating as the subject disc. Push the button on the front of the drive; if the tray was removed, this will do very little. This tells the drive that a new disc is being inserted. If the tray was removed:

- Place the disc on the spindle
- Put the magnetic spindle clamp on
- Press the button

If the tray was not removed:

- Place the disc in the tray
- Press the button
- Quickly place the spindle clamp on the spindle (that this may take some practice)

The drive will spin up and examine the disc. Windows should be able to confirm that the replacement disc is present. Wait for the disc to spin down; grabbing it will result in injury. Remove the spindle clamp and the disc, replace the disc with the subject disc, and replace the spindle clamp. Do not press any buttons on the drive. This allows quick-erased discs and discs with a damaged lead-in to be read using CD/DVD Inspector.

Downloading Additional Materials

All materials described in this book can be downloaded from the InfinaDyne public web site. To get a list of what is available, open the URL http://www.infinadyne.com/pub/CDDVDForensics. This will show a list of the materials that go with this book and can be freely downloaded.

Any materials downloaded from the InfinaDyne web site are specifically intended for purchasers of this book, copying and redistribution is prohibited.

Glossary

"." directory

This is the name given to a directory for HSG, ISO 9660 and Joliet file systems to reference the current directory.

".." directory

This is the name given to a directory for HSG, ISO 9660 and Joliet file systems to reference the previous directory.

!00

A special construction used with the search in the Sector Display tool in CD/DVD Inspector. This literally means to search for "not 00" or searching for any byte that is not binary zero.

1/4 wave plate

Part of the optical assembly on the sled for reading CDs or DVDs. Quarter wave plate is used to turn plane-polarized light into circularly polarized light and vice versa.

ASCII

The American Standard Code for Information Interchange defines the code assignments for text in nearly all computers today. It was first defined in 1967. ASCII defines code positions 0-127.

8-bit ASCII character set

Defines the extended set of code definitions for all values from 0–255 which can be represented by 8 bits. This is technically an extension of the definition of ASCII which only requires 7 bits. All current computers use the 8-bit extended form of ASCII today.

8-bit bytes

A "byte" is the fundamental unit of storage in current computers. It is made up of 8 bits and can take on any value from 0 to 255.

8-bit 1 MHz microprocessors

When CD audio discs were new the state of the art at the time consisted of large mainframe computers, minicomputers made up of many integrated circuits, and single-chip microprocessors. Single-chip microprocessors had a data width of 8 bits meaning they accessed memory one byte at a time and ran with a clock speed of 1 MHz or less. Contrast this with today's microprocessors which run at speeds up to 3,000 MHz and access data 4 or 8 bytes at a time.

16-bit Unicode

An alternate representation of characters which uses 16 bits to represent each character instead of only 8 as is done for ASCII. This allows up to 65,535 different characters to be represented. This is how file names in the Joliet, UDF and HFS+ file systems are stored.

AA (Apple Extensions)

A System Use Sharing Protocol (SUSP) code which identifies data specific to the Apple Macintosh operating system.

abCD

A drag-and-drop CD writing application formerly published by Prassi.

Absolute Time In Pre-groove (ATIP)

Information which is stored in the pre-groove of recordable and rewritable discs.

abstract file

The ISO 9660 specification allows for the specification of the name of a file to be placed in the volume descriptor which contains information about the content of a disc. This file must be placed in the root directory. There is no definition of what the file should contain in the standard.

AccessData FTK

A product of AccessData Corp. which is a commonly used forensic application.

Adaptec/Roxio/Sonic

The publishers of the one of the more common CD and DVD writing software products. This product was originally called Easy CD Creator and is now known as Easy Media Creator.

This product has some interesting quirks in that versions 4 and 5 had a bug which would respond to certain errors by terminating writing the disc apparently successfully but without writing all of data on the disc. No error message was given to the user, so they believed the disc was completed successfully.

Advanced PhthaloCyanine

A modification of the phthalocyanine dye by Mitsui Toatsu Chemicals. This is used for recordable CDs and is designed to have longer life than previous cynanine-based recordable discs.

allocation blocks

The unit of allocation on HFS and HFS+ file systems. An allocation block is required to be a power-of-2 multiple of 512 bytes. Commonly 2048, 4096 and 8192 are used for allocation block sizes on CD and DVD media.

The HFS and HFS+ volume information report the number of allocation blocks for a file system.

allocation size

The volume information for HFS and HFS+ file systems reports the size of the allocation blocks being used. See allocation blocks for more information.

allocation table

This term refers to a data structure, usually a bitmap of some sort, used to control allocation of space on hard disks and the like. The term "allocation table" is also used with the UDF file system to refer to the Virtual Allocation Table or VAT. The VAT is a construct which allows virtualization of pointers on recordable (write-once) media.

In general CD and DVD file systems do not have any sort of space management data structure because the file system does not allow for updating. This is considerably different from hard disks and flash drives where such updating is expected.

ammonia-based cleaners

Generally known as window cleaners or multi-surface cleaners, this term is referring to any sort of cleaning solvent with an ammonia base. Ammonia can "fog" polycarbonate making it less transparent. These types of cleaning solvents should not be used with CDs and DVDs.

amorphous

One of the two states of rewritable media, as opposed to crystalline. When the alloy material is in the amorphous state it is less reflective than in the crystalline state.

Analog

A continuous representation of a signal by voltage or current rather than "sampled" where it is represented in discrete units. Audio CDs represent the original analog signal in digital samples which are then converted back to analog form.

analog audio

The output from a CD player after conversion of the digital samples into analog form.

analog output connector

The connector on a computer CD or DVD drive which enables audio discs to be played directly without interaction with the computer. Modern CD and DVD drives have both analog and digital audio connectors.

Analysis

A tool in CD/DVD Inspector which creates a summary report of all of the content on the disc.

Analysis Dialog

The dialog displaying the output of the Analysis tool.

Analysis Report

The report created by the Analysis tool in CD/DVD Inspector.

anomalous data

A term which refers to data which does not fit in context with the rest of the data. An example of this is an ice cube in a pot of boiling water.

CD/DVD Inspector has a number of tools such as the Disc Map and Sector Display for finding, identifying and extracting such anomalous data.

Anchor Volume Descriptor Pointer (AVDP)

The pointer located at sector 256, 512 or the end of the disc which points to the volume descriptors for a UDF file system.

Anneal

The process of heating just below the melting point and allowing to slowly cool a spot on a rewritable disc. This is use to erase areas and return the material to a crystalline state.

Apple Extensions

The AA System Use Sharing Protocol (SUSP) data structure containing information specific for the Apple Macintosh operating system is referred to as the "Apple Extension" to the ISO 9660 standard.

Application field

The field in the ISO 9660 Primary Volume Descriptor (PVD) or Joliet Supplementary Volume Descriptor (SVD) where the computer application the disc is intended for can be indicated. This is also sometimes used to contain the name of the writing software application.

The content of this field is displayed by the Volume information tool and the Analysis tool.

ART

The file extension for AOL graphic images. These are compressed using the Johnson-Grace compression algorithm which AOL purchased.

Asarte Toast

The original product for creating Apple Macintosh CDs. This was later purchased by Adaptec and passed on to Roxio when it was split off. This product is now published by Sonic.

Assertions

This term is specifically used in reference to Regular Expressions. An assertion specifies a condition that has to be met at a particular point in a match, without consuming any characters from the subject string.

For complete information about regular expressions and their construction a tutorial about the PERL language is recommended as there are many good references about this subject. CD/DVD Inspector implements regular expressions in a form compatible with PERL.

ATAPI (ATA Packet Interface)

ATA or AT Attachment was the successor to the ST506 and ESDI hard disk interfaces for small hard drives. This was extended in the early 1990's to allow CD-ROM drives to be connected to the same parallel data bus as hard drives thus eliminating the requirement for a separate interface card.

Most CD and DVD drives sold today use the ATAPI interface, although in the future this may be replaced by SATA or Serial ATA interface.

ATIP Reference Power

A field in the ATIP information for CD-RW discs which specifies the power level for writing speed determinations.

Audio track

Also known as a Red Book track, this refers to a track on a CD which contains no file system but just audio samples.

AVDP (Anchor Volume Descriptor Pointer)

See Anchor Volume Descriptor Pointer.

backslashed assertions

Regular Expression assertions which are specified by a single character following a backslash. There are only two defined for CD/DVD Inspector (\b and \B) which refer to being at or not being at a word boundary.

Other, more complicated assertions are possible. A tutorial on PERL regular expressions is suggested for further study on this topic.

bar code reading

Some CD writers in the mid-1990 had the ability to read a circular bar code in the mirror band of a recordable disc. This allowed the writing software to identify the blank disc that was used and to preserve this information.

This capability has not been preserved in modern CD and DVD drives.

Basic mode

This is an install-time option for CD/DVD Inspector which sets the option "Recover without prompts."

bibliography file

The ISO 9660 specification allows for the specification of the name of a file to be placed in the volume descriptor which contains information about the origin of the content of a disc. This file must be placed in the root directory. There is no definition of what the file should contain in the standard.

Big endian

The characteristic of some microprocessors of storing binary integers with the most significant bit first, followed by bits of lesser significance. This is the order in which integers are stored in Apple Macintosh (non-Intel) computers.

The origin of the term comes from the novel "Gulliver's Travels" by Jonathan Swift. A war was being fought be two groups which had different opinions on which end of a soft-boiled egg to open, the big end or the little end.

BIOS

The software in a Windows computer which controls the startup. Originally, this software was responsible for all I/O interactions with peripheral devices, such as the keyboard, display and serial ports.

bi-stable alloy

The alloy used in rewritable media which can be in either of two states: amorphous or crystalline.

bi-stable dye

The any of a number of organic dyes used in recordable media which can be changed to being less transparent by the application of heat.

bi-stable metallic alloy

See bi-stable alloy above.

bit map

On CDs and DVDs there is generally not a bit map representing allocated and unallocated space. Such a bit map does exist for HFS and HFS+, but the bit map is of no consequence because the file system is read-only. The UDF file system on rewritable media will often have such a bit map and it is often corrupted causing lost space and overwritten files.

Block size

The block size for an ISO 9660 or Joliet file system is generally required to be 2048 bytes. This information is contained in the Primary Volume Descriptor (for ISO 9660) or Supplementary Volume Descriptor (for Joliet).

For HFS the issue of block sizes is rather confused because there are three different size structures that interact. The fundamental size of a "sector" for HFS and HFS+ is 512 bytes which corresponds with hard disks. Physical sectors on CDs and DVDs are 2048 bytes or four of HFS sectors. Finally, there are allocation blocks which may not be aligned on physical sector boundaries and are a power-of-two multiple of HFS sectors. Allocation blocks on CD and DVD media are generally 2048, 4096 or 8192 bytes but other sizes are possible.

BMP

The most basic, uncompressed bitmap representation used by Microsoft Windows.

Border zone

This is the name for a group of sectors on DVD media. This corresponds to a track on CD media.

Boot

The process of starting up a computer, a shortened form of "bootstrapping." This comes from the usual procedure to get an operating system running on a computer where the hardware reads a small amount of data and instructions which then causes some additional data and instructions to be read which then reads more in and so on.

Boot volume descriptor

A volume descriptor defined by El Torito for CD and DVD media which allows CDs and DVDs to be directly "booted" for installing operating systems and the like.

This descriptor is required to be in sector 17 of the disc or 17 sectors after the first sector in the last session on the disc.

Bootable

The condition of disc having a properly constructed El Torito bootable volume descriptor. Bootable discs are described by the Analysis tool.

Booting catalog

Part of the El Torito standard which lists the available boot images. In general, the BIOS only supports a single boot image on a disc for each hardware platform type.

BSD

Berkley Software Distribution. This is one of the original contributors to the UNIX operating system. The University of California at Berkley created much of what is considered to be "BSD UNIX" today and released it under an open license which allowed it to be reused and redistributed. The basis for the Apple OSX operating system is derived from a version of BSD UNIX.

Buffer underrun

A condition which occurs when writing CDs and DVDs because the drive requires a continuous stream of data. If sufficient data is not available to the drive writing is interrupted which can mean a wasted disc also known as a "coaster". This is not as severe a problem today because with faster computers it is less likely that data will not be available for writing continuously.

Buffing tools

Tools for polishing the bottom (polycarbonate) side of a CD or DVD to remove scratches. This can work because removing a small amount of material does not affect the usability of the disc – the laser can still focus on the pit and lands or the dye layer of the disc.

Consumer tools generally do not remove much material and can be safe to use. Professional tools are capable of removing much more polycarbonate and because of this are substantially riskier to use in forensic situations.

Business card disc

A CD or DVD which is approximately the size of a US business card. There are two basic types, those with rounded ends and those with square ends. These discs hold significantly less information than a standard disc does, but they are quite useful for passing out information.

It is unusual to find these size discs as manufactured – they are almost always recordable discs.

C2 error pointer

When reading a CD some drives provide the functionality of being able to return a map of incorrect data that could not be corrected. These "error pointers" are a result of failures of the level 2 of error correction or C2. This capability does not exist for DVD media.

Caddy

Some early CD drives used a "caddy" to hold discs to prevent them from being damaged by frequent use. This was a good idea, but it was inconvenient for users and was soon dropped.

Calculate MD5 hash

MD5 hash values are one standard for determining a cryptographic signature for the purposes of comparing files and detecting alterations.

Calculating an MD5 hash value for files is directly supported within CD/DVD Inspector. Right click any file, folder or session and select "Calculate MD5 hash" or select the file, folder or session and choose the "Calculate MD5 hash" item in the File menu.

CD

Any of the class of media to which CD Audio, CD-ROM, CD-R, CD-RW discs belong. CD stands for "Compact Disc" which is the original name under which audio discs were marketed. Philips and Sony still hold trademark rights to this name.

CD Audio

A disc or track that contains "Red Book" audio samples. See Red Book for a complete definition of this.

CD-DA

This term refers to the digital audio samples which are used in a "Red Book" audio track. CD Digital Audio samples are 16 bits for the left and right channel at a sample rate of 44,100 Hz or samples per second. If these samples are saved to a file, this file is said to contain CD-DA data.

CDDB key or CDDB code

CDDB (or CD DataBase) was an application that worked with several computer CD players in an attempt to get around the fact that audio CDs do not have digital information about the album title or track names. Therefore, when copying music discs (see pirating) the user often ends up with a disc with no labeling to indicate what is on the disc. The CD DataBase was a community-based effort to construct a comprehensive database of CD audio discs.

A CDDB-enabled application would assemble the lengths of the tracks and the number of tracks and perform a calculation to compute a single 32-bit value. This value was the key for looking up the album title and track names.

It was a reasonably good idea and for a period of time from around 1995 to 1999 or so it was strictly a community effort. If your album was not in the database you could add the information for your disc, if you had it. The relative success of this led to the formation of a company to commercially exploit this data and the technique. This company, Gracenote, now competes with a number of community-based free alternatives.

CD-i

Refers to a disc meant for playing in a CD-i system. The term "CD-i" means "CD Interactive" and players for media and games were introduced beginning around 1992. They never really caught on and only a small number of players were ever sold.

The discs used the ISO 9660 file system with MPEG-2 video. Today the form survives somewhat as VCD or "Video CD" which allows up to an hour of video on a CD. These are far more popular in Asian countries than in the US or Europe.

CD-R

Acronym for "Compact Disc – Recordable" which applies to any write-once CD disc.

CD-ROM

Acronym for "Compact Disc – Read Only Memory" which applies to any data CD disc. All CDs are either CD Audio or CD-ROM discs.

CD-ROM Mode 1

One of the two modes of writing data discs. Mode 1 is the most compatible with all devices and provides 2048 byte data sectors only. There is also a mode 2 (separate from XA) but it is not generally used.

CD-ROM XA

One of the two modes of writing data discs. There are two forms with form 1 supporting multiple "streams" of multimedia data and form 2 exchanging some of the error correction/error detection bytes for additional data in each sector. XA form 2 is used for VCD and SVCD discs.

"CD-RTOS CD-BRIDGE"

This string is placed in the System Use field of the ISO 9660 Primary Volume Descriptor to indicate the disc has been written in XA mode and XA directory extensions will be present. This string is supposed to be present in Unicode form in a Joliet Supplementary Volume Descriptor but some writing software places this string in the System Use area in ASCII instead.

CD-RW

Acronym for "Compact Disc – Read/Write" which refers to CD discs that are rewritable. CD-RW discs can be rewritten an average of 1,000 times in each sector. This being an average means that some sectors will fail long before 1,000 rewrites are reached and some will not fail after 10,000 rewrites.

CD+G

Acronym for "Compact Disc plus Graphics". This refers to audio discs that have additional information for displaying graphics in the R through W subchannels. This is most often used for Karaoke discs which display the lyrics as graphics on a television set while the music is playing.

CD Text

The term "CD Text" refers to either of two standards for storing textual information on audio CDs. The more common is the Sony standard which is today used on most audio discs to store the album and artist names and track names. Sony-type CD Text is stored in the lead in area of the disc. Philips has a different CD Text standard which is intended to store the lyrics with the audio in the same R through W subchannels that are used for CD+G graphics data.

cdrecord

This is the name of a freely distributed program for writing CDs and DVDs. It was originally designed for Linux only but has been ported to Windows as well. This program is currently the only common means of creating a disc with Rock Ridge extensions.

CD Writing Wizard

The Microsoft Windows XP tool that helps users create data discs.

CE (continuation of extension data)

A Rock Ridge directory extension which is used to continue directory extensions into an additional sector.

CeQuadrat

A software company that published a drag-and-drop writing product named PacketCD. This company also published the WinOnCD product. The company was purchased by Roxio and the products are now owned by Sonic.

CD-XA001

A marker that is present in ISO 9660 Primary Volume Descriptor and Joliet Supplementary Volume Descriptor when the disc has been written in XA mode and XA directory extensions are expected on files.

changer (cartridge)

CD-ROM drives that would hold multiple discs were somewhat common in the late 1990s and there were two basic types: those that accepted a preloaded cartridge of discs and those that were loaded using individual discs. Drives report what type of mechanism they have and "changer with cartridge" is one of these types.

changer (individual discs)

CD-ROM drives that would hold multiple discs were somewhat common in the late 1990s and there were two basic types: those that accepted a preloaded cartridge of discs and those that were loaded using individual discs. Drives report what type of mechanism they have and "changer with individual discs" is one of these types.

checkpoint facility

Often with computer programs that take considerable time a technique is used where information is saved periodically to allow the lengthy process to be resumed from the last saved point. This is done by CD/DVD Inspector using the Disc Memory to prevent lengthy disc re-examinations if something interrupts the examination process.

checksum errors

If data structures in a UDF file system are not constructed properly or are corrupted it is likely that the checksum will be incorrect. This is detected and reported on in the Analysis report.

CL (child link)

A Rock Ridge directory extension.

Clamping ring

The inner part of a CD or DVD where the drive clamps the disc between the spindle and a bearing. There is no data in this area and it is safe to write here with CD-safe markers. Hub labels can also be applied here which can be either preprinted or written on.

clock unit

A time measurement that is determined by the rate of changes in the bit patterns being read from a CD or DVD drive. This varies with the rotational velocity of the disc and the position of the laser along the radius of the disc. Decoding the 14 bit pattern that makes up each byte on the disc requires the drive determine how long pit is in time units which translate directly to the number of zero bits between the beginning and end of the pit.

Cluster

A group of sectors allocated to a file together to reduce fragmentation. FAT32 and NTFS file systems for hard disks allocate space in clusters. Clustering is not used by any CD or DVD file system. This means that any strategy for forensically examining hard disks which is based on the concept of cluster allocation is not valid for CDs or DVDs.

collimator lens

Part of the optical assembly moved across the radius of a CD or DVD. This lens helps to focus the laser on an extremely small spot on the disc.

compressed data

Some drag-and-drop file systems compress the data being written to the disc to reduce the space it takes and allow more data to be written. There are two competing products that did this, one from CeQuadrat called PacketCD and the other from Roxio called DirectCD and later Drag2Disc.

CeQuadrat was purchased by Roxio and the PacketCD product discontinued. Very few working copies of PacketCD still exist today.

DirectCD and Drag2Disc are current products from Sonic (who purchased them from Roxio) and do offer the user the possibility of compressing data on discs.

CD/DVD Inspector supports the compression present in both products.

Compute disc MD5

As part of any good forensic procedure it is important to be able to prove that the media has not been altered as a result of the forensic examination. An accepted method of doing this is to collect an MD5 hash value from the media as early as possible in the process and then be able to compare this to a later MD5 hash value. If they match, no changes have occurred.

With CD/DVD Inspector, use the "Compute disc MD5" menu selection in the Pro Tools menu to generate a hash value of the entire disc.

computer peripherals

This term refers to any device which is connected to a computer, usually through a data bus that allows it to communicate with the computer. Examples are keyboards, monitors, modems, printers and so on.

concave singlet lens

A lens in the optical assembly for reading or writing CDs and DVDs. This optical assembly is carried by a larger structure called the sled which is moved across the radius of the disc.

Constant Angular Velocity (CAV)

A technique whereby the disc is spun at a fixed rate of speed (the angular velocity) and the data passes by the optical assembly at a variable speed depending on the distance from the center of the disc. As the sled moves outward the data rate increases.

All modern drives use a CAV technique to avoid having to change the rotational speed of the disc as the sled moves across the radius of the disc.

For writing purposes full CAV is unusual – the writer usually implements something called Zoned CAV where multiple fixed speeds are used.

Contrast this with the Constant Linear Velocity (CLV) which is how audio discs are read and how the first CD-ROM drives worked.

Constant Linear Velocity (CLV)

A technique whereby the disc is spun at a speed determined by the radial position of the sled thereby keeping the rate at which data passes by the optical assembly fixed.

This is how audio CDs are read and how the entire CD mechanism was originally designed. It makes the data handling circuitry far less complicated but requires the spindle motor to change the speed of the disc rapidly. Eliminating the need for this speed change significantly improves the access time of data on different parts of the disc.

Contrast this with Constant Angular Velocity (CAV) which is the way modern drives operate.

Copy Directory

A function in CD/DVD Inspector which is accessed by selecting a folder or session and either right-clicking and choosing "Copy directory ..." from the context menu or selecting "Copy File(s) ..." from the File menu.

All of the files within the selected folder and subfolders are copied to the location selected.

The destination for the files and folders is prompted for.

Copy File

A function in CD/DVD Inspector which is accessed by selecting one or more individual files and either right-clicking and choosing "Copy file ..." from the context menu or selecting "Copy File(s) ..." from the File menu.

The destination for the files is prompted for.

Copy sectors

The function in CD/DVD Inspector which is used to copy individual sectors from the disc without regard for any file system that may be there. The user is prompted for the sectors to copy, the format of the data to be copied and the destination.

Copy Text button

All of the dialogs in CD/DVD Inspector have a "Copy Text" button which copies the contents of the dialog in textual form to the clipboard where it can be pasted into a report document.

copyright file

The ISO 9660 specification allows for the specification of the name of a file to be placed in the volume descriptor which contains information about the copyright of the content of a disc. This file must be placed in the root directory. There is no definition of what the file should contain in the standard.

Copyright Management information

Copyright management information is present on "protected" movie DVD discs.

Cross-Interleaved Reed-Solomon Code (CIRC)

CIRC is the third and final layer of error correction technique used for CD-ROM data. This corrects single-bit errors when a data sector is read.

crystalline

This is one of the two states of the metallic alloy used for rewritable media, the opposite of amorphous. When the alloy is in a crystalline state it is more reflective than when in the amorphous state.

CSS-protected DVD movie discs

DVD movie discs that are manufactured commercially are protected using a system called CSS which makes copying the content difficult. CD/DVD Inspector does not normally operate on CSS protected movie discs but an optional component is available which allows it to do so. The distribution of this optional component is restricted. Please contact InfinaDyne sales for more information if you believe you need this component.

cyanine

The name of a family of organic dyes which are used for recordable media. The dye is heat-sensitive and becomes less transparent when heated by the laser when a disc is being written.

cyanine organic dye

See cynanine above.

cyanoacrylate (superglue) process

A chemical fingerprint developing process for revealing latent fingerprints. This should not be used with CDs and DVDs if at all possible and never allow the bottom (data side) of a disc to be exposed to cyanoacrylate fumes if the disc is to be examined for data.

This technique was first used by the Criminal Identification Division of the Japanese National Police Agency in 1978.

cylinders

The arrangement of data in concentric circles on a hard disk or floppy diskette. CDs and DVDs have the data arranged in a spiral pattern, not in concentric circles. The term "track" is used for both magnetic media (hard disks, floppy diskettes) and CDs and DVDs but there is no similarity between a track on a hard drive and a track on a CD.

cylindrical lens

A lens in the optical assembly for reading or writing CDs and DVDs. This optical assembly is carried by a larger structure called the sled which is moved across the radius of the disc.

data area

The area between the mirror band and the outer edge of the disc where data is on a CD or DVD. See the illustration of this in Figure 2 on page 3.

data bytes

The data that was originally stored on the disc, recovered after processing all of the decoding and error correction.

data carving

A forensic technique whereby files are broken out of a continuous stream of bytes by recognizing headers and other structures within the files contained in the stream. An example of this is separating a large amount of data into individual JPEG pictures based on locating the beginning of each picture.

data frame

> On DVDs the data frame contains the user data and other control information for handling positioning and error correction. Sixteen data frames are assembled into an ECC block which is the smallest amount of data that can be read from a DVD disc. ECC blocks are not accessible using consumer drives, just the 2048 bytes in each user data sector.

data/control bus

> The digital interface between the computer and the CD or DVD drive. There are several different types, such as IDE, SATA, USB, FireWire and SCSI.

data pane

> An optional pane in CD/DVD Inspector where the data for the currently selected file is displayed.

data preparer

> The field in the ISO 9660 Primary Volume Descriptor (PVD) or Joliet Supplementary Volume Descriptor (SVD) where up to 128 bytes of text about the preparer of the disc can be placed. This is often the name of the company that created the disc.

> The content of this field is displayed by the Volume information tool and the Analysis tool.

Decoding

> The process by which information is translated from one form to another. For CDs the data bytes are encoded into a form more easily read and then must be decoded back to the original data.

de-interleave

> The R through W subchannels contain data which, for error correction purposes, is spread over three sectors and is interleaved with the information from other sectors as well. The result of this is that physical damage, such as scratches on the disc, has less of an impact on a single sector which will often allow the error correction process to reconstruct the original data.

Details view

One of the four selectable views for the File pane in CD/DVD
Inspector. This view shows the file name, the starting sector of
the first extent, the size of the file, the last modified date and time
and the MD5 hash value.

device buffer size

The Hardware information display shows the size of the buffer in
the device in K. This is not necessarily used for caching data for
reading but is instead used when writing to a disc.

device capabilities

All modern CD and DVD devices have a standard mechanism by
which they report the capabilities of the device, such as what
types of discs can be read and written, what speeds are available
and so on.

device name

The name of the device assigned by the manufacturer. Note that
the device name shown by CD/DVD Inspector may not be the
same as either the name on the front of the device or even the
name on a sticker on the outside of the drive.

diffraction grating

A part of the optical assembly for reading or writing CDs and
DVDs which is used to split the beam. This optical assembly is
carried by a larger structure called the sled which is moved across
the radius of the disc.

digital audio interface

Many modern CD and DVD drives have a digital audio connector on the back of the drive which allows the digital samples
from an audio CD to be directly sent to a digital audio device for
processing. This is in addition to any analog audio interfaces on
the back of the drive and/or a headphone jack on the front.

digital data/control bus

> The digital interface between the computer and the CD or DVD drive. There are several different types, such as IDE, SATA, USB, FireWire and SCSI.

digital output

> If the drive supports direct digital audio output, this is reported in the Hardware information display described on page 3.

DirectCD

> An application from Adaptec and later Roxio for drag-and-drop CD writing that made creating discs more accessible to the average consumer. This product was released in 1997 and was shipped with many CD-RW drives. The same product is now called Drag2Disc and is published by Sonic.

> There are a number of problems with this software and losing files or the entire content of a disc occurs frequently. In a forensic setting it is important that these discs be recovered as completely as possible because you may be able to retrieve data the user thought was forever lost.

directory entry

> A file system directory is made up of many directory entries, each of which represents a file or folder in the file system.

Disc

> The generic name for a piece of optical media. The spelling was arrived at by Philips when they created the name Compact Disc.

Disc at Once recording

> A recording technique whereby all of the content for the disc is sent to the drive from the computer at one time in a continuous stream.

This is the recording technique most commonly used for music CDs.

Disc Contents by Folder

One of the report formats supported by CD/DVD Inspector.

disc drive motor

This is the motor that spins the disc in the drive. Also called the spindle motor.

Disc Map

A display of how the space on a disc is utilized generated by CD/DVD Inspector.

Disc Memory

A feature of CD/DVD Inspector which "remembers" all of the directory information about a disc after it has been obtained once. This is also used as a checkpoint facility to allow a lengthy scan to be resumed without having to start over.

Disc Memory catalog

The catalog of Disc Memory items displayed by the Preferences dialog page.

Disc Report

Any of the reports capable of being created by CD/DVD Inspector.

disc swap

A technique whereby a good disc is examined by the drive and then an inaccessible disc is substituted.

disc swap drive modifications

The modifications which are necessary to a CD or DVD drive to enable it to be used for disc swapping are described in Appendix A – Disc Swap Modifications.

disc triage

> The process by which discs which can be processed quickly are identified and discs which cannot be processed quickly are put aside for later processing.

discrete logic chips

> When audio CD players first appeared on the consumer market they were constructed using discrete logic chips rather than a single VLSI (Very Large Scale Integration) chip. Using 30 to 40 separate integrated circuits was often necessary to perform all of the decoding and processing that was necessary. Today, an audio CD player is contained in a single integrated circuit.

disk

> The generic term for magnetic media, such as hard disks and floppy diskettes. Contrast this with the generic term "disc" used for optical media.

display sectors

> Use of the Sector Display tool in CD/DVD Inspector to show the contents of individual sectors in hex and character form.

DLA

> A drag-and-drop writing application originally written by Veritas and distributed by HP with their computers.
>
> This application is similar to DirectCD and other drag-and-drop writing tools and suffers from a number of problems which make it likely that users will lose files and entire discs. It is important in a forensic setting to be able to recover these lost files.

DMA

> Direct Memory Access, a technique which allows devices to directly write to the computer's memory without requiring the processor to be involved. This significantly speeds up data transfer to and from CD and DVD devices.

dmem

>The file extension given to exported disc memory files and the description files which are part of a Disc Image file set.

dongle

>Generically, a dongle is a hardware device used for license validation and authorization. CD/DVD Inspector is most commonly licensed using a dongle assigned to a single user.

drag–and–drop

>A writing technique using incremental or packet writing which was introduced in 1997. Software which uses this technique allows the user to write to a CD or DVD the same way that any other removable storage is used – "just like a big floppy."

>The problem is that most of this software is poorly interfaced with Microsoft Windows and has file system implementation issues both of which cause data loss. This data loss is good for forensic examiners in that users may believe they have destroyed every copy of a file only to have the forensic examiner recover it from a supposedly inaccessible disc.

Drag2Disc

>Originally named DirectCD, this application is now published by Sonic and provides the capability for drag-and-drop writing of CDs and DVDs. DirectCD was originally from Adaptec and later Roxio.

>There are a number of problems with this software and losing files or the entire content of a disc occurs frequently. In a forensic setting it is important that these discs be recovered as completely as possible because you may be able to retrieve data the user thought was forever lost.

drive buffer

>The memory contained in a CD or DVD drive that is used as a write buffer and to a lesser extent, a cache for data that has been read.

drive firmware

The programming that is contained within a CD or DVD drive that enables it to operate. The very first CD-ROM drives had as little as 32KB of firmware whereas today a recent DVD writer can have 32MB of firmware.

drive read speed

The speed at which data can be read from a completely readable disc – i.e. a disc that does not have read errors. The maximum read speed is reported in the Hardware information display.

drive serial number

Every CD or DVD drive has a serial number assigned by the manufacturer. In some cases this serial number can be requested from the drive and is displayed by CD/DVD Inspector.

Computer CD and DVD writers do not as a general rule write the serial number of the writer on the disc. There are some exceptions to this, but they are not common.

drivers

Software needed to assist the operating system in communicating with a device. In general Microsoft Windows does not need any special drivers to communicate with any CD or DVD device today and neither does CD/DVD Inspector.

DVD

Originally, "DVD" was an acronym for Digital Video Disc and then later Digital Versatile Disc. Today it is generally agreed that DVD is not an acronym for anything.

DVD Data Frames

The container for the 2048 byte user data sector which is the smallest unit accessible from a computer.

Sixteen data frames are assembled into a single ECC block which is the smallest unit of information which can be read from a DVD.

DVD-R

Stands for DVD minus Recordable. Such discs belong to the "DVD minus" family. A DVD-R disc will hold up to 4.35GB of data.

DVD+R

Stands for DVD plus Recordable. Such discs belong to the "DVD plus" family. A DVD+R disc will hold up to 4.35GB of data.

DVD+R DL (dual layer)

An extension of the DVD standard to allow for dual-layer recording. Previously the only dual-layer discs were those manufactured that way. This allows up to 8.5GB of data to be written to a disc.

Most current DVD drives support reading and writing DVD+R DL discs.

DVD-Audio

A DVD which contains audio to be played on a DVD audio player. This is a music format which has not achieved wide acceptance.

DVD-Video

A DVD containing a movie or other video presentation. Commercially produced DVD-Video discs are generally CSS protected.

DVD-RAM

A relatively obsolete media format which emphasized rewritable discs that could be written to more than 10,000 times. There were considerable interoperability issues with these discs and they never really caught on.

DVD-ROM

A DVD which contains data, as opposed to a DVD-Video or DVD-Audio disc.

DVD-RW

Stands for "DVD minus Read Write." This, like CD-RW discs, allows an average of 1,000 writes in each location on the disc before failing. Such discs belong to the "DVD minus" family. A DVD-RW disc will hold up to 4.35GB of data.

DVD+RW

Stands for "DVD plus Read Write." This, like CD-RW discs, allows an average of 1,000 writes in each location on the disc before failing. Such discs belong to the "DVD plus" family. A DVD+RW disc will hold up to 4.35GB of data.

Dye

The bi-stable organic compound which is placed between the polycarbonate and reflector of recordable (or write-once) media. Most dyes in use today are based on either cynanine or phthalo-cyanine.

ECC

Stands for Error Correction Code, a technique whereby a small amount of additional data can assist in correcting minor errors in a larger section of data.

ECC Blocks

The smallest unit of data stored on DVD discs. An ECC block is composed of sixteen data frames, each containing a 2048 byte user data sector. User data sectors are the only data that is accessible using consumer drives.

ECMA

Ecma International is an industry association founded in 1961 and dedicated to the standardization of Information and Communication Technology (ICT) and Consumer Electronics (CE). They can be found at www.ecma-international.org

There are freely available standards documents at the ECMA web site which parallel many ISO standards. For example, ECMA-119 is the same as ISO 9660. A copy of the ISO 9660 standard costs $250 but ECMA-119 can be downloaded as a PDF file from the ECMA web site.

ECMA Standard 119

A parallel standard to ISO 9660. The ECMA standard is freely downloadable from the ECMA web site at www.ecma-international.org.

EDC

Error Detection Code, part of the error correction and detection on CDs.

Eight into Fourteen Modulation (EFM)

The translation of 8-bit data bytes to 14-bit patterns which are actually written to a CD. The original EFM definition is in the Philips/Sony Red Book standard which describes CD audio.

electromagnetic

Employing both electricity and magnetism. Electric motors are electromagnetic devices. Hard disks and floppy diskettes are electromagnetic in that they store information magnetically and it is read and written using electricity. CDs and DVDs are not electromagnetic as there is no magnetism involved in writing or reading CDs or DVDs.

Electro-Magnetic Pulse (EMP)

A strong electromagnetic effect that is the result from a high-altitude nuclear detonation. This was first observed EMP incident occurred as a result of a high-altitude nuclear test in the South Pacific. Since then, EMP and EMP effects have been a primary concern of military and national data systems.

CDs and DVDs are immune to EMP effects whereas hard disks are not.

electro-optical

The nature of CDs and DVDs is that they are not like other electromechanical devices that are more common. They use optics rather than magnetism and are therefore electro-optical in nature.

electrostatic technique

During the manufacture of CDs and DVDs various techniques are used to deposit thin films of reflector materials (gold and silver) onto the discs and to do so evenly. One such technique is vacuum electrostatic deposition where a small amount of metal is vaporized and then condensed onto the surface of the disc forming the reflector.

El Torito

The standard for making a bootable CD or DVD. The name was derived from the name of the restaurant in southern California where meetings where held to discuss this subject.

emulated media type

A designation in the El Torito boot descriptor which identifies the type of media which is being emulated by the boot image on the CD or DVD. This allows a floppy diskette image to be saved on the CD and when the disc is booted the BIOS emulates a floppy diskette to enable access to the content of the files in the boot image.

EnCase

A forensic investigation and case management tool from Guidance Software, Inc.

end piece

A clear piece of polycarbonate without any information or pregroove molded into it and no reflector. Such discs are used to protect other discs on a spindle and are placed on the ends.

EPROM erasers

> A small ultraviolet light source that supplies enough energy to erase the contents of UV-erasable EPROM (Erasable Programmable Read Only Memory) integrated circuits. Such lamps can provide enough energy to affect both recordable and rewritable discs.

ER (extension reference)

> This is an extension type defined by the System Use Sharing Protocol and used with Rock Ridge extensions.

Error Detection Code (EDC)

> Part of the error correction and detection on CDs.

ES (extension selector)

> This is an extension type defined by the System Use Sharing Protocol and used with Rock Ridge extensions.

evidence

> Data, which when presented in court or other proceeding is either in support or not in support of other facts being asserted.

expert mode

> This is an install-time option for CD/DVD Inspector which clears the option "Recover without prompts."

extended attributes

> Additional data present in a UDF file system which extends the original definition of the UDF file system to include other file attributes. Most commonly, this includes creation date and time for files.

FAT

> Generically, the format of the original file system used on the IBM PC. Today the formats FAT12, FAT16 and FAT32 are in common use. FAT12 is the original IBM PC format, FAT16 is an extension to that and FAT32 is commonly used on hard disks.

This is gradually being replaced by NTFS which provides for additional attributes and security.

Neither NTFS or FAT are used on CDs or DVDs.

father disc

One step n the manufacture of CDs and DVDs. See the discussion on page 3.

file allocation

The technique of assigning space on media (hard disks, floppy diskettes, CDs, DVDs, etc.) to individual files. For media that is read-write, such as hard disk, this often involves allocating more than is actually needed to prevent fragmentation from occurring or at least limiting it. Fragmentation is not a consideration for read-only file systems on CDs and DVDs.

file header information

The unique characteristics of files which make it possible to identify the type of a file simply by a few bytes in the beginning. For example, all BMP files have the characters BM in the first two positions of the file data.

file pane

One of the panes of CD/DVD Inspector. This pane shows the files that are in a folder or session which is selected in the left or folder pane.

file permissions

For UDF and Rock Ridge file systems there are specific permissions in the usual POSIX everyone-group-user form. On POSIX-compliant systems this can be used to control access to files and folders. Microsoft Windows does not have individual file permissions like this.

file set descriptor

A data structure in the UDF file system which describes the contents of the UDF file system.

file system

Generically, a set of data structures which allow a large amount of storage to be subdivided, assigning space to individual files and providing a means to access them usually by name. There are a large number of different file systems, some used on hard disks and some only used on CDs and DVDs.

Finder

Part of the user interface for the Macintosh operating system.

FireWire

A serial data bus that operates at high speed for connecting peripheral devices to a computer.

firmware

Program code which is stored in a peripheral device to control it. This can be as simple as the keyboard controller in a keyboard or as complicated as the firmware in a DVD writer.

flags

This refers to a convention of using a small amount of storage to contain binary "switches" which can be on or off. An example of this are the flags in the ISO 9660 directory entry which indicate various attributes.

floppy disk controllers

A floppy disk drive requires a controller to perform tasks such as arranging and encoding the data for recording, decoding the data that has been read, moving the read/write head assembly and starting and stopping the spindle motor. All of this functionality was possible to implement using discrete logic integrated circuits but today has largely been replaced by VLSI (Very Large Scale Integration) circuits which perform this function as well as a number of others at the same time.

focal plane

In optics, this is the distance from the lens to the object when the object is in focus. For CDs and DVDs this is below the surface of the polycarbonate such that minor scratches on the polycarbonate are out of focus and have a limited effect on reading and writing data.

folder pane

The leftmost pane in CD/DVD Inspector which controls the content of the file pane.

forensic binary images

The practice of copying all of the data from media before examination and conducting the examination on the copied data rather than the original. It is extremely important that the entire content of the original media be copied as a "forensic binary image" or evidence can be missed.

forensic examiner

A person trained to perform forensic examinations on computers and other digital devices and media.

forensic software

Software that has been tested and qualified for use in forensic examinations.

forensic workstation

A computer workstation which has been configured, tested and qualified for use in forensic examinations.

Formazan

A hybrid Cyanine/PhthaloCyanine dye which was developed by Kodak for use on recordable CDs.

fragmentation

The condition whereby a single file is split into multiple parts.

When this occurs on a hard disk it can affect performance. It does not generally occur with read-only file systems such as ISO 9660 and Joliet but is possible with UDF.

fragment

A piece of a file which has been fragmented into multiple parts in multiple physical locations.

frames

The lowest level of organization on CD media. Subcode frames are assembled to play audio samples or to form data sectors.

free blocks

When space is reserved on a CD or DVD it is possible that some or all of it has not been written to yet. These sectors (or blocks) are free.

This is also used in reference to HFS and HFS+ file systems where the file system identifies a number of free allocation blocks. Since these are read-only file systems on CD and DVD media such free blocks are not significant.

FTK

This is the common name for the Forensic ToolKit product from AccessData Corp.

FTP

Acronym for File Transfer Protocol, a common technique for transferring files over the Internet.

full erase

When a rewritable disc is "full erased", every part of the disc is written over. It is not possible to recover any data from a disc which has been "full erased".

However, because this can take 45 minutes for a CD-RW and even longer for DVD media, commonly users will only do a "quick erase" which does not write over the entire surface of the disc. A quick erased disc can be recovered using the disc swap technique but it is necessary to modify a CD or DVD drive to access such a disc.

gap size

The gap size is a field that is present in the ISO 9660 directory entry but has no use today. The intent was to allow two or more files to be interleaved together. However, support for such interleaving has apparently never been present in any operating system. This is used together with the field "unit size".

gate-level integrated circuits

A low level of integration where individual integrated circuits have discrete gates and other logic building blocks. Such integrated circuits are often used in discrete logic to construct all of the necessary processing required.

Today such integrated circuits are not as common with VLSI (Very Large Scale Integration) combining many, many gates and other logic building blocks into a single chip. Often such VLSI chips will include a complete microprocessor, RAM and bus controllers replacing hundreds of separate gate-level integrated circuits.

GIF

A graphics file format defined by CompuServe in the 1980s. It is restricted to a total of 256 separate colors in an image. It is used today primarily for non-photographic web graphics and can include animation.

glass master disc

The initial step in manufacturing a CD or DVD where the data is written with a Laser Beam Recorder to a "glass master" which is a piece of polished glass with a photoresist coating on one side.

GMT

An acronym for Greenwich Mean Time which is the basis for worldwide time zones. Also called UTC or Universal Coordinated Time (the acronym comes from the French spelling).

Some file systems record times as either local time or GMT time and have a time zone expressed as minutes from GMT.

Guidance Software

The publisher of the EnCase forensic software product.

hard disk

An electromagnetic high speed read-write device capable of storing a great deal of information magnetically. Because it is a read-write device the requirements for a file system on a hard disk are quite different from those on a CD or DVD.

hard link

A technique for allowing a single file to have multiple names. This is similar to symbolic links but can generally only be used for files.

UDF allows for hard links in the directory structure by simply allowing multiple names to point to the same file.

hardware platform

Generically the combination of the processor, memory and at least data buses for a computer. Today it is common to talk about the Windows hardware platform or Macintosh hardware platform when referring to generic properties which apply to all such computers.

hash matching

A technique of comparing files by actually comparing their hash signatures. MD5 is one such hash signature, SHA1 is another.

hash set

A set of hash values which are assembled together in a meaningful set for matching purposes. For example, there are hash sets available which will quickly allow identification of files belonging to various releases of Microsoft Office. Other hash sets can be used to identify known child pornography files.

hash value

The hash value or hash signature is the result from processing the file using the MD5, SHA1 or other algorithm.

Hashkeeper-style CSV format

The format used by the HashKeeper project and National Software Reference Library (NSRL).

header

The beginning of a file, especially when it contains a unique signature which makes it possible to identify the type of file from just the beginning of the file.

hex

A shortened form of the word hexadecimal, meaning 16. A convention of expressing 8-bit bytes (or characters) using two digits where each digit has 16 values from 0 to 9 and A through F.

hexadecimal specification

A search specification for CD/DVD Inspector which consists of one or more two-digit hexadecimal values.

HFS file system

The file system which was used on the first Macintosh computers, later replaced by HFS+. CDs and DVDs can be written with either HFS or HFS+ file systems.

HFS+

The successor to the HFS file system which appeared with the Macintosh OS 8.2.

–hide–joliet

An option which can be specified for the "cdrecord" program to remove files from the Joliet directory structure. Files can also be hidden from the ISO 9660 directory structure as well, thus leaving some space used on the disc which is not referenced by the file system.

HSG (High Sierra Group)

A group of companies which got together in 1986 and 1987 to create the High Sierra Group standard for CD-ROM discs. This was the first public standard for making CD-ROMs usable across multiple computer systems.

HTML

HyperText Markup Language, the definition language that is used for documents on the World Wide Web. It is also a convenient way to describe pages which can be printed and contain a mix of text and graphics.

The image reports produced by CD/DVD Inspector are created using HTML.

hygroscopic

The property of absorbing humidity. CDs, especially those with heavy silk-screened labels tend to be rather hygroscopic, that is they absorb humidity and become sticky. DVDs are hygroscopic to a lesser extent because of their construction but still can become "sticky" with heaving silk-screened labels.

IEC 908

A "translation" of the Philips/Sony Red Book standard by the IEC in 1987.

IEEE P1281 System Use Sharing Protocol document

The description of the System Use Sharing Protocol which is used by Apple (for ISO 9660 extensions) and by Rock Ridge. This document may be downloaded from the InfinaDyne public FTP site (http://www.infinadyne.com/pub)

IEEE P1282 Rock Ridge Interchange Protocol

The description of the Rock Ridge extensions to ISO 9660 to contain POSIX file attributes.

iLook

A forensic software product distributed by the IRS.

image

This can refer to either: a forensic image capturing the content of digital media or a graphic image.

Forensic images can be captured in several different ways with CD/DVD Inspector.

Graphic files in the formats ART, BMP, GIF, JPEG, PNG, and TIFF are supported by CD/DVD Inspector. Graphic images can be reported on with CD/DVD Inspector with the HTML image reports.

image detail report

One of the HTML image reports in CD/DVD Inspector.

image selection report

One of the HTML image reports in CD/DVD Inspector.

IMAPI

Acronym for Image Mastering API, a component of Windows XP. This is the writing software that comes with Windows XP.

implementation identifier

A field in UDF data structures which identifies the writing software that created the data structures. In general, there will be only a single implementation identifier present for an entire disc because UDF implementations are not perfectly interoperable. Thus, trying to write to a disc written with one application using another will likely destroy the disc.

The implementation identifier from when the disc was created is reported in the Analysis report for UDF file systems.

in phase

In reading CDs and DVDs the optical system can differentiate between in-phase reflections and out-of-phase reflections from the disc. Lands generate in-phase reflections and pits generate out-of-phase reflections. This only happens with manufactured discs. With recordable discs the dye actually blocks some of the reflected laser light.

inactivity spin-down

The spin-down time is the duration a CD or DVD drive waits after the last command before turning off the spindle motor. This is controllable on a small number of drives. Many drives simply report "infinite" and do not allow the time to be changed.

InCD

A drag-and-drop writing application published by Ahead Software. This is bundled with the Nero product.

This application is similar to DirectCD and other drag-and-drop writing tools and suffers from a number of problems which make it likely that users will lose files and entire discs. It is important in a forensic setting to be able to recover these lost files.

incremental recording

A recording technique which allows the laser to be turned off after writing a single packet of data. This is an alternate name for packet writing and more commonly used with DVD writing.

integrated circuit mask

In the process of creating integrated circuits a photographic mask is used as part of the process to control the exposure to light which in turn makes changes in the photoresist used for etching the circuitry in the integrated circuit. This is similar to how CDs and DVDs are manufactured except that instead of a photographic mask a laser system is used to expose the photoresist chemical on the glass master.

The results, which are areas which are etched by chemicals and areas which are left alone is the same. And in both cases the photoresist is a chemical which is altered by being exposed to light.

Intel byte order (I)

Also known as little endian.

Intel-style processor

Processors which operate with little endian byte order.

Intel x86

The family of processors that Intel originated and now is also manufactured by AMD, VIA and a number of other companies.

interchange level

A designation in the UDF file system indicating if the file system is intended for read-only use or read-write use by other applications.

interleaving

The technique of weaving two or more sets of data bits or data bytes together. This can be done for a number of reasons, but it is done on CD and DVD media to limit the damage to a single set of data in case of physical damage. The error correction that is incorporated into CD and DVD media can recover transparently from a small number of defects in a single sector so it is better to distribute a single large defect over multiple sectors through interleaving rather than have it affect a single sector such that it cannot be recovered.

IR (infrared light)

The infrared spectrum covers light in the range between 3000 nm and 500 nm. While much of this spectrum is not visible to humans, it is often used for various data applications because it has been easy to create solid-state infrared laser diodes for a number of years. Only recently has higher frequency laser diodes been able to be manufactured.

ISO

International Standards Organization, a body which oversees the creation and distribution of standards worldwide.

ISO 9660

The standard that defines the most common CD file system.

ISO 13346

A file system that was defined in the mid-1990s that forms the basis for the UDF file system. This is also known as ECMA-167.

ISOBuster

A shareware application for examining and possibly recovering data from CDs and DVDs. The author added some forensic features to the product and some forensic examiners use this instead of CD/DVD Inspector.

ISO image file

A quasi-standard format which supports a single session, single track data disc being described by a binary file.

ISRC

This is an acronym for International Standard Recording Code which is an identification method for music. Audio CD tracks will often have an ISRC code present in the Q subchannel. CD/DVD Inspector will read this and display the ISRC code when it is present for an audio track.

Joliet file system

A Microsoft extension to the ISO 9660 standard that was defined in 1995. This is described in greater detail on page 3.

Joliet Volume Information

The output of the Volume information display for a Joliet file system.

JPEG

A graphic file format that uses "lossy" compression to achieve greater compression than would otherwise be possible. This is designed for photographic images rather than computer graphics. This is defined by and named for the Joint Photographic Experts Group.

.JPG

The file extension used with the JPEG file format.

kernel module

CD/DVD Inspector uses a kernel module to allow it to access CD and DVD devices without requiring Administrator rights.

KHz

Abbreviation for KiloHertz meaning thousands of Hertz or cycles per second.

lacquer

The protective coating over the reflector on CD-R and CD-RW discs. This is essentially a thin layer of paint and can easily be damaged destroying some or even all of the data on the disc.

lands

The areas on a manufactured CD which are closer to the laser and reflect in-phase light.

Laser Beam Recorder

The device used in CD and DVD manufacturing to expose the glass master to light.

laser diode

A solid-state semiconductor device which emits coherent light when current is supplied to it. The frequency of the light remains constant and the power of the light emitted is dependent on the amount of current. This is how a CD or DVD writer changes between reading and writing – by changing the amount of current to the laser diode.

laser lens

part of the optical assembly that moves across the radius of disc in a CD or DVD drive. When modifying a drive for use with the disc swap technique the final lens of the optical assembly is exposed and is pointing upward. This can present the opportunity for accidentally looking into the laser and receiving enough laser energy into an eye to seriously damage it or even cause blindness.

Follow all of the recommended safety precautions when using a modified drive.

laser pick up assembly

The entire optical and focusing assembly that moves across the radius of the disc. This is also known as the sled because it moves across the disc on rails.

lead-in

The beginning part of a session on a CD.

lead-out

The end of a session on a CD. T

L-format path table

Part of the ISO 9660 file system which is a list of all of the directories present on the disc. The L-form path table contains integers in the Intel or little endian byte order.

Linux®

A alternative operating system that was developed by the Finnish professor Linus Torvalds. It is popular in many areas today because it is free and in some respects more reliable than Microsoft Windows.

list view

One of the four formats of displaying files in the file pane. In this view only the icon and file name are displayed.

little endian form

When the volume information is displayed for ISO 9660 file systems, all of the little endian forms of the information are displayed first followed by all of the big endian forms.

Load Hash set

A function in the Pro Tools menu for loading hash sets for comparison to the content on a disc.

loading mechanism

CD and DVD drives have had several different types of disc loading mechanisms over the years. The tray type is the most common with the notebook manual tray mechanism being a close second. There are also caddy loading drives and slot loading drives. Previously, changer type devices were available but these seem to have all disappears from the market.

The Hardware information display shows the mechanism type that the drive is reporting, but this is not always accurate. Note that there is no designation for a notebook type of drive and these are generally lumped in as tray type mechanisms.

logical file system

The organization of files and directories over a storage medium which is for the most part separate and independent of the physical organization of the medium. For example, the HFS file system can be used on either read-only CDs or read-write hard disks.

lookup table

Part of the Red Book standard shows the conversion between eight bit bytes and the fourteen bit patterns that are recorded on a CD. A suggested implementation is a lookup table to translate between these forms.

LSI (Large Scale Integration) chip

An integrated circuit which has at least a thousand logic gates. This is considered to be the fourth generation of integrated circuits. Today, most electronic devices use VLSI integrated circuits which have many tens of thousands of logic gates.

Macintosh

The computer family produced by Apple Computers. The Macintosh family was known especially for its use of big endian processors and a single button mouse. Recently Apple has begun using the Intel processor which is little endian for some computers.

Make Zip Image

A function in the Pro Tools menu of CD/DVD Inspector. This creates a ZIP file containing all of the contents of all sessions and all file systems found on a disc.

Master Directory Block

Part of the structure of the HFS and HFS+ file systems.

mastered

A technique of disc creation in which all of the files are gathered at one time and the entire session is then written.

Contrast this with drag-and-drop disc writing where each file is separately presented to be written to the disc.

maximum reading speed

The Hardware information display reports the maximum reading speed that the drive reports. There are conditions where the drive cannot achieve this speed. For most CLV drives today this applies only to data at the outer edge of the disc.

Maximum recording speed = nnX

This value is reported in the Analysis report for rewritable media. The maximum speed is manufactured into CD-RW discs in the ATIP or Absolute Time in Pregroove. For DVDs this information is in data structures manufactured into the disc in the lead-in area.

MD5

A popular cryptographic hash function for reducing all of the characteristics of a message to a single 128-bit value. This is commonly used in forensic analysis for ensuring that media has not been altered and for comparing files in a high speed manner.

It is being replaced to some extent by the SHA1 256 bit hash value. CD/DVD Inspector does not yet support SHA1 hash values.

media

The generic term for all types of CDs and DVDs.

Media Catalog Number (MCN)

A numeric value that is assigned to a commercially produced audio disc by the publisher.

The space for this value was originally called UPC code but it was quickly realized that the UPC code is not a fixed thing for audio discs. It was changed in the 1990s to be called MCN instead.

ME–320U2

A USB 2.0 adapter case which can be used to convert internal IDE CD and DVD drives into external USB 2.0 drives. This particular case is available from a number of vendors and is very inexpensive.

Media Sciences

A company specializing in quality testing CDs and DVDs. Dr. Jerome Hartke is a respected authority on CD and DVD manufacturing.

metacharacter

Any of a number of characters which have special meaning apart from representing the character itself in a regular expression.

metallic alloy

Rewritable media use a bi-stable metallic alloy instead of dye. This can be in either of two states: amorphous or crystalline.

Metallized Azo

A class of CD-R discs originated by Verbatium.

metalized glass master

One step in the manufacturing of CDs and DVDs. This is after the glass master has been recorded, etched and then plated.

metallization

One step in the manufacturing of CDs and DVDs. This is the step during which the glass master is plated with nickel after etching.

M-format path table

Part of the ISO 9660 file system which is a list of all of the directories present on the disc. The M-form path table contains integers in the Motorola or big endian byte order.

MHz

Abbreviation for MegaHertz meaning millions of Hertz or cycles per second.

microprocessor

In common use, this means a single VLSI chip which contains all of the parts of a computer except for the memory.

Minimum recording speed = nnX

This value is reported in the Analysis report for rewritable media. The minimum speed is manufactured into CD-RW discs in the ATIP or Absolute Time in Pregroove. For DVDs this information is in data structures manufactured into the disc in the lead-in area.

minutes

Because CDs originated with audio discs, all CDs can be addressed by a minute-second-frame (MSF) address. It is also common to refer to the capacity of a CD in minutes rather than megabytes or number of sectors.

mirror band

The region between the clamping area and the data area of a disc.

mkisofs program

Part of the cdrecord set of tools for creating discs under Linux. This program creates the image file to be recorded to the disc. It will create an ISO 9660 file system with Rock Ridge as well as a

Joliet file system. Some versions include the capability to build a hybrid disc with an HFS file system as well.

Mode 2 Form 1

One of the XA recording modes which has 2048 byte data sectors with full error correction.

Mode 2 Form 2

One of the XA recording modes which has 2336 byte data sectors and omits the last layer of error correction.

mother disc

One of the last steps in the manufacturing of a CD. See the information on page 3.

Motorola byte order (M)

Also known as big endian. This is the byte order used by processors from Motorola rather than the byte order used by processors from Intel.

Motorola-style processor

Motorola has historically produced big endian byte order processors while Intel has produced little endian byte order processors.

mount the disc

When a CD or DVD is placed into a drive the first step is to read the information in the lead-in of the disc. This is the table of contents for a CD and the index of border zones and other data for DVDs. If this cannot be read, the disc is not "mounted" in the drive and cannot be accessed.

The drive makes this determination by itself and cannot be forced to accept a disc.

MSCDEX (MicroSoft CD Extension)

For MS-DOS and Windows up until Windows 95 this was required to access CDs. This implements the ISO 9660 and HSG file systems.

MS-DOS 2.0

In 1983 Microsoft began distributing MS-DOS 2.0 which defined partition tables for hard disks and the subdirectory structure. This was the operating system that enabled the IBM PC XT to make effective use of the 10MB hard disk it was sold with.

Multi-Read compliant

CD-ROM drives which can read CD-RW discs with fixed-length packets are known as Multi-Read compliant. Not all CD-ROM drives can do this although some could be updated by flashing the firmware to and updated level.

This is mostly a non-issue since this transition occurred in 1997.

multisession capable

Many CD-ROM drives made before 1994 could not read discs with multiple sessions. Those that could were labeled as "multi-session capable".

nanometer (nm)

A "nanometer" is a measure of length. It is equal to one billionth of a meter. One million (1,000,000) nanometers equal one millimeter.

NM (alternate long name)

A Rock Ridge directory extension which hold an alternate (long) name for a file. The format for this extension is presented in the Rock Ridge section on page 3.

Nero Burning ROM®

A CD and DVD writing product published by Ahead Software. The full version of this product is bundled with InCD, a drag-and-drop writing program.

Nickel Sulfamate

A chemical used to electroplate an etched glass master with a thin layer of nickel to make a metalized glass master.

not bootable

A setting in the El Torito boot entry that indicates there is a emulated device image present but that it is not bootable.

notebook drive

A thin form-factor CD or DVD drive which is designed to fit
into a notebook computer. Many of these drives, even the ones
that are not removable, are in fact using a standardized shape. This
allows such drives to be easily replaced often with only some
outer plastic needing to be moved from one drive to another.

NTFS

Acronym for New Technology File System. This was introduced
by Microsoft for Windows NT 3.1 in 1993.

objective lens

The final lens in the optical assembly which focuses the laser at
the focal plane. This is also called the focusing lens.

octal coding

An alternative to decimal or hexadecimal using base 8 instead of
10 or 16. Early minicomputers from Digital Equipment
Corporation and some others used octal notation instead of hexadecimal and because of this octal is closely associated with
UNIX.

offset

A number of bytes indicating the displacement from the beginning of a data structure or sector. All offsets in this book are relative to zero, so the first position of any data structure has an offset
of zero.

OPC (Optimal Power Calibration)

The process by which a CD or DVD writer determines the
proper current for writing. This is done by initially writing to a
reserved area of the disc and checking the results. Modern CD
and DVD writers also use a technique called running OPC where

the laser power is adjusted continuously to deal with changes in dye density and other factors that affect write quality.

optical media

Generically, this term refers to all types of optical media, including CDs, DVDs and even DVD-RAM discs.

Optical Storage Technology Association (OSTA)

The industry association responsible for Multi-Read certification and the UDF specification. They can be found on the Internet at www.osta.org.

optional path table L

An optional additional table of path information for the ISO 9660 or Joliet file system. The L-format path table has little endian integers.

It is not clear what the function of the optional path table is, but for modern systems it apparently has no function.

optional path table M

An optional additional table of path information for the ISO 9660 or Joliet file system. The M-format path table has big endian integers.

It is not clear what the function of the optional path table is, but for modern systems it apparently has no function.

organic solvents

A class of chemicals which are used to dissolve other compounds and are formed from organic compounds with a low boiling point. Such chemicals are generally very destructive to the lacquer and reflector of a CD.

orgy of evidence

The most recent reference for this term is the movie "Minority Report" where it is offered that too much evidence is a clear sign that everything is not as it seems. It has also been used to reference situations where no matter where you turn everything seems to be evidence.

Often with computer forensic cases there is only a single piece of media with all of the evidence on it. Having pertinent evidence on nearly every disc collected is not a situation you should hope for.

OS 8

The Apple Macintosh operating system release where support for HFS+ was added.

OSX

The current operating system for Apple Macintosh computers. This operating system is built on a UNIX-like base.

out of phase

In reading CDs and DVDs the optical system can differentiate between in-phase reflections and out-of-phase reflections from the disc. Lands generate in-phase reflections and pits generate out-of-phase reflections. This only happens with manufactured discs. With recordable discs the dye actually blocks some of the reflected laser light.

ownership

Refers to POSIX-compliant file systems, such as UDF or Rock Ridge, where a user and group identifier is present to indicate the ownership of a given file or directory.

packet

A single group of sectors written to a disc. Packets can be fixed-length or variable-length depending on the parameters sent to the drive.

PacketCD

A drag-and-drop writing application formerly published by CeQuadrat. This product was discontinued when Adaptec bought CeQuadrat in 1999.

This application is similar to DirectCD and other drag-and-drop writing tools and suffers from a number of problems which make it likely that users will lose files and entire discs. It is important in a forensic setting to be able to recover these lost files.

packet writing

A recording technique which allows the laser to be turned off after writing a single packet of data. This is an alternate name for incremental recording and more commonly used with CD writing.

parallel directory structure

When both ISO 9660 and Joliet file systems are present on a disc, it is common that for every entry in the Joliet file system there is an identical file with a short name in the ISO 9660 file system. The short name fits the limits of ISO 9660 level 1 which restricts file names to 8 characters with a three character extension.

When every file in the Joliet file system is mirrored in the ISO 9660 file system with the only difference being the name, it is said that a parallel directory structure exists.

parallel IDE bus

The standard 40-pin IDE bus that is common for hard disks, CD and DVD drives and some other devices.

This is being replaced by SATA, a 7-pin serial bus that can transfer data as fast or faster than the parallel bus.

parent directory

In a directory structure where there are multiple directories, the parent is the directory "above" the current directory in the hierarchy.

Partition Map Block

In HFS and HFS+ file systems this contains information about the partition containing the file system.

partition name

For an HFS or HFS+ file system, this is the name of the partition, generally assigned by the writing software.

path table

A table in an ISO 9660 or Joliet file system which lists all of the folder names and what the parent folder is. There are two path tables required, one with all integers in little endian byte order and one with all integers in big endian byte order.

path table size

A field in the ISO 9660 Primary Volume Descriptor and Joliet Supplementary Volume Descriptor which contains the length of the path table.

PC BIOS

The software in a Windows computer which controls the startup. Originally, this software was responsible for all I/O interactions with peripheral devices, such as the keyboard, display and serial ports.

PCM

Acronym for Pulse Coded Modulation. This is a representation of audio signals where each sample is represented by a numeric value. CD Audio consists of a left and right sample 44,100 times per second with each sample occupying 16 bits. This adds up to a total of approximately 10 MB per minute of audio.

PD (padding field)

This is an extension type defined by the System Use Sharing Protocol and used with Rock Ridge extensions.

PERL

Acronym for Practical and Easy Reporting Language. This is an interpreted language that has many features for processing strings. It has become the de facto standard for Regular Expression processing.

Many books are available as well as web tutorials to assist in understanding PERL and Regular Expressions.

petroleum solvents

A class of chemicals which are used to dissolve other compounds and are formed from organic compounds with a low boiling point. Examples are gasoline, kerosene, and naphtha. Such chemicals are generally very destructive to the lacquer and reflector of a CD and should not be used anywhere near CDs or DVDs.

Philips CD Text

A standard that was introduced in 1997 for incorporating song lyrics onto Red Book audio discs. The R through W subchannel data is used for storing this information.

This has never found acceptance in the commercial music business.

Contrast this with Sony CD text which is used very widely on commercial music CDs.

photodetector

Part of the photodetector array for sensing the direct and reflected laser light in a CD or DVD drive. Photodetectors are small semiconductor devices which will block current until they are exposed to light and then pass current.

photodetector array

A set of four or more photodetectors for sensing the direct and reflected laser light in a CD or DVD drive. This is part of the optical assembly contained on the sled.

PhthaloCyanine

An organic dye introduced by Mitsui Toatsu Chemicals. The benefit over cynanine dyes was that it would be more stable thus media using it would have a longer life.

Pioneer Axx and 1xx

> A series of Pioneer DVD writers that have been tested and found to produce high quality discs. Unfortunately, these drives have a firmware bug which makes it impossible to get a consistent MD5 hash of a CD-R which has been written using packet writing.

> Such drives should be avoided for forensic use.

pits

> The areas of a manufactured CD or DVD where the laser light is reflected out of phase, thus making them distinguishable from the "lands."

PL (parent link)

> This is an extension type defined by the System Use Sharing Protocol and used with Rock Ridge extensions.

Plextor(®

> The manufacturer of high quality CD and DVD drives. InfinaDyne has found that the Plextor 12x CD-RW drives are capable of reading marginal CDs that other drives cannot access. These are strongly recommended for forensic use.

PN (POSIX device number)

> This is an extension type defined by the System Use Sharing Protocol and used with Rock Ridge extensions.

PNG

> Acronym for Portable Network Graphic, a graphic file format. This was intended to be a replacement for GIF because of patent issues but it still has not achieved wide acceptance.

polarizing beam splitter

> Part of the optics assembly on the sled for reading CDs and DVDs. This splits the beam from the laser diode into four parts and reflects one of these directly towards the photodetector array.

polycarbonate

A durable thermoplastic material used for everything from CDs to bullet-proof glass. It is also used for eyeglass lenses. While it is very durable, it can be scratched and deep scratches will affect the readability of CDs and DVDs.

Also, the polycarbonate discs are made from will shatter of stressed sufficiently and when it shatters it tends to break into a small number of large pieces and a very large number of barely visible fragments which are extremely dangerous.

pop-up

A style of CD drive where the spindle clamp is manually actuated. Many audio players work this way and some small DVD players but computer peripherals no longer use this type of mechanism.

port

(a) An electrical connector for data, (b) to change a computer program to support a different hardware or software platform, such as to port a program from Windows to Linux.

POSIX

A set of application programming interface standards defined by IEEE. This is currently implemented by Linux and other UNIX and UNIX-like system vendors. Windows NT at one time had a POSIX subsystem but this has been abandoned.

post-gap

A group of 150 sectors trailing the data or audio which are required for CDs and not required for DVDs.

PowerPC

A processor architecture that Apple has been using for a number of years. The PowerPC can be configured as either big or little endian but Apple chose to use big endian to be compatible with the previous processor architecture they were using.

Apple has recently been shipping Intel-based computers which hare little endian.

pre-emphasis

Audio tracks on CDs can be identified as being recorded with or without pre-emphasis. Pre-emphasis is a technique to reduce noise introduced into the recording.

The assumption is that the source material has no noise or distortion and that any noise introduced by the conversion to digital form and conversion back to analog will introduce only high frequency noise. The high frequencies of the original material are amplified and the music is converted to digital form and placed on a CD. When a track is played that is marked as having pre-emphasis, the high frequencies are attenuated (volume reduced) to remove the added amplification introduced during the recording process. The result is that any high frequency noise added during conversion or playback is reduced in volume.

pre-groove

A "blank" disc is not really blank at all – there is a pre-groove spiral which is manufactured into the disc that the laser follows while writing. This also has information encoded into it such as the distance along the spiral (absolute time) and other information about the disc itself. This information is collectively called "Absolute Time In Pre-groove" or ATIP.

Primary Volume Descriptor

Part of the ISO 9660 specification which defines the volume. This is required to be placed at sector 16 or (for the second and later sessions) 16 sectors after the beginning of the track.

printed circuit board

A usually stiff piece of fiber or plastic upon which there are interconnections "printed" on the board. In reality a printed circuit starts out as a solid sheet of copper foil over the board and where interconnections are not desired the copper is chemically removed.

The technique for ensuring the correct copper paths remain is done photographically. A drawing of the finished circuit pathways is made into a transparency with the pathways opaque. The board with a solid sheet of copper is coated with a light-sensitive solution called photoresist and light is passed through the transparency onto the photoresist. Where ever the light strikes the photoresist it is chemically changed so that it can be washed away with a solution called the developer or etchant. The result of this is the finished board with the pathways that appeared on the transparency.

This is very similar to the way in which CDs are manufactured in that again light is used to control the etching of the photoresist and it is developed.

Pro Tools Menu

One of the menus in the menu bar on CD/DVD Inspector.

proprietary operating system

An operating system generally designed for dedicated control computers. An example would be an elevator control system.

proprietary raw camera formats

Most digital cameras record only JPEG format pictures, but some will also record a "raw" format that is specific to the camera and its image sensor. These formats are generally not documented. CD/DVD Inspector supports many of these raw image formats and will display such pictures directly.

publisher

The field in the ISO 9660 Primary Volume Descriptor (PVD) or Joliet Supplementary Volume Descriptor (SVD) where up to 128 bytes of text about the publisher of the disc can be placed. This is often the name of the company that created the disc.

The content of this field is displayed by the Volume information tool and the Analysis tool.

PX (POSIX file attributes)

This is an extension type defined by the System Use Sharing Protocol and used with Rock Ridge extensions.

quick erase

An alternative to a full erase that takes considerably less time – generally less than five minutes. When a rewritable disc is "full erased", every part of the disc is written over. It is not possible to recover any data from a disc which has been "full erased".

However, because this can take 45 minutes for a CD-RW and even longer for DVD media, commonly users will only do a "quick erase" which does not write over the entire surface of the disc. A quick erased disc can be recovered using the disc swap technique but it is necessary to modify a CD or DVD drive to access such a disc.

radial tracking signal

A signal derived from the photodetector by the drive electronics which keeps the sled positioned along the spiral path of the data on a CD or DVD.

When writing this is derived from following the pre-groove.

When reading this is determined by locating leading pits (or less reflective areas) along the track of the spiral.

raw 16-bit audio samples

CD audio tracks contain PCM-encoded audio samples without any additional information. This is often referred to as "raw 16-bit audio samples." See the item PCM above for additional information.

RAW format

See the item "proprietary raw camera format" above.

Raw sector search

A tool in CD/DVD Inspector for searching sector data without regard to how the sectors are used. This is done from within the Sector Display tool.

RE (relocated directory)

This is an extension type defined by the System Use Sharing Protocol and used with Rock Ridge extensions.

This extension is used when the total directory depth exceeds the ISO 9660 limit of 8 and the directory structure is continued into a different path nearer the root of the directory structure.

readability test

A media test in CD/DVD Inspector for the overall readability of a disc under "baseline" conditions. This test is hidden when the "Forensic use" option is selected as it does not have any significance for forensic examiners.

real-time operating system

An operating system designed to handle events quickly. This is the sort of operating system that you find in dedicated computers in control applications, such as elevator controllers, alarm systems, and manufacturing systems. Microsoft Windows is not such an operating system.

rear-facing analog output

Most CD and DVD drives have an analog output connector on the rear of the drive. This is designed to be connected to the motherboard or audio card so that the audio from playing a CD can be routed to the speakers connected to the computer.

recovered disc

Any disc that was previously inaccessible or had files recovered on it.

Red Book

The standard defined by Philips in 1982 for how audio CDs work.

Red Book Audio

An audio track that conforms to the Red Book standard on a CD.

Reed–Solomon Product Code (RS-PC)

An error correction strategy used on CDs.

Reference Speed

A speed encoded in the ATIP for CD-RW discs. This speed is the one at which the write power calibration was determined for.

reflector

The molecules-thick metal in a recordable disc that reflects the laser light. If the reflector is damaged this also affects the dye beneath it and destroys data. Damage to the reflector can be "read around" if it is not too severe but the data at the location of the damage cannot be recovered.

replacement disc

A disc used in place of a damaged or quick erased disc in order to allow the drive to read a valid table of contents and calibrate to the reflectivity of the disc. The disc must be chosen to be roughly the same as the damaged disc and written in the same manner.

reserved

This refers to space on a disc or in a data structure which has not yet been assigned a use but is kept as a placeholder for future use. An example of this is the space reserved for the lean-in when writing a disc using Track At Once. The lead-in is written after the session is closed but the space is held for it when writing begins.

Revision

The last firmware update applied to the drive. Some drives can be updated after they are sold via flash memory updates. It can be important with some drives to know the revision level of the firmware because of behavior differences.

RID

Acronym for Recorder Identification. This is recorded on audio discs by stand-alone CD recorders. Computer CD and DVD writers do not generally record any information about the drive for CDs or DVDs.

Rock Ridge

A standard introduced in 1993 for extending ISO 9660 to support POSIX file and directory attributes. This makes use of another standard called System Use Sharing Protocol for sharing the directory extension space in an ISO 9660 file system.

root directory

The highest level directory (or folder) in a file system.

root directory sector

The sector holding the beginning of the root directory structure. This is shown in the Volume information display for ISO 9660 and Joliet file systems.

Other file systems have a root directory, but it is not as useful to examine it with the Sector Display tool.

root directory timestamp

The timestamp in the "." directory entry for ISO 9660 and Joliet file systems. This timestamp may be more accurate than the recording date and time in the Primary and Supplementary Volume Descriptors because some software offers the user the choice of setting these to specific values. The root directory timestamp in the "." directory entry is constructed by the writing software and will almost always reflect the time set on the computer when the disc is created.

Of course, the person creating the disc may be very clever and set the computer time to something different as well as taking other steps to modify the apparent date the disc was created. However, this trick alone will often disclose the real time the disc was created.

Roxio Easy CD Creator® 4 and 5

This software is known for creating "partial" discs where the entire directory structure is present but only a portion of the files are actually written to the disc. No error message is given to the user when writing ends prematurely, thus leading the user to think the disc was completed successfully.

RRIP112.DOC

The file name of the Rock Ridge specification. This can be downloaded from the InfinaDyne public FTP server. See Appendix B – Downloading Additional Materials.

R-W subchannel data

Additional data space on CDs outside of the normal user data area. This exists for both data and audio discs and up to 35MB can be stored on a disc in this area.

RZone

The name for a group of sectors on DVD media. This is an alternate name for a border zone. This corresponds to a track on a CD.

SATA

Serial AT Attachment, a new data bus for connecting hard disks, CD and DVD devices to computers. This replaces the parallel ATA or IDE bus.

SATA interface

If a hard disk, CD or DVD drive or other device has a connector for attaching an SATA cable, it is said to have a SATA interface.d

Scan Files

A function in the File menu on CD/DVD Inspector. This searches for matches of simple strings, hexadecimal strings or Regular Expressions over all of the files on the media.

SCSI

An acronym for Small Computer System Interface. This was originally the primary way to connect CD devices to computers. It is a high speed data bus that uses 25 or 50 separate connections. Today this has been mostly replaced by IDE, USB, FireWire and SATA data buses.

SCSI drive

A hard disk, CD or DVD drive which has a SCSI data bus connector.

SCSI enclosure

An external enclosure with a power supply for a SCSI drive. Prior to the introduction of USB 2.0 and FireWire this was the only way to have an external CD or DVD device.

sector

The fundamental unit of data transfer between a CD or DVD device and the computer.

Sector Display

A CD/DVD Inspector tool that displays individual sectors in hex and character form. This is opened by either clicking the toolbar button for it or selecting it from the File menu.

seconds

Because CDs originated with audio discs, all CDs can be addressed by a minute-second-frame (MSF) address. It is also common to refer to the capacity of a CD in minutes rather than megabytes or number of sectors.

Select Device Dialog

The dialog that is presented to the user when CD/DVD Inspector starts up or when explicitly invoked to change devices.

setname

The name of a character set used in an ISO 9660 file system. This is replaced in the message by either ISO 9660 or MS-DOS, depending on the characters found in file names.

SF (file data in sparse format)

This is an extension type defined by the System Use Sharing Protocol and used with Rock Ridge extensions.

session

A group of sectors on a CD or DVD usually recorded at the same time.

Session At Once recording

A CD recording technique similar to Disc At Once but not closing the disc and allowing later sessions to be added. This is not supported by all CD and DVD writers.

SHA1

A cryptographic hash algorithm that results in a 256-bit value which can be used for validation and file comparisons.

single laser diode

All CD and DVD devices use only a single laser diode even though multiple "beams" are used for tracking and reading the disc. All of the separate "beams" are split from a single source.

SL (symbolic link)

This is an extension type defined by the System Use Sharing Protocol and used with Rock Ridge extensions.

sled

The mechanical assembly inside a CD or DVD drive that holds the optics and is moved across the radius of the disc.

slot-loading drive

CD and DVD drives can come with a variety of ways to place the disc in the drive. A slot-loading drive has a slot on the front and a motor will grab the disc and pull it into the drive. This is very similar to an automobile CD player.

Such drives are no longer very common.

Sodium Hydroxide

The caustic developer agent used to etch the glass master and remove the photoresist that was not exposed to light.

solvent-based markers

Markers that have a definite and strong odor are generally Xyelene based. Such markers will almost instantly destroy the reflector if the data area of a disc is written on using one of these.

Solvent-based markers have no place in a forensic lab dealing with CD and DVD media.

Sony CD Text

A standard for placing the names of the album, artist and individual track names on an audio music disc. This was introduced in 1997 by Sony about the same time that Philips introduced their own CD Text standard. The Sony CD Text information is stored in the lead-in with the table of contents information.

This has received wide acceptance and many music writing CD applications will also write CD Text information using the Sony technique.

SP (system use sharing protocol indicator)

This is an extension type defined by the System Use Sharing Protocol and used with Rock Ridge extensions. The presence of this extension in the root directory "." entry indicates that System Use Sharing Protocol extensions are present on the disc.

space allocation

The problem of allocating space to files is quite different from that used on read-write hard disks when dealing with CDs and DVDs, even those that can be rewritten.

sparable partition

A UDF file system for which media errors are handled by replacing sectors individually with other sectors located elsewhere on the disc. This process sometimes handled automatically by the drive.

A sparable partition must have a sparing information table.

sparing information table

The table that contains the error sector to new sector correspondence list in a UDF file system.

spindle hole

The 15 cm hole at the center of a CD or DVD.

spindle motor

The motor which rotates the disc. This is also called the disc drive motor.

splitter cursor

A cursor shape that indicates the user can move a bar between two panes of a window. CD/DVD Inspector uses this when the user is resizing the various panes of the display.

sputtering

A technique for electrostatically depositing metal in a thin film on a CD or DVD.

ST (system use sharing protocol terminator)

This is an extension type defined by the System Use Sharing Protocol and used with Rock Ridge extensions.

stacking ring

The ring on the bottom of a CD or DVD designed to keep discs stacked on a spindle apart. This is to prevent them from sticking together, especially after silk-screening the label on the top of the disc.

Discs with heavy printed labels are also somewhat more hygroscopic (absorbs humidity) than blank discs.

Discs should be carefully aligned when being transported so the stacking rings will keep the discs separate. If this is not done the top of one disc can stick to the bottom of another and remove part of the reflector when they are separated.

stamper

The result of metalizing and transforming the glass master. This is then used to mold CDs or DVDs.

The term "stamper" originated from the manufacture of vinyl records. The process involved heating the vinyl record and stamping it with the recording.

steganography

Is a technique by which messages are hidden in another medium, such as a graphic image, music or even an executable program file.

CD/DVD Inspector does not analyze files for potential use of steganography.

subchannels

CDs have multiple data streams including the main data channel. These subchannels are assigned the letters P through W and have a total of 96 bytes per CD sector.

subcode blocks

Part of the low level structure of CDs. Roughly, one subcode block is processed into one user data sector.

subcode information

In general, the organization of low level CD data which is processed to form user data sectors and other control information.

subdirectory

A folder within another folder in a file system.

subheader

In XA CD sectors this carries two copies of the channel and program information. This can be used to separate multiple multimedia data streams, such as audio and video.

subpatterns

Parts used to construct assertions in a Regular Expression.

Sun

A computer company known for their high performance computers and Solaris operating system. Solaris is a derivative of UNIX.

Supplementary Volume Descriptor

Part of the ISO 9660 standard that enables the use of alternate character sets for file names. Joliet is defined using a Supplementary Volume Descriptor with a system use field that identifies the character set being used as 16–bit Unicode. The Supplementary Volume Descriptor is written following the Primary Volume Descriptor.

SUSP

See System Use Sharing Protocol below.

SUSP112.DOC

The file name of the document describing the System Use Sharing Protocol specification. This can be downloaded from the InfinaDyne public FTP server. See Appendix B – Downloading Additional Material for more information.

SVCD

Acronym for Super Video CD. An SVCD is a CD with 30-60 minutes of moderate-resolution video. While this format did not catch on in the US or Europe, it is extremely popular in Asian countries.

symbolic links

A technique to enable a single file or folder to have multiple names, potentially in different places in the directory structure. A symbolic link is similar to a hard link with the exception that symbolic links can be used for files or folders whereas a hard link can generally only be used for files.

Rock Ridge support symbolic links.

sync

A specific bit pattern at the beginning of a subcode block that the drive can recognize as the beginning point. Finding the sync for is necessary before the drive can begin reading data.

system ID

A field in the ISO 9660 Primary Volume Descriptor and Joliet Supplementary Volume Descriptor which is available for providing information about the system that the disc is intended to be used with. Sometimes this has information in it which indicates the software that created the disc.

system use

A field in the ISO 9660 Primary Volume Descriptor which has no defined use. For a Joliet Supplementary Volume Descriptor this field identifies the character set used in the file system.

System Use Sharing Protocol

A method by which the optional area following an ISO 9660 directory entry can be shared between multiple uses. This is used by Rock Ridge for the directory extensions used. See the SUSP112.DOC entry above for information about this specification.

"T"

CD pit sizes are defined as being 3T to 11T where T is one clock unit. The duration of a "clock unit" can depend on the rotational speed of the disc and the radius of the spiral at that point. With a 1X CLV drive the linear velocity is always between 1.2 and 1.4 meters per second. At 1X the data transfer rate is 179200 bytes per second which translates to roughly 2,600,000 clock units per second. Therefore, a clock unit for this 1X CLV drive is approximately $1/2,600,000^{th}$ of a second or about 0.0000038 seconds. As drive speeds increase this decreases similarly.

Table of Contents (TOC)

The list of tracks on a CD. For a DVD the index of border zones is translated by the drive into a Table of Contents and this is returned in response to requesting the Table of Contents.

TF (additional POSIX time stamps)

This is an extension type defined by the System Use Sharing Protocol and used with Rock Ridge extensions. The format for this extension is presented in the Rock Ridge section.

TIFF

Acronym for Tagged Image File Format. This graphic file format is a generic container for a variety of formats with and without compression.

timestamp

A time and date attribute of a file or folder.

toolbar

> A graphic user interface component that presents iconic buttons to invoke commonly used functions.

track

> A group of sectors generally written at one time on a CD.

Track at Once recording

> A recording technique where the drive generates a table of contents entry for the track that was written. This is the most common writing technique for data tracks.

track pitch

> The separation between "wraps" of the spiral on a CD or DVD. The track pitch for CDs is 1.8nm and 0.8nm for DVDs.

tracking drive

> The mechanism that moves the sled across the radius of the disc.

tracking motor

> The motor that moves the sled across the radius of the disc.

trailing version identifier

> The marker ";1" that is required by the ISO 9660 standard at the end of every file name. This was required to make the file names compatible with the VMS operating system where multiple versions of files can co-exist.

Transfer Block

> Some CD and DVD drives have the capability to return partly incorrect data when errors occur. This is controlled by the "TB" (Transfer Block) bit in the error recovery control information. If the drive does not support the Transfer Block setting, the drive cannot return any sector which is not completely correct.

transition

Obtaining the EFM symbol from a CD is done by identifying the transitions between lands and pits.

transition decoding

Reading from a CD consists of decoding transitions between lands and pits into EFM symbols. The EFM symbols are then decoded into data bytes and de-interleaved.

tray

CD and DVD drives can come with a variety of ways to place the disc in the drive. The most common mechanism is a sliding tray.

UCS-2

A form of 16-bit Unicode used for the Joliet and HFS+ file system.

UDF file system

A file system derived from the ISO 13346/ECMA 167 specification. UDF is capable of storing files larger than 2GB and is therefore often used with DVD media. UDF is required for DVD Video and DVD Audio discs.

Unattached items

A folder created by CD/DVD Inspector to hold files which have been recovered but the folder they belong in cannot be determined. The presence of this folder indicates that an intensive UDF examination has been performed.

Unicode

A standardized set of character sets using 8, 16 and 32 bits. Full UCS-4 (32 bit) Unicode supports more than 2 million unique character assignments. CD and DVD file systems use UCS-2 (16 bit) characters which supports 65536 unique character assignments.

unit size

The unit size is a field that is present in the ISO 9660 directory entry but has no use today. The intent was to allow two or more files to be interleaved together. However, support for such interleaving has apparently never been present in any operating system. This is used together with the field "gap size".

UNIX

An operating system developed at Bell Laboratories in the early 1970s. It serves as the basis for most microcomputer and mini-computer operating systems today. For example, Linux and Solaris are both derived from UNIX.

UNIX file names

UNIX file names are allowed to be any length and in general restricted to printable ASCII characters.

Unnamed_nnnn

The form of names assigned to files recovered from a UDF file system. The "nnnn" is replaced by a numeric value from 0001 to 9999. If more than 9999 files are found, additional digits are added as needed.

UPC

Uniform Product Code, a standard from the Uniform Code Council. Originally the UPC for music CDs was envisioned as being recorded on the CD but because a single CD may be sold under a number of different UPCs this was not really practical. This field was renamed to MCN or Media Catalog Number.

USB

Universal Serial Bus, a data bus standard.

USB 1.1

The first implementation of the USB standard which could transfer data at up to 12Mb per second. This is limits the speed at which peripherals can operate. For example, the maximum data rate for a CD drive connected on a USB 1.1 data bus is approximately 6X.

USB 2.0

The high speed implementation of USB which can transfer data at up to 480Mb per second. CD and DVD devices on a USB 2.0 data bus are not limited by this type of connection.

USB bridge

Usually a single chip which "bridges" between USB and a different type of data bus. The most common form of this is bridging between an IDE drive and the USB bus.

user data

The 2048 bytes in a CD or DVD data sector. CDs have other sector formats which can support larger amounts of user data per sector.

UV (ultraviolet light)

Light at a wavelength shorter than can be seen by humans. UV light generally has a higher concentration of energy and can be used for a variety of purposes. Some of these involve sufficiently intense light that CDs and DVDs can be affected.

A significant source of UV light is the sun which under the right conditions can affect CDs and DVDs.

vacuum chamber

Part of the configuration for sputtering or vacuum deposition of metal onto a CD or DVD.

Validation

The process by which forensic software and hardware is tested to verify correct operation.

VCD

Acronym for Video CD. A VCD is a CD with 30-60 minutes of low-resolution video. While this format did not catch on in the US or Europe, it is extremely popular in Asian countries.

vertical market

A a group of similar businesses or customers with specialized needs. The first CD-ROM applications were for vertical markets with specific needs for access to large amounts of data. Considering the largest practical hard drive at the time was around 200MB, a CD could contain three times that amount of data and an unlimited number of CDs could be used.

View Image

A feature of CD/DVD Inspector for displaying ART, BMP, GIF, JPEG, PNG or TIFF images.

virtual allocation table (VAT)

A data structure used with the UDF file system to allow files to be updated and deleted on write-once media.

volume created

The timestamp when an ISO 9660 or Joliet volume was written.

volume descriptor

A data structure that hold information about a file system. Each file system has its own unique data structure or data structures for this purpose.

volume effective

The timestamp when an ISO 9660 or Joliet volume is to be considered effective. This timestamp is almost never filled in or always set to the same time as the volume creates time.

volume expires

The timestamp when an ISO 9660 or Joliet volume is considered to have expired. This timestamp is almost never filled in or simply set to some time in the far future.

Volume ID

The name of the volume which is displayed by most operating systems.

volume in set

For ISO 9660 and Joliet this field is intended to be set to the number of the volume within a set of volumes (discs). There is no operating system support for this and the value will always be 1.

volume information

Information displayed by the Volume information display specific to the file system selected.

volume modified

The timestamp that the volume was last modified. This is intended as a revision date but in practice it will always be set to either the volume create date and time it will not be set.

volume set name

An alternate name apart from the volume name for a UDF file system. This is often simply set to the volume name when the disc is formatted. This is useful because it cannot be changed on write-once media whereas the volume name can be.

volume set size

For ISO 9660 and Joliet this field can be set to the number of volumes (discs) in a set of discs. This is not supported by any current operating system and can be considered to be obsolete. It will always be 1.

volume size

The size of the volume for ISO 9660 or Joliet file systems. This value will usually be equal to the last sector written in the session.

washable markers

Markers which do not use solvents and are safe for use on CDs and DVDs. These are often water-based.

water–based markers

Markers based on water rather than a solvent. This type of marker is safe to use on CDs a DVDs.

.WAV

An audio file format for Microsoft Windows. CD/DVD Inspector can copy all or part of an audio track to a .WAV file so it is directly playable on Microsoft Windows.

Windows Vista

The next version of Windows from Microsoft due to be released in late 2006 or early 2007.

Windows XP CD writing capability

Windows XP is distributed by Microsoft with a CD writing tool that is a mastering-style writing application. The user must first assemble a list of files to be written to a CD and then instruct Windows XP to write the files to the disc.

This is not a drag-and-drop writing application although Microsoft called it that before Windows XP was released.

wrap

Each full circle of the spiral on a CD or DVD is referred to as a "wrap".

XA format

The second mode of data writing on CDs. This allows additional features and can be used to intermix multimedia streams although this is not commonly done.

XA Mode 2 Form 1

The second mode of data writing on CDs where user data sectors are 2048 bytes and there is additional program and channel information for separating intermixed multimedia streams.

XA Mode 2 Form 2

The second mode of data writing on CDs where user data sectors are 2336 bytes and there is reduced error correction. This allows greater data rates because more user data bytes are transferred with each read. This format is used for VCD and SVCD discs.

Xenon flash lamp

A source of UV light which is used to "cure" the lacquer on CDs. Such lamps are also used with adhesives used for bonding DVDs.

.ZIP

The file extension for a ZIP archive. The ZIP archive format was originally defined by PKWare but is now supported by various libraries.

ZIP Archive

A compressed archive file using the ZIP archive format.

ZIP Image

A file created by CD/DVD Inspector which contains all of the files and all of the file systems found on a disc. This can then be imported into other forensic tools.

Zoned CAV

A strategy used by CD and DVD writers for fixing the rotation speed of the disc at a few fixed values corresponding to various "zones" along the radius of the disc. This eliminates the need for the data rate to change drastically as the write location on the disc changes from the inside to the outside.

Index

A

AccessData Full Tune-Up Kit (FTK), 65
accessibility problems, 50, 186
amorphous state, 11
Analysis report, 97, 183
Analysis tool (CD/DVD Inspector), 83, 103–149, 161
Anchor Volume Descriptor Pointe (AVDP), 44
application information, 105, 165
  ISO-9660 and, 136
  Joliet and, 144
  UDF and, 149
ATIP reference power, 106
audio, 2, 96, 123
  CDDB key and, 106, 110
  file systems and, 32–43
  ISRC/RID codes and, 114
  manufacturing process and, 20
  Red Book and, 54, 121
  sectors and, 14, 15
  tracks and, 14
  writing to discs and, 30
Audio Play Supported item, 130
audio subcode blocks, 15
AVDP (Anchor Volume Descriptor Pointe), 44

B

Bar Code Reading Supported item, 128
beginning of data area, 5
big-endian block size, 109
binary images, 53–56
  CD/DVD Inspector 3.0 and, 94, 163
  forensic images and, 92–95
blank discs, 106, 186
blank tracks, 122
block size, 114
blue star icon, 171
boot catalog, 108, 109, 118
bootable disc information, 106
border zones, 12, 14
buffing tools, 69

C

C2 Error Pointers item, 128
CD Audio sectors, 15
CD/DVD Inspector, 55, 65–67, 159–167
  advanced tasks and, 169–180
  basics and, 73–157
  Data window of, 80
  Disc Memory and, 81, 101
  disc triage and, 68
  examining discs
    at startup, 100

step-by-step guide for,
160–163

forensic images, creating with,
92–95

installing, 74

main window of, 77, 98

preferences for, 96–103

quick description of, 74

starting, 160

tools with, 83–86

CD+G Graphics for Karaoke
Discs, 16

CDDA positioning, 130

CD-DA sectors, 15

CDDB key, 106

CD-R discs, 7, 9–11

CD-ROM drives, 23–26

CD-ROM Mode 1, 15

CD-ROMs, 3
binary images and, 54
manufacturing process for,
20–23

CD-RW discs, 2, 7, 106

CDs
binary images and, 53–56
collecting evidence from, 57–62
colors and, 8
differences vs. DVDs, 19
documenting/fingerprinting, 61
file systems and, 35–48
identifying, 58
information storage on, 11

logical structures of, 29–51

physical features of, 1–28

preparing for examination,
63–71

sizes/shapes of, 6

space allocation and, 48

types of, 7

writing to, 2, 30

See also discs

CD-Text/CD+G CDDA
Supported item, 130

CD-Text/CD+G Decoded item,
130

character classes, 89–92

CIRC (Cross-Interleaved Reed-
Solomon Code), 19

clamping ring, 4, 6

cleaning discs, 61, 65
cautions for, 62, 68
disc triage and, 67–69

colors, 8, 186

commands, 127

Compact Discs. *See* CDs

Compact Discs-Rewritable
(CDs-RW), 2, 7, 106

Compact Disk-Read Only
Memory. *See* CD-ROMs

compressed data, 120

Compute Disc MD5 (CD/DVD
Inspector), 83

Compute MD5 Hash (CD/DVD
Inspector), 84

contaminants, 62, 68, 186

copying
  disc contents, 95
  files, 99
creating
  binary images, 94, 163
  forensic images, 92–95
  InfinaDyne image files, 94, 164
Cross-Interleaved Reed-Solomon
  Code (CIRC), 19
crystalline state, 11
CSV files, hash sets and, 170
CSV Format Export report, 155
cyanoacrylate processes, 61

D

data area, beginning/end of, 5
data frames, DVD sectors and, 16
data preparer information, 107
  ISO-9660 and, 136
  Joliet and, 143
date information, 165
Device Buffer Size (in K) item,
  131
Device Capabilities item, 131
device names, 126
Digital Output on Port 1 item,
  129
Digital Output on Port 2 item,
  129
Digital Versatile Discs. *See* DVDs
directories, 118
  depth and, 112

ISO-9660 directory analysis
  and, 176–179
missing directory entries and,
  114
setname and, 115
sorting by name, 98
directory entry, ISO-9660 and,
  37
Disable Disc Memory feature,
  101
disc-at-once writing, 30
Disc Contents by Extension
  report, 153
Disc Contents by Folder report,
  151, 182
Disc Contents by Name report,
  152
Disc Map (CD/DVD Inspector),
  84, 162, 171–175
Disc Memory feature, 81
  disabling, 101
  settings for, 102
Disc Report (CD/DVD
  Inspector), 84, 149–157
discs, 120
  accessibility problems and, 50,
    186
  blank, 106, 186
  bootable information and, 106
  cleaning, 61, 65, 67–69
  copying contents of, 95
  documenting/fingerprinting, 61
  examining, 160–167

at CD/DVD Inspector startup, 100

with Disc Memory, 81

step-by-step guide for, 160–163

father, 21

handling, 58

marking, 59

mother, 21

ordering by decreasing readability, 67–71

preparing for examination, 63–71

searching for keywords/data, 86–92, 163

stacking/storing, 59

swapping technique for, 70

tips about, 186

transporting, 60

XA mode and, 115

See also CDs; DVDs

documenting discs, 61

Drive Serial Number item, 131

DVD+R discs, 7

DVD+R/RW discs, 8

DVD+RW discs, 2

DVD-R discs, 7

DVD-ROM drives, 7

DVD-RW discs, 2

DVDs

binary images and, 53–56

collecting evidence from, 57–62

colors and, 8

differences vs. CDs, 19

documenting/fingerprinting, 61

DVD kind and, 107

dyes and, 10

file systems and, 35–48

identifying, 58

information storage on, 11

logical structure of, 29–51

physical features of, 1–28

preparing for examination, 63–71

sizes/shapes of, 6

space allocation and, 48

types of, 7

writing to, 2, 30

See also discs

dye layers, 3

dyes, 3, 8, 11

E

ECC (Error Correction Code), 16

ECC blocks, 16, 20

EFM (Eight into Fourteen Modulation), 12

El Torito boot catalog, 108, 109

El Torito standard, 47, 118

electromagnetic radiation, 2

EnCase (Guidance Software), 65, 101

end of data area, 5

erasing data, 31

Error Correction Code (ECC), 16

error messages, 98, 108

evidence collection, 57–62

binary images and, 53–56

preparing discs for examination and, 63–71

reporting and, 181–184

examining discs, 100, 160–163

with Disc Memory, 81

preparing for, 63–71

extents, 101

external interfaces, 26

F

FAT (File Allocation Table), 32

father disc, 21

File Allocation Table (FAT), 32

file systems, 32, 186

CD/DVD, 35–48

disc accessibility problems and, 50

files/directories and, 118

information for, 131–149

logical, 32–35

messages and, 104, 108, 111, 124

missing files and, 166

number of on disk, 120

space allocation and, 48

unknown data tracks and, 179

files, 118

copying, 99

full list of, 182

mismatched counts and, 111

missing, 166

MS–DOS separator characters and, 112

overlapping, 116

sessions and, 105, 112

version identifiers and, 113, 117

version markers and, 97

Files with MD5 Hash Value report, 154

findings, reports of, 181–184

fingerprinting discs, 61

firmware, 27, 126

forensic hardware, 64, 67

forensic images, creating, 92–95

reproducing, 55

forensic software, 65, 67

Forensic Use option, 101

forensic workstation, 66

installing CD/DVD Inspector on, 74

validating, 67

free sectors, 119

FTK (AccessData Full Tune-Up Kit), 65

full erase operations, 31

G

Guidance Software's EnCase, 65, 101

H

handling discs, 58–60, 62, 186
hard drives, binary images and, 53–56
hardware, for forensics, 64, 67
hardware information, 126
Hardware Information (CD/DVD Inspector), 84
hash matching, 170
hazardous substances, 62
HFS (Hierarchical File System), 33, 46
  displaying name of, 109
  volume information for, 147
HFS+, 47
  displaying name of, 109
  volume information for, 147
HSG (High Sierra Group), 34, 36, 148

I

ILook Investigator, 65
Image Detail report, 156
image files, 109, 162
image reports, 156, 183
Image Selection report, 156

image viewer (CD/DVD Inspector), 79, 85
Inactivity Spin-down item, 131
incremental recording, 30, 43
InfinaDyne image files, 94, 164
InfinaDyne's CD/DVD Inspector. *See* CD/DVD Inspector
Information Security Research Center (ISRC), 108, 111
information storage on CDs/DVDs, 11
installing CD/DVD Inspector, 74
interfaces, 26
ISO 9660, 32–35, 37–39, 117
  directory analysis and, 176–179
  disc accessibility problems and, 50
  volume information for, 132–139
ISRC code, 108, 111
ISRC Code is Read item, 128

J

Joliet, 39
  disc accessibility problems and, 50
  volume information for, 139–147

K

keywords, searching for, 86–92, 163

L

lands, 11
laser beam recorders, 21
lead-in area, 13
lead-out area, 13
lead-out track, 109, 116
little-endian block size, 109
Loading Mechanism, 128
logical file systems, 32–35

M

main window (CD/DVD
    Inspector), 77, 98
manufacturer information, 107,
    111
mastering program, 117
Maximum Reading Speed item,
    129
MCN (Media Catalog Number),
    110
MD5 (Message Digest 5), 54
MD5 hash values, 126, 170
MDG (Mobile Data Gateway),
    83
media
  full list of files on, 182
  type and, 104
  See also discs
Media Catalog Number (MCN),
    110
Message Digest 5 (MD5), 54
messages, 98, 104, 108, 111, 124

metalized glass master, 21
metallic alloys, 11
metallization, 22
Microsoft CD EXtension
    (MSCDEX), 34
minimum/maximum recording
    speeds, 110
mirror band, 5, 6
mismatched file counts, 111
Mobile Data Gateway (MDG),
    83
Mode 2 Form 1 Supported item,
    129
Mode 2 Form 2 Supported item,
    129
mother disc, 21
MSCDEX (Microsoft CD
    EXtension), 34
MS-DOS separator characters,
    112
Multi-session Capable item, 129
multi-session discs, 186
multi-session hiding, 167

N

next writeable location, 111
NTFS (New Technology File
    System), 32

O

overlapping files, 116

P

packet writing, 30, 43
partition names, 113
path table, ISO-9660 and, 37
Philips CD Text, 13, 17, 33
pits, 11
platform information, 165
POSIX (Portable Operating
        System Interface), 40
POSIX character classes, 92
post-gaps, 105, 117
publisher information, 113
    ISO-9660 and, 136
    Joliet and, 143
P-W subchannels, 15

Q

quick erase operations, 31

R

RAW read command, 127
raw sector searching, 86, 184
Read CDDA command, 127
readability of discs, disc triage for,
        67–71
Readability Test Reason code,
        128
Reading CDDA Supported item,
        130
reading speed, maximum, 129
recording speeds, 110

recovery operations, CD/DVD
        Inspector and, 100
Red Book audio, 35, 121
Reed-Solomon Product Code
        (RS-PC), 19
reflector, 3, 8
    damaged, 69
    marking discs and, 60
    missing, 59, 70
    protecting, 68
    solvents and, 69
reports, 181–184
    Disc Report and, 84, 149–157
    extents and, 101
rewritable discs, 2, 7, 106
Rock Ridge, 40–43, 113
root directory information, 125
RS-PC (Reed-Solomon Product
        Code), 19
R-W subchannels, 16
RZones, 13-15

S

Scan Files tool (CD/DVD
        Inspector), 84, 86, 87–92
    keywords and, 163
    reports and, 184
scratches, 4, 68
    buffing out/filling, 65, 69
    location of, 58, 186
searching discs for
        keywords/data, 86–92, 163

Sector Display tool (CD/DVD Inspector), 84, 179

sectors, 14, 104, 108, 109
  free, 119
  types of, 15

Secure Hashing Algorithm 1 (SHA1), 54

sessions, 14
  linked/not linked files and, 105, 112, 119
  tracks and, 109

setname, 115

SHA1 (Secure Hashing Algorithm 1), 54

software, for forensics, 65, 67

Sony CD Text, 13, 14, 33

space allocation, 48

space utilization analysis, 171–175

sparing information, 125

special features, CD/DVD Inspector and, 100

spindle hole, 4

spiral pattern, 2

sputtering, 22

stacking ring, 5, 58

stampers, 21

step-by-step guide for examining discs, 160–163

subchannels, 15

subcode blocks, 15

superglue processes, 61

SUSP (System Use Sharing Protocol), 40

swapping discs, 70

SYNC (synchronous) subcode information, 19

System Use Sharing Protocol (SUSP), 40

T

terminology, 12–15

tips, 185

TOC Toolbar (CD/DVD Inspector), 85

TOCs, 14, 113, 116

tools, 55, 65, 69
  Analysis, 83, 103–149
  CD/DVD Inspector, 83–86
  Disc Report, 84, 149–157
  Scan Files, 84, 86, 87–92, 163, 184

track-at-once writing, 30

Track Information command, 127

tracks, 3, 14, 104, 121–123
  blank, 122
  ISRC/RID codes and, 114
  lead-out, 109, 116
  messages and, 108, 109
  unknown data tracks and, 179

Transfer Block Supported item, 131

U

UDF (Universal Disk Format), 30, 32, 43–46, 124
  disc accessibility problems and, 51
  intensive examination and, 99
  volume information for, 148
unknown data tracks, 179
UPC Code is Read item, 128
Using 10 Byte command, 127

V

validation, 67
VAT (Virtual Allocation Table), 125
VCDs (Video Compact Discs), 20
version identifiers, 113, 117
version markers, files and, 97
Video Compact Discs (VCDs), 20
Virtual Allocation Table (VAT), 125
volume descriptor, ISO-9660 and, 37
volume identifiers, 118
volume information display, 131–149

W

warning messages, 124

workstations, for forensic examinations, 66
  installing CD/DVD Inspector on, 74
  validating, 67
Write Image file (CD/DVD Inspector), 86

X

XA mode, 115

Z

Zip image files, creating, 93
.zip64 extension and, 101

Syngress: *The Definition of a Serious Security Library*

Syn·gress (sin-gres): *noun, sing.* Freedom from risk or danger; safety. See *security.*

AVAILABLE NOW
order @
www.syngress.com

BigNum Math: Implementing Cryptographic Multiple Precision Arithmetic
Tom St Denis

BigNum Math takes the reader on a detailed and descriptive course of the process of implementing bignum multiple precision math routines. The text begins with a coverage of what "bignum math" means and heads into the lower level functions. Subsequent chapters add on to what has already been built right through to multiplication, squaring, modular reduction and ultimately exponentiation techniques.

ISBN: 1-59749-112-8

Price: $49.95 US $64.95 CAN

Syngress Force Emerging Threat Analysis: From Mischief to Malicious
David Maynor, Lance James, Spammer-X, Tony Bradley, Frank Thornton, Brad Haines, Brian Baskin, Anand Das, Hersh Bhargava, Jeremy Faircloth, Craig Edwards, Michael Gregg, Ron Bandes

AVAILABLE NOW
order @
www.syngress.com

Each member of the Syngress Force authoring team is a highly regarded expert within the IT Security community. These are the "first responders" brought in when things go wrong at the largest corporations and government agencies. In this book, they have distilled years of field experience with an intimate knowledge of next generation threats to provide practitioners with a response strategy.

ISBN: 1-59749-056-3

Price: $49.95 US $64.95 CAN

Network Security Assessment: From Vulnerability to Patch
Steve Manzuik, Ken Pfeil, Andre Gold

AVAILABLE NOW
order @
www.syngress.com

This book will take readers from the discovery of vulnerabilities and the creation of the corresponding exploits, through a complete security assessment, all the way through deploying patches against these vulnerabilities to protect their networks. This book is unique in that it details both the management and technical skill and tools required to develop an effective vulnerability management system. Business case studies and real world vulnerabilities are used through the book.

ISBN: 1-59749-101-2

Price: $59.95 U.S. $77.95 CAN

SYNGRESS®

Syngress: *The Definition of a Serious Security Library*

Syn·gress (sin–gres): *noun, sing.* Freedom from risk or danger; safety. See *security*.

AVAILABLE NOW
order @
www.syngress.com

Sockets, Shellcode, Porting, and Coding: Reverse Engineering Exploits and Tool Coding for Security Professionals

James C. Foster

In this ground breaking book, best-selling author James C. Foster provides never before seen detail on how the fundamental building blocks of software and operating systems are exploited by malicious hackers and provides working code and scripts in C/C++, Java, Perl and NASL to detect and defend against the most dangerous attacks. The book is logically divided into the Five, main categories representing the major skill sets required by security professionals and software developers: Coding, Sockets, Shellcode, Porting Applications, and Coding Security Tools.

ISBN: 1-59749-005-9

Price: $49.95 US $69.95 CAN

Buffer Overflow Attacks: Detect, Exploit, Prevent

James C. Foster, Foreword by Dave Aitel

The SANS Institute maintains a list of the "Top 10 Software Vulnerabilities." At the current time, over half of these vulnerabilities are exploitable by Buffer Overflow attacks, making this class of attack one of the most common and most dangerous weapon used by malicious attackers. This is the first book specifically aimed at detecting, exploiting, and preventing the most common and dangerous attacks.

ISBN: 1-93226-667-4

Price: $39.95 US $59.95 CAN

AVAILABLE NOW
order @
www.syngress.com

AVAILABLE NOW
order @
www.syngress.com

Writing Security Tools and Exploits

James C. Foster

Writing Security Tools and Exploits will be the foremost authority on vulnerability and security code and will serve as the premier educational reference for security professionals and software developers. The book will have over 600 pages of dedicated exploit, vulnerability, and tool code with corresponding instruction. Unlike other security and programming books that dedicate hundreds of pages to architecture and theory based flaws and exploits, this book will dive right into deep code analysis. Previously undisclosed security research in combination with superior programming techniques will be included in both the Local and Remote Code sections of the book.

ISBN: 1-59749-997-8

Price: $49.95 U.S. $69.95 CAN

SYNGRESS®

Syngress: *The Definition of a Serious Security Library*

Syn·gress (sin–gres): *noun, sing.* Freedom from risk or danger; safety. See *security*.

AVAILABLE NOW
order @
www.syngress.com

Hacking the Code:
ASP.NET Web Application Security
Mark Burnett

Are Your Web Applications Really Secure? This unique book walks you through the many threats to your web application code, from managing and authorizing users and encrypting private data to filtering user input and securing XML. For every defined threat, it provides a menu of solutions and coding considerations. And, it offers coding examples and a set of security policies for each of the corresponding threats.

ISBN: 1-93226-665-8

Price: $49.95 US $69.95 CAN

Nessus, Snort, & Ethereal Power Tools:
Customizing Open Source Security
Applications

AVAILABLE NOW
order @
www.syngress.com

Brian Caswell, Gilbert Ramirez, Jay Beale, Noam Rathaus, Neil Archibald

If you have Snort, Nessus, and Ethereal up and running and now you're ready to customize, code, and torque these tools to their fullest potential, this book is for you. The authors of this book provide the inside scoop on coding the most effective and efficient Snort rules, Nessus plug-ins with NASL, and Ethereal capture and display filters. When done with this book, you will be a master at coding your own tools to detect malicious traffic, scan for vulnerabilities, and capture only the packets YOU really care about.

ISBN: 1-59749-020-2

Price: $39.95 US $55.95 CAN

AVAILABLE NOW
order @
www.syngress.com

Hack the Stack:
Using Snort and Ethereal to Master
the 8 Layers of An Insecure Network

Michael Gregg

Remember the first time someone told you about the OSI model and described the various layers? It's probably something you never forgot. This book takes that same layered approach but applies it to network security in a new and refreshing way. It guides readers step-by-step through the stack starting with physical security and working its way up through each of the seven OSI layers. Each chapter focuses on one layer of the stack along with the attacks, vulnerabilities, and exploits that can be found at that layer. The book even includes a chapter on the mythical eighth layer. It's called the people layer. It's included because security is not just about technology it also requires interaction with people, policy and office politics.

ISBN: 1-59749-109-8

Price: $49.95 U.S. $64.95 CAN

SYNGRESS®

Syngress: *The Definition of a Serious Security Library*

Syn·gress (sin–gres): *noun, sing.* Freedom from risk or danger; safety. See *security.*

AVAILABLE NOW
order @
www.syngress.com

Buffer OverFlow Attacks:
Detect, Exploit, Prevent

James C. Foster, Foreword by Dave Aitel

The SANS Institute maintains a list of the "Top 10 Software Vulnerabilities." At the current time, over half of these vulnerabilities are exploitable by Buffer Overflow attacks, making this class of attack one of the most common and most dangerous weapons used by malicious attackers. This is the first book specifically aimed at detecting, exploiting, and preventing the most common and dangerous attacks.

ISBN: 1-932266-67-4

Price: $34.95 US $50.95 CAN

Programmer's
Ultimate Security DeskRef

James C. Foster

AVAILABLE NOW
order @
www.syngress.com

The Programmer's Ultimate Security DeskRef is the only complete desk reference covering multiple languages and their inherent security issues. It will serve as the programming encyclopedia for almost every major language in use.

While there are many books starting to address the broad subject of security best practices within the software development lifecycle, none has yet to address the overarching technical problems of incorrect function usage. Most books fail to draw the line from covering best practices security principles to actual code implementation. This book bridges that gap and covers the most popular programming languages such as Java, Perl, C++, C#, and Visual Basic.

ISBN: 1-932266-72-0

Price: $49.95 US $72.95 CAN

AVAILABLE NOW
order @
www.syngress.com

Hacking the Code:
ASP.NET Web Application Security

Mark Burnett

This unique book walks you through the many threats to your Web application code, from managing and authorizing users and encrypting private data to filtering user input and securing XML. For every defined threat, it provides a menu of solutions and coding considerations. And, it offers coding examples and a set of security policies for each of the corresponding threats.

ISBN: 1-932266-65-8

Price: $49.95 U.S. $79.95 CAN

SYNGRESS®

"Thieme's ability to be open minded, conspiratorial, ethical, and subversive all at the same time is very inspiring."—Jeff Moss, CEO, Black Hat, Inc.

Richard Thieme's Islands in the Clickstream: Reflections on Life in a Virtual World

Richard Thieme is one of the most visible commentators on technology and society, appearing regularly on CNN radio, TechTV, and various other national media outlets. He is also in great demand as a public speaker, delivering his "Human Dimension of Technology" talk to over 50,000 live audience members each year. *Islands in the Clickstream* is a single volume "best of Richard Thieme."

ISBN: 1-931836-22-1

Price: $29.95 US $43.95 CAN

"Thieme's Islands in the Clickstream is deeply reflective, enlightening, and refreshing." —Peter Neumann, Stanford Research Institute

"Richard Thieme takes us to the edge of cliffs we know are there but rarely visit ... he wonderfully weaves life, mystery, and passion through digital and natural worlds with creativity and imagination. This is delightful and deeply thought provoking reading full of "aha!" insights."—Clinton C. Brooks, Senior Advisor for Homeland Security and Asst. Deputy Director, NSA

"WOW! You eloquently express thoughts and ideas that I feel. You have helped me, not so much tear down barriers to communication, as to leverage these barriers into another structure with elevators and escalators."
—Chip Meadows, CISSP, CCSE, USAA e-Security Team

"Richard Thieme navigates the complex world of people and computers with amazing ease and grace. His clarity of thinking is refreshing, and his insights are profound."—Bruce Schneier, CEO, Counterpane

"I believe that you are a practioner of wu wei, the effort to choose the elegant appropriate contribution to each and every issue that you address." —Hal McConnell (fomer intelligence analyst, NSA)

"Richard Thieme presents us with a rare gift. His words touch our heart while challenging our most cherished constructs. He is both a poet and pragmatist navigating a new world with clarity, curiosity and boundless amazement."—Kelly Hansen, CEO, Neohapsis

"Richard Thieme combines hi-tech, business savvy and social consciousness to create some of the most penetrating commentaries of our times. A column I am always eager to read."—Peter Russell, author "From Science to God"

"These reflections provide a veritable feast for the imagination, allowing us more fully to participate in Wonder. This book is an experience of loving Creation with our minds."—Louie Crew, Member of Executive Council of The Episcopal Church

"The particular connections Richard Thieme makes between mind, heart, technology, and truth, lend us timely and useful insight on what it means to live in a technological era. Richard fills a unique and important niche in hacker society!"—Mick Bauer, Security Editor, Linux Journal

SYNGRESS®

Syngress: *The Definition of a Serious Security Library*

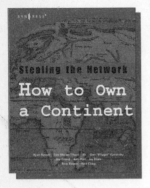

AVAILABLE
APRIL, 2004
www.syngress.com

Stealing the Network: How to Own a Continent

Ryan Russell, FX, Dan "Effugas" Kaminsky, Joe Grand, Tim Mullen, Jay Beale,
Russ Rogers, Ken Pfeil, Paul Craig

The first book in the "Stealing the Network" series was called a "blockbuster" by
Wired magazine, a "refreshing change from more traditional computer books" by
Slashdot.org, and "an entertaining and informative look at the weapons and tactics
employed by those who attack and defend digital systems" by Amazon.com. This
follow-on book once again combines a set of fictional stories with real technology to
show readers the danger that lurks in the shadows of the information security
industry... Could hackers take over a continent?

ISBN: 1-931836-05-1

Price: $49.95 US $69.95 CAN

Special Ops: Host and Network
Security for Microsoft, UNIX, and Oracle

Erik Pace Birkholz

AVAILABLE NOW!
ORDER at
www.syngress.com

"Strap on the night vision goggles, apply the camo pain, then lock and load.
Special Ops is an adrenaline-pumping tour of the most critical
security weaknesses present on most any corporate network today, with some of
the world's best drill sergeants leading the way."
—Joel Scambray, Senior Director, Microsoft's MSN

ISBN: 1-928994-74-1

Price: $69.95 USA $108.95 CAN

AVAILABLE NOW!
ORDER at
www.syngress.com

Stealing the Network:
How to "Own the Box"

Ryan Russell, FX, Joe Grand, and Ken Pfiel

Stealing the Network: How to Own the Box is NOT intended to be an "install, con-
figure, update, troubleshoot, and defend book." It is also NOT another one of the
countless Hacker books out there now by our competition. So, what IS it? *Stealing
the Network: How to Own the Box* is an edgy, provocative, attack-oriented series of
chapters written in a first-hand, conversational style. World-renowned network security personalities present a series of chapters written from the point of an attacker
gaining access to a system. This book portrays the street fighting tactics used to
attack networks.

ISBN: 1-931836-87-6

Price: $49.95 USA $69.95 CAN

SYNGRESS®